THE KLUWER INTERNATIONAL SERIES IN ENGINEERING AND COMPUTER SCIENCE

KNOWLEDGE REPRESENTATION, LEARNING AND EXPERT SYSTEMS

Consulting Editor

Tom Mitchell

Other books in the series:

ROBOT LEARNING, J.H. Connell, S. Mahadevan
ISBN: 0-7923-9365-1
GENERATING ABSTRACTION HIERARCHIES: An Automated Approach to Reducing Search in Planning, C. A. Knoblock
ISBN: 0-7923-9310-4
REINFORCEMENT LEARNING, T. S. Sutton
ISBN: 0-7923-9234-5
AN INTRODUCTION TO FUZZY LOGIC APPLICATIONS IN INTELLIGENT SYSTEMS, R. Yager, L. Zadeh
ISBN: 0-7923-9191-8
CONNECTIONIST APPROACHES TO LANGUAGE LEARNING, D. Touretzky
ISBN: 0-7923-9216-7
STRUCTURE LEVEL ADAPTATION FOR ARTIFICIAL NEURAL NETWORKS, T. C. Lee
ISBN: 0-7923-9151-9
COMPETITIVELY INHIBITED NEURAL NETWORKS FOR ADAPTIVE PARAMETER ESTIMATION, M. Lemmon
ISBN: 0-7923-9086-5
INCREMENTAL VERSION-SPACE MERGING: A General Framework for Concept Learning, H. Hirsh
ISBN: 0-7923-9119-5
LEARNING WITH NESTED GENERALIZED EXEMPLARS, S. L. Salzberg
ISBN: 0-7923-9110-1
KNOWLEDGE ACQUISITION: Selected Research and Commentary, S. Marcus
ISBN: 0-7923-9062-8
CHANGE OF REPRESENTATION AND INDUCTIVE BIAS, D. P. Benjamin
ISBN: 0-7923-9055-5
MACHINE LEARNING, META-REASONING AND LOGICS, P. B. Brazdil, K. Konolige
ISBN: 0-7923-9047-4
AUTOMATING KNOWLEDGE ACQUISITION FOR EXPERT SYSTEMS, S. Marcus
ISBN: 0-89838-294-7
MACHINE LEARNING OF ROBOT ASSEMBLY PLANS, A. M. Segre
ISBN: 0-89838-269-6
LEARNING FROM GOOD AND BAD DATA, P. D. Laird
ISBN: 0-89838-263-7
A CONNECTIONIST MACHINE FOR GENETIC HILLCLIMBING, D. H. Ackley
ISBN: 0-89838-236-X
MACHINE LEARNING OF INDUCTIVE BIAS, P. Utgoff
ISBN: 0-89838-223-8
MACHINE LEARNING: A Guide to Current Research, T. Mitchell, J. Carbonell, R. Michalski
ISBN: 0-89838-214-9
UNIVERSAL SUBGOALING AND CHUNKING OF GOAL HIERACHIES, J. Laird, P. Rosenbloom, A Newell
ISBN: 0-89838-213-0

Contents

ISBN 978-0-7923-9374-0   ISBN 978-1-4615-3202-6 (eBook)
DOI 10.1007/978-1-4615-3202-6

Library of Congress Cataloging-in-Publication Data

A C.I.P. Catalogue record for this book is available from
the Library of Congress.

Printed on acid-free paper.

Contents

ISBN 978-0-7923-9374-0 ISBN 978-1-4615-3202-6 (eBook)
DOI 10.1007/978-1-4615-3202-6

Library of Congress Cataloging-in-Publication Data

A C.I.P. Catalogue record for this book is available from the Library of Congress.

Printed on acid-free paper.

Machine Learning, 11, 109–110 (1993)

Introduction

Most machine learning research has been primarily concerned with the development of systems that implement one type of inference within a single computational paradigm. Such systems, which can be called *monostrategy* learning systems, include those for empirical induction of decision trees or rules, explanation-based generalization, neural net learning from examples, genetic algorithm-based learning, and others. Monostrategy learning systems can be very effective and useful, if the learning problems they are applied to are sufficiently narrowly defined.

Many real-world applications, however, pose learning problems that go beyond the capability of monostrategy learning methods. In view of this, recent years have witnessed a growing interest in developing *multistrategy systems* that integrate two or more inference types and/or computational paradigms in one learning system. Such multistrategy systems take advantage of the complementarity of different inference types of representational mechanisms. Therefore, they have a potential to be more versatile and more powerful than monostrategy systems. On the other hand, due to their greater complexity, their development is significantly more difficult and represents a new great challenge to the machine learning community.

This special issue contains a sample of articles characteristic of the current research in this area. Most of the articles in this issue are improved and updated versions of papers that were originally presented at the *First International Workshop on Multistrategy Learning* (MSL-91), organized by George Mason University in Harpers Ferry, WV, November 7–9, 1991. The Workshop Proceedings contained a great number of excellent contributions to this area; therefore it was not possible to select papers that could qualify as the "best." The papers included in this issue were selected to illustrate well the diversity and richness of the current research in this area. To assure the superior quality of the contributions, all papers have been rigorously reviewed for the special issue. The review of the editor's article was handled by T. Dietterich and G. Tecuci. The editor expresses his sincere thanks to all the reviewers for their diligent and careful reviews.

The opening article by the editor serves as an introduction and presents a general conceptual framework for analyzing inferential capabilities of learning methods and for developing multistrategy learning systems. Saitta and Botta describe the system WHY, which combines symbolic deduction, inductive generalization, and abductive derivation strategies and which uitlizes a causal model of the application domain.

Maclin and Shavlik explore "knowledge-based" neural networks, which resulted from their attempt to combine explanation-based learning with neural learning. Pazzani's article investigates an incremental, theory-driven method for creating rules that predict effects of actions.

Morik describes a system for supporting a "balanced cooperation" among different learning mechanisms, including the user as one of them, in the process of building a model or knowledge base. Finally, Tecuci describes a multistrategy task-adaptive method that aims at integrating a range of learning strategies based on a justification tree approach.

Presenting this first special issue on multistrategy learning, its editor hopes that it will stimulate the reader's interest in this novel and remarkably challenging subarea of machine learning.

Ryszard S. Michalski
George Mason University

Reference

Michalski, R.S., & Tecuci, G. (Eds.), *Proceedings of the First International Workshop on Multistrategy Learning*, Fairfax, VA: Center for Artificial Intelligence, George Mason University.

Machine Learning, 11, 111-151 (1993)

Inferential Theory of Learning as a Conceptual Basis for Multistrategy Learning

RYSZARD S. MICHALSKI MICHALSKI@AIC.GMU.EDU
Center for Artificial Intelligence, George Mason University, Fairfax, VA 22030

Abstract. In view of a great proliferation of machine learning methods and paradigms, there is a need for a general conceptual framework that would explain their interrelationships and provide a basis for their integration into multistrategy learning systems. This article presents initial results on the *Inferential Theory of Learning* that aims at developing such a framework, with the primary emphasis on explaining logical capabilities of learning systems, i.e., their *competence*. The theory views learning as a goal-oriented process of modifying the learner's knowledge by exploring the learner's experience. Such a process is described as a search through a *knowledge space*, conducted by applying knowledge transformation operators, called *knowledge transmutations*. Transmutations can be performed using any type of inference—deduction, induction, or analogy. Several fundamental pairs of transmutations are presented in a novel and very general way. These include generalization and specialization, explanation and prediction, abstraction and concretion, and similization and dissimilization. Generalization and specialization transmutations change the *reference set* of a description (the set of entities being described). Explanations and predictions derive additional knowledge about the reference set (explanatory or predictive). Abstractions and concretions change the level of detail in describing a reference set. Similizations and dissimilizations hypothesize knowledge about a reference set based on its similarity or dissimilarity with another reference set. The theory provides a basis for *multistrategy task-adaptive learning* (MTL), which is outlined and illustrated by an example. MTL dynamically adapts strategies to the *learning task*, defined by the input information, the learner's background knowledge, and the learning goal. It aims at synergistically integrating a wide range of inferential learning strategies, such as empirical and constructive inductive generalization, deductive generalization, abductive derivation, abstraction, similization, and others.

Keywords. Learning theory, multistrategy learning, inference, classification of inference, deduction, induction, abduction, generalization, abstraction, analogy, transmutation.

For every belief comes either through syllogism or from induction.
Aristotle, Prior Analytics, Book II, Chapter 23 (p. 90)
ca 330 BC.

1. Introduction

Most research in machine learning has been oriented toward the development of *monostrategy* methods that employ one type of inference and a single computational mechanism. Such methods include, for example, inductive learning of decision rules or decision trees, explanation-based generalization, empirical discovery, neural net learning from examples, genetic algorithm-based learning, conceptual clustering, and others. The research progress on these and related topics has been reported by many authors, among them Laird (1988), Touretzky, Hinton, and Sejnowski (1988), Goldberg (1989), Schafer (1989), Segre (1989),

Rivest, Haussler, and Warmuth (1989), Fulk and Case (1990), Porter and Mooney (1990), Kodratoff and Michalski (1990), Birnbaum and Collins (1991), Warmuth and Valiant (1991), and Sleeman and Edwards (1992).

With the growing understanding of capabilities and limitations of monostrategy methods, there has been an increasing interest in *multistrategy learning* systems that employ two or more inference types and/or computational mechanisms. Multistrategy systems can have potentially for much greater *competence*, that is, the ability to solve a much wider range of learning problems than monostrategy systems, because they take advantage of the complementarity of individual learning strategies. On the other hand, they are also potentially significantly more complex, and thus their implementation presents a much greater challenge. Therefore, a decision on their application to a given range of problems should reflect the above trade-off. Since human learning is clearly multistrategy, research on multistrategy systems is of significant relevance to understanding human learning, and thus has a great importance regardless of the practical applications of the work.

Among early well-known multistrategy systems (sometimes called "integrated learning systems") are UNIMEM (Lebowitz, 1986), Odysseus (Wilkins, Clancey, & Buchanan, 1986), Prodigy (Minton et al., 1987) DISCIPLE (Kodratoff & Tecuci, 1987), Gemini (Danyluk, 1987, 1989, 1993), OCCAM (Pazzani, 1988), IOE (Dietterich & Flann, 1988), and KBL (Whitehall, 1990). Most of these systems are concerned with integrating symbolic empirical induction with explanation-based learning. Some, like DISCIPLE, also include a simple method for analogical learning. The integration of the strategies is often done in a predefined, problem-independent way, and without clear theoretical justification. Some recent multistrategy systems are described by De Raedt and Bruynooghe (1993) and Mooney and Ourston (1993).

An open and challenging problem is how to integrate a whole spectrum of learning strategies in a problem-dependent way, and on the basis of sound and general theoretical foundations. By a problem-dependent integration we mean an integration in which a learning strategy, or a combination of them, is automatically adapted to different learning situations.

The articles in this special issue represent novel and diverse efforts in this general direction. The present article investigates principles characterizing diverse inferential learning strategies and proposes a general conceptual framework for developing multistrategy systems. Its central part is devoted to *Inferential Theory of Learning* (*ITL*), which analyzes learning processes in terms of generic operators for knowledge transformation, called *knowledge transmutations* or *knowledge transforms*.

A knowledge transmutation is a conceptually simple, high-level knowledge transformation pattern that derives a piece of knowledge from a given input and background knowledge. A transmutation is an operator on knowledge that can employ any type of inference. Among major research topics studied in the theory are an analysis of the properties of different knowledge transmutations, their interrelationships, and their role in different learning algorithms, methods, and paradigms.

The main objective of the theory is to characterize the logical capabilities of learning methods and processes, that is, their *competence*. To this end, the theory addresses such questions as what types of knowledge transformation occur in learning processes; what is the "truth" status of knowledge generated by them; what knowledge transmutations occur in different types of learning; how prior knowledge is used; what types of logical relationships inputs, all of the learner's background knowledge, and all knowledge that the learner can potentially generate. In the context of empirical inductive learning, the knowledge space is usually called a *description space*.

For illustration, here are a few examples of transmutations. An *inductive generalization* takes one or more concept examples and creates a general description of them. An explanation-based generalization is a form of deductive generalization that takes an example from an "operational" description space, a concept description from an "abstract" description space, and relevant domain knowledge, and derives from them a concept description in the operational description space (see, e.g., Mitchell, Keller, & Kedar-Cabelli, 1986). Sections 4 to 7 define and discuss several fundamental knowledge transmutations, such as generalization, abstraction, and similization, and their counterparts, specialization, concretion, and dissimilization. Other types of transmutations, due to space limitations, are discussed only very briefly.

The analysis and explanation of diverse learning processes in terms of underlying knowledge transmutations is a major topic of the Inferential Theory of Learning. The transmutations represent transformations of various aspects of knowledge, and they can be implemented in many different ways. Depending on the knowledge representation and the computation mechanism, knowledge transmutations can be performed explicitly or implicitly. In symbolic learning systems, transmutations are usually (but not always) implemented in a more or less explicit way and executed in steps that are conceptually comprehensible. For example, the INDUCE learning system performs inductive generalization according to certain generalization rules—selective or constructive—where each rule represents a conceptually simple transformation (Michalski, 1983; Bloedorn & Michalski, 1991; Wnek & Michalski, 1991a).

In neural networks, transmutations are performed implicitly, in steps dictated by the underlying computational mechanism. These steps may not correspond to any conceptually simple operations or rules of inference. For example, a neural network may generalize an input example by performing a sequence of small modifications of weights of internode connections. Individual weight modifications may be difficult to explain in terms of explicit inference rules. Nevertheless, they can produce a global effect equivalent to generalizing a set of examples.

Such an effect can be easily demonstrated by a method for *diagrammatic visualization* (DIAV). In DIAV, concepts are mapped into sets of cells in a planar diagram, which represents a multidimensional space spanned over multivalued attributes. Operations on concepts are visualized by changes in the configurations of the corresponding sets of cells. Examples of diagrammatic visualization of inductive generalizations performed by a neural network, a genetic algorithm, and symbolic learning systems are presented by Wnek and Michalski (1991b, 1993).

A learning goal is a necessary component of any learning process. Given an input, and some nontrivial background knowledge, a learner could potentially generate an unbounded number of inferences. To limit the proliferation of choices, a learning process is constrained and/or guided by the learning goal. A learning goal determines what parts of prior knowledge are relevant, what knowledge is to be acquired, in which form, and how the learned knowledge is to be evaluated. There can be many different types of learning goals, and they can be expressed explicitly or implicitly. Goals can be classified roughly as domain independent or domain dependent.

and an attribute evaluation method. The knowledge created is in the form of a decision tree. In a "self-contained" rule-learning system, all background knowledge and learned knowledge would be in the form of rules. A learning process would involve modifying prior rules and/or creating new ones. The ultimate learning capabilities of a learning system are determined by what it can or cannot change in its knowledge base, and by what kinds of inference and knowledge transformations it is capable of performing.

The Inferential Learning Theory postulates that a learning process depends on the input information (input), background knowledge (BK), and learning goal. These three components constitute a *learning task*. The learning task determines what type of learning strategy or strategies need to be employed (by "learning strategy" is roughly meant a combination of the type of inference employed and the computational and the representational mechanism used to implement it). An input to any step of learning can be sensory observations, knowledge communicated by a source (e.g., a teacher), or knowledge generated by the previous learning step. Although most learning systems assume that input is in the form of facts or concept examples, a learning system should be able to learn from any type of knowledge, including previously formed generalizations, conceptual hierarchies, mathematical equations, knowledge at any level of abstraction, estimates of certainty of given knowledge, or any combination of various types.

The key idea of the theory is that processes involved in accomplishing a learning goal can be characterized in terms of generic patterns of inference, called knowledge transmutations. A knowledge transmutation takes an input and background knowledge as arguments and generates a new piece of knowledge. It represents conceptually simple and comprehensible units of knowledge transformation, and it can employ any type of inference. Specifically, the theory views a learning process as a search through a knowledge space, conducted by applying knowledge transmutations as search operators:

Given:
- Input knowledge (I)
- Goal (G)
- Background knowledge (BK)
- Transmutations (T)

Determine:
- Output knowledge O that satisfies goal G, by applying transmutations from the set T to input I and/or background knowledge BK.

By the input knowledge (I) is meant here any information (facts, examples, general knowledge, etc.) that the learner receives from the environment or as results of previous steps of learning. Goal (G) specifies criteria to be satisfied by the Output Knowledge (O) in order that learning is accomplished. Background knowledge (BK) is a part of learner's prior knowledge that is relevant to a given learning process. While complete and formal definition of "relevant" knowledge goes beyond the scope of this article, as a working definition the reader may assume that it is a part of prior knowledge that can be useful at any stage of a given learning process.

Transmutations are operators that make knowledge changes in the knowledge space. The knowledge space is a space of knowledge representations that can represent all possible

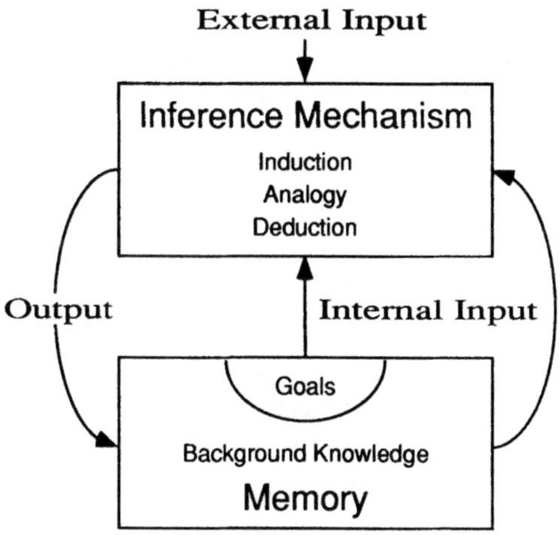

Figure 1. An illustration of a general learning process.

that is, the relevant parts of the learner's prior knowledge. Consequently, the information flow in a learning process can be characterized by a general schema shown in figure 1. In each learning cycle, the learner analyses the input information in terms of its background knowledge and its goals, and performs various inferences to generate new knowledge and/or a better form of knowledge. The "new knowledge" may be provided from the outside, or may be generated by induction, deduction, or analogy. It can be additional knowledge, or a change in the belief in the knowledge already possessed. (For further discussion of this topic, and a distinction between different types of new knowledge—"intrinsic" vs. "derived"—see section 4.) If the results of a given learning act are satsifactory from the viewpoint of the learning goal(s), they are assimilated within the learner's memory and become available for use in subsequent learning processes.

The basic premise of the Inferential Learning Theory is that in order to learn, an agent has to be able to perform inference and to have memory that both stores the background knowledge (BK) needed for performing the inference and records "useful" results of inference. Without either of the two components—the ability to reason and the ability to memorize and retrieve information from memory—no learning can be accomplished. Thus, one can write an "equation":

Learning = Inferencing + Memorizing

It should be noted that the term "inferencing" is used here in a very general sense, meaning any type of reasoning or knowledge transformation. The double role of memory, as a supplier of background knowledge and as a depository of results, is often reflected in the organization of a learning system. For example, in a neural net, background knowledge resides in the structure of the network, i.e., in the type and the number of units used, in the way they are interconnected, and in the initial weights of the connections. The learned knowledge usually resides only in the new values of the weights. In decision tree learning, the BK includes the set of attributes used to describe objects, the domains of the attributes, exist between the learned knowledge, the input information, and the learner's prior knowledge; how learning goals and their structure influence learning processes; how learning processes can be classified and evaluated from the logical viewpoint; what is the validity of the learned knowledge; etc. The theory stresses the use of multitype inferences in learning processes, the role of the learner's prior knowledge, and the importance of learning goals. Although the primary goal is not to develop a cognitive learning theory, the conceptual framework presented does try to formally capture the intuitive perceptions of different forms of human inference and learning, and suggests solutions that could be used as a basis for developing cognitive models. A number of ideas presented here stem from research on the core theory of human plausible inference (Collins & Michalski, 1989).

The above goals distinguish the Inferential Theory of Learning (ITL) from the Computational Learning Theory (COLT), which focuses on the *computational complexity* and *convergence* of learning algorithms, particularly those for empirical inductive learning. COLT has not yet been much concerned with multistrategy learning, the role of the learner's prior knowledge, or the learning goals (e.g., Fulk & Chase; 1990; Warmuth & Valiant, 1991). The above should not be taken to mean that the issues studied in COLT are unimportant, but only that they are different. A "unified" theory of learning should take into consideration both competence and complexity of learning processes.

This article outlines basic ideas of ITL and presents a novel and more general view of several fundamental knowledge transmutations, such as generalization, abduction, abstraction, similization, and their opposites. The last section describes briefly an application of the theory to the development of a methodology for *multistrategy task-adaptive learning*. Many ideas are presented in prefatory and illustrative fashion, with the emphasis on developing a general perspective of the whole subject. Various details and a better formalization of various concepts await further research. To make the article easily accessible to the AI and Cognitive Science communities, as well as to readers who are not regularly using predicate logic, expressions in predicate logic are usually accompanied by a natural language interpretation. The presented work is a significant extension or refinement of ideas described in earlier publications (Michalski, 1983, 1990a,b, 1991).

2. Basic tenets of the inferential theory of learning

Learning has been traditionally characterized as an improvement of a system's behavior or knowledge due to its experience. While this view is appealing due to its simplicity, it does not provide many clues about how to actually implement a learning system. To build a learning system, one needs to understand, in computation terms, what types of behavior or knowledge changes occur in learning, and how they are accomplished in response to different types of experience. (Here "experience" means the totality of information generated in the course of performing some actions, not a physical process.)

To provide answers to such questions, the Inferential Theory of Learning assumes that learning is a goal-guided process of modifying the learner's knowledge by exploring the learner's experience. Such a process can be viewed as a search through a *knowledge space*, defined by the knowledge representation used. The search can employ any type of inference—any form of deduction, induction, or analogy. It involves "background knowledge,"

Domain-independent goals call for a certain type of learning activity, independent of the topic of discourse, e.g., to acquire a general rule for classifying given facts, to confirm a given piece of knowledge, to derive from it some other knowledge, to concisely describe given observations, to discover a regularlity in a collection of data, to find a causal explanation of a found regularity, to acquire control knowledge, to reformulate given knowledge to a more effective form, to solve a problem of a given type, to plan what to learn, etc. Domain-dependent goals call for acquiring a problem of a given type, to plan what to learn, etc. Doman-dependent goals call for acquiring a specific piece or type of domain knowledge. A learner may pursue more than one goal, and the goals may be conflicting. When they are conflicting, their relative importance controls the amount of effort that is extended to pursue any of them. The relative importance of specific goals depends on the importance of higher-level goals. Thus, learning processes are controlled by a hierarchy of goals and the estimated degrees of their importance.

Most machine learning research has so far given relatively little consideration to the problem of learning goals and how they affect learning processes. As a result, many developed systems are method oriented rather than problem oriented. There have been, however, several investigations of the role and the use of goals in learning and inference (e.g., Stepp & Michalski, 1983; Hunter, 1990; Ram, 1991; Ram & Hunter, 1992). Among the important research problems related to this topic are the development of methods for goal representation, for using goals to guide a learning process, and to understand the interaction and conflict resolution among domain-independent and domain-specific goals. These issues are of significant importance to the understanding of learning in general, and interest in them will likely increase in the future.

In sum, Inferential Learning Theory states that learning is a goal-guided process of deriving desired knowledge by using input information and background knowledge. Such a process involves a search through a knowledge space, using knowledge transmutations as operators. Knowledge transmutations can involve any type of inference.

3. Types of inference

The central property of any knowledge transmutation is the type of underlying inference. The inference type characterizes the transmutation along the truth–falsity dimension, and thus determines the validity of the knowledge derived by it. For this reason, before discussing different knowledge transmutations, we will first analyze basic types of inference that can be involved in them.

Any type of inference can produce some useful knowledge worth remembering for future use. Consequently, a complete learning theory has to include a complete theory of inference. Such a theory of inference has to account for all possible types of inference. To this end, figure 2 presents an attempt to illustrate schematically all major types of inference. The first classification divides inferences into two fundamental types: deductive and inductive. In defining these types, many conventional approaches do not distinguish between the input information and the reasoner's prior knowledge. Such a distinction, however, is important from the learning theory viewpoint, because in a given learning process, there is clearly a difference between the knowledge already possessed by the learner and the information communicated from the outside.

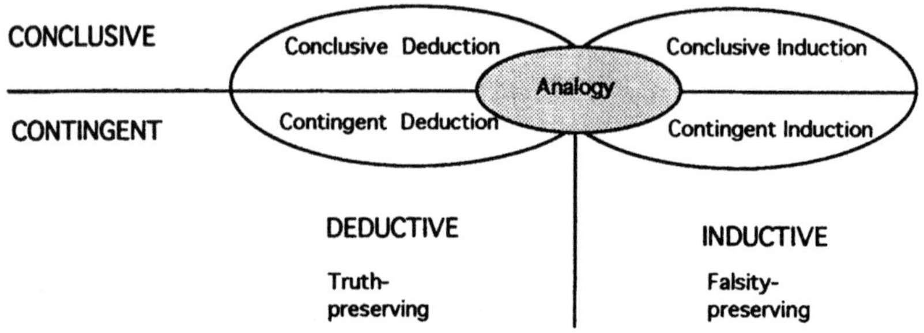

Figure 2. A classification of major types of inference.

To characterize basic types of inference in a general, language-independent way, consider the entailment

$$P \cup PK \models C \tag{1}$$

where P stands for a set of statements, called the *premise*, BK stands for a set of statements representing the reasoner's background knowledge, and C stands for a set of statements, called the *consequent*. P is assumed to be consistent with BK.

Deductive inference is deriving consequent C, given P and BK. Inductive inference is hypothesizing premise P, given C and BK. Thus, deduction can be viewed as "tracing forward" the relationship (1), and induction as "tracing backward" this relationship. Because (1) succinctly explains the relationship between two fundamental forms of inference, it is called the *fundamental equation* for inference.

Deduction is truth-preserving, i.e., C must be true if P and BK are true, and induction is falsity-preserving, i.e., if C is false, then P must be false also, if BK is true. (The latter property applies to every type of induction such as inductive generalization, abduction, inductive specialization, concretion, and others—see section 5).

In a general view of deduction and induction that also captures their approximate or common sense forms, the "strong" entailment $\models$ in (1) may be replaced by a "weak" entailment. A weak entailment includes cases in which C is only a *plausible, probabilistic, or partial* consequence of P and BK. The difference between a "strong" (valid) and "weak" (plausible) entailment leads to another major classfication of types of inference.

Specifically, inferences can be *conclusive* or *contingent*. Conclusive inferences assume "strong" entailment; they are true in every possible situation. Contingent inferences assume only "weak" entailment; they may be true in some situations and not true in others. Conclusive deductive inferences are "strongly" truth-preserving, and conclusive inductive inferences are "strongly" falsity-preserving. Contingent deductive inferences are "weakly" truth-preserving, and contingent inductive inferences are "weakly" falsity-preserving.

If inductive inference produces a statement that characterizes a larger set of entities than the input statement (C), then it is called an *inductive generalization*. As shown below, such an inference is based on tracing backward a domain-independent (tautological) implication, known as the rule of *universal specialization*. If it hypothesizes a premise that explains the input, then it is called *abduction*. Abduction is based on tracing backward domain-dependent implications. These distinctions are illustrated by the examples below.

A conclusive deductive inference is illustrated by the following transmutation:

Input	$\mathfrak{A} \in X$	($\mathfrak{A}$ is an element of X.)
BK	$\forall x \in X, q(x)$	(All elements of X have property q.)
	$(\forall x \in X, q(x)) \Rightarrow (\mathfrak{A} \in X \Rightarrow q(\mathfrak{A}))$	(If all elements of X have property q, then any element of X, e.g., $\mathfrak{A}$, must have property q.
Output	$q(\mathfrak{A})$	($\mathfrak{A}$ has property q.)

If Input is the premise P, and Output is the consequent C, then the fundamental equation (1) is clearly satisfied. In constrast, the following transmutation illustrates conclusive induction:

Input	$q(\mathfrak{A})$	($\mathfrak{A}$ has property q.)
BK	$\mathfrak{A} \in X$	($\mathfrak{A}$ is an element of X.)
	$(\forall x \in X, q(x)) \Rightarrow (\mathfrak{A} \in X \Rightarrow q(\mathfrak{A}))$	(If all elements of X have property q, then any element of X, e.g., $\mathfrak{A}$, must have property q.
Output	$\forall x \in X, q(x)$	(*Maybe* all elements of X have property q.)

The Output is obtained by tracing backward a tautological implication (listed as part of BK), known in logic as the rule of universal specialization. If Input is the consequent C and the Output is the premise P, then the fundamental equation (1) is satisfied, because the union of sentences in Output and BK entails the Input. The inference is falsity-preserving, because if the Input were not true (it did not have the property q), then the hypothetical premise (Output) would have to be false. This form of induction is called *generalization* because it hypothesizes a statement in which the property that characterized only one element ($\mathfrak{A}$) now characterizes a larger set (X). The output from induction is uncertain, which here, and henceforth is indicated by the qualifier "*Maybe.*"

To proceed, we will introduce two important concepts, a *reference set* and a *descriptor.* A reference set of a statement (or set of statements) is an entity or a set of entities that this statement(s) describes or refers to. A descriptor is an attribute, a relation, or a transformation whose instantiation (value) is used to characterize the reference set or the individual entities in it. For example, consider a statement: "Nicholas is of medium height, has a Ph.D. in astronomy from the Jagiellonian University, and likes travel." The reference set here is the singleton "Nicholas." The sentence uses three descriptors: a one-place attribute, "height(person)"; a binary relation, "likes(person,activity)"; and a four-place relation, "degree-received(person, degree, topic, university)."

Consider another statement: "Most people on Barbados and Dominica have beautiful dark skin." Here the reference set is "Most people on Barbados and Dominica," and the descriptors are "skin-color(person)" and "skin-attractiveness(person)." What is the reference set and what are descriptors in a statement or set of statements may be a matter of interpretation and/or context. However, once the interpretation is decided, other concepts below can be consistently applied.

Using the above concepts, a generalization is characterized as a transmutation that extends the reference set of the input statement(s). Abduction (also called *explanation*) is characterized as a transmutation that hypothesizes explanations of the properties of the reference set, but does not change the set. An opposite of abduction is *prediction*, which derives consequences of the properties of the reference set. Here is an illustration of an abduction:

Input	$q(\mathfrak{A})$	($\mathfrak{A}$ has property q.)
BK	$\forall x \in X, q(x)$	(All elements of X have property q.)
	$(\forall x \in X, q(x)) \Rightarrow (\mathfrak{A} \in X \Rightarrow q(\mathfrak{A}))$	
Output	$\mathfrak{A} \in X$	(*Maybe* $\mathfrak{A}$ is an element of X.)

The *Input* states that the reference set $\mathfrak{A}$ has the property q. The abductive transmutation hypothesizes that $\mathfrak{A}$ is an element of X, which is the context of BK can be viewed as an explanation of the Input: $q(\mathfrak{A})$ *because* $\mathfrak{A} \in X$. The fundamental equation (1) holds, because, if Output is true, then Input must also be true in the context of BK. Again, if Input were not true, then Output could not be true; thus the inference preserves falsity. As in generalization, Output was obtained by "tracing backward" a rule in BK ($\mathfrak{A} \in X \Rightarrow q(\mathfrak{A})$).

In both cases above, generalization and abduction, Output plus BK (strongly) entails Input. These forms are therefore called *conclusive induction* and *conclusive abduction*, respectively (as opposed to *contingent induction and contingent abduction*, described below).

In the literature, some authors restrict abduction to processes of creating the "best" explanation of a given fact, i.e., to inferences involving "tracing backwards" the "strongest" implication, whose right-hand side states the given fact. A difficulty with this view is that it is not always easy to determine which explanation among the alternative ones is the "best." If producing an alternative but not the "best" explanation is not abduction, then what is and what is not abduction depends on the measure of "goodness" of explanation, rather than on logical properties of inference. Some authors also require that the explanation is "causal." Since the rule "All elements of X have property q" (or, "If an entity belongs to X, then it has property q") does not express a causal relationship, then the reasoning illustrated in the example above would not be classified as abduction.

This article views the concept of abduction in a more general sense. Specifically, abduction is viewed as an inference that generates explanations of a given reference set, and is done by tracing backward certain domain-dependent implications. If these implications represent causal relationships, then abduction produces causal explanations. Peirce (1965), who originally introduced the concept of abduction, did not restrict it to reasoning producing only the "best" or only "casual" explanations (for a discussion on the relationship between abduction and deduction, see Console, Theseider, & Torasso, 1991). Some theoretical views on abduction are found in Zadrozny (1991). For an analysis and development of casual reasoning in humans, see Shultz and Kestenbaum (1985).

Conventional definitions of abduction describe it as "tracing backwards" an implicative rule. We will now show that such a view makes a tacit assumption that, if violated, allows abduction to produce completely implausible inferences. Consider, for example, the following inference:

Input	Color(My-Pencil, Green)	(My pencil is green.)
BK	Type (object, Grass) ⇒ Color(object, Green)	(If an object is grass then it is green.)
Output	Type(My-Pencil, Grass)	(*Maybe* my pencil is grass.)

Although the implication in BK is quite strong, the abductive derivation based on it is implausible. The reason for this is that the implication

Color(object, Green) ⇒ Type(object, grass) (If an object is green then it is grass.)

normally holds only with an infinitesimal likelihood. Thus, abduction can produce an implausible hypothesis if the reverse implication has insufficient "strength." This simply means that abductive derivation makes an assumption about the "reverse strength" of an implication employed in it. To make this issue explicit, we introduce a more general form of implication as a basis for abductive derivation.

Definition. A *mutual implication* or, for short, an *m-implication*, describes a logical dependency between statements (well-formed predicate logic expressions) in both directions:

$$A \Leftrightarrow B: \alpha, \beta \quad (2)$$

where α and β, called *merit parameters,* express the *forward strength* and the *backward strength* of the m-implication, respectively.

An m-implication can be used for reasoning by tracing it in either direction. Tracing it forward (from the left to the right) means that if A is known to be true, then B can be asserted as true with the degree of belief α, if no other information relevant to B is known that affects this conclusion. Tracing an m-implication backward means that if B is known to be true, then A can be asserted as true with the degree of belief β, if no other information relevant to A is known that affects this conclusion. The m-implication reduces to a logical implication if α is 1 and β is unknown (in which case it is written as A ⇒ B).

If any of the parameters α or β takes value 1 (which represents a complete belief), then the m-implication is *conclusive* (or *demonstrative*) in the direction for which the merit parameter equals 1; otherwise it is called *mutually-contingent* (or *m-contingent.*) In many situations, it is convenient to express an m-implication that has merit parameters (or only one) sufficiently high to merit their consideration without stating their precise values. For this purpose, we use symbols ↔ (or →), without listing α and β. Thus, an m-implication A ⇔ B: α, β, in which α and β are unspecified but are above some "threshold of acceptability," is alternatively written A ↔ B, or A → B. The concept of mutual implication was originally postulated in the theory of plausible reasoning (Collins & Michalski, 1989), which was developed by analyzing protocols recording examples of human reasoning.

Based on the above definition, one can say that abduction produces a plausible conclusion, if it traces backward a mutual implication in which β is sufficiently high. Thus, if abduction is based on a standard implication (in which β is unknown), then it can be quite haphazard reasoning. Section 7 shows that a generalized form of mutual implication provides a formal basis for analogical inference.

The concept of an m-implication raises two basic problems: how merit parameters are determined, and how they are combined and propagated in reasoning through a network of m-implications. Regarding the first problem, the simplest interpretation of them is to assume that $\alpha = p(B \mid A)$ and $\beta = p(A \mid B)$. However, to make the concept of m-implication applicable for expressing many kinds of dependencies (including those occuring in human plausible reasoning), it is assumed that merit parameters do not have only one interpretation or representation. In a general view of m-implication, they can be precise values or only estimates of conditional probability, ranges of probabilities, degrees of dependency based on a contingency table (e.g., Goodman & Kruskal, 1979; Piatetsky-Shapiro, 1992), characterizations of the "strength" of dependency provided by an expert, or some other measures of dependency.

As to the second problem (how to combine merit parameters in reasoning with multiple m-implications), a comprehensive study of ideas and methods for the case of the probabilistic interpretation of merit parameters is presented by Pearl (1988). He uses "Bayesian networks" for updating and propagating beliefs based on a probabilistic model.

The fundamental difficulty in solving the second problem generally is that all logics of uncertainty, such as multiple-valued logic, probabilistic logic, fuzzy logic, etc., are not *truth-functional*, which means that there is no definite function for combining uncertainties. The reason is that the certainty of a conclusion from uncertain premises does not depend solely on the certainty (or probability) of the premises, but also on their meaning and their semantic interrelationship. The ultimate solution of this open problem will require methods that take into consideration both merit parameters and the meaning of the sentences. The results of research on human plausible reasoning conducted by Collins and Michalski (1989) show that people derive a combined certainty of a conclusion from uncertain premises by taking into consideration structural (or semantic) relations among the premises, based on a hierarchical knowledge representation, and involve also other types of merit parameters, such as typicality, frequency, dominance, etc.

Conclusive inferences are those that involve tracing mutual implications in which one merit parameter equals 1 (assuming that the input statement is true and perfectly matches the premise). Tracing mutual implications in which both merit parameters are below 1 (or when the above assumptions are not true) produces contingent inferences. In natural language, the contingency of a conclusion is expressed by a qualitative or quantitative degree of "strength" or "truth" (e.g., "maybe," "probably," "likely," "with probability of .7," with a "degree of belief," "certainty," or "confidence," etc.), or by a contingent quantifier (e.g., "most," "frequently," "usually," "90% of . . .," etc.). Suppose, for example, that BK contains a statement "Most elements of X have property q" and input is "x is a member of X." Deriving the statement "x likely has the property q" is a contingent deduction.

Let us consider more examples of contingent inferences. Consider a statement: "Fire usually produces smoke." This statement can be viewed as a weak mutual implication (both merit parameters are below 1). If one sees fire, then by contingent deduction one may derive a conclusion that there may be smoke. If one observes smoke, then by contingent induction ("tracing backward" the m-implication), one may hypothesize that there may be fire. Since the m-implication represents domain knowledge, this form of induction is contingent abduction. It explains "fire" by hypothesizing "smoke." Notice that if the input is false (there is no smoke), the uncertainty degree (falsity) of the hypothesis depends on the forward strength of the mutual implication.

In the above example, reasoning in both directions of the m-implication is uncertain. This might suggest that there is no intrinsic difference between contingent deduction and contingent induction (in the case above, abduction). A usual way of distinguishing between the two types of inference is to check if the entailment $|=$ in a given instantiation of (1) represents as a causal ordering, i.e., if P can viewed as a cause and C as an effect. In such a situation, contingent deduction (or contingent prediction) derives a plausible consequent, C, of the causes represented by P. Abduction derives plausible causes, P, of the consequent C. Since we can say that "fire causes smoke," and not the converse, then the above rule allows us to make a qualitiative distinction between inferences that trace this implication in one or another direction. Contingent deduction (prediction) can thus be viewed as "tracing forward" and abduction as "tracing backward" contingent, causally ordered dependencies.

This distinction, however, is not generally sufficient. The problem is that there are mutual implications that do not represent causal dependencies. For example, consider the statement "Prices at Tiffany's tend to be high." This statement expresses a non-causal mutual implication:

$$\text{Purchased-at(item, Tiffany's)} \Leftrightarrow \text{Price(item, High)}: \alpha, \beta \tag{3}$$

If one is told that an item, e.g., a crystal vase, was purchased at Tiffany's, then one may conclude, with confidence α, that the price of it was high (if no other information about the price of the vase is known). The conclusion is uncertain if $\alpha < 1$ (which reflects, e.g., the possibility of a sale). If one is told that the price of an item was high, then one might hypothesize, with confidence β (usually low) that perhaps the item was purchased at Tiffany's. The confidence β depends on our knowledge about how many expensive shops are in the area where the item was purchased. Both inferences above are uncertain (assuming α, $\beta < 1$), and there is no clear causal ordering underlying the m-implication. Which inference is then contingent deduction, and which is contingent induction (or abduction)?

The way we propose to resolve this problem is based on the observation that a conclusive deduction traces an implication in the "strong" direction (with the degree of strength 1), and abduction traces such an implication in a "weaker" direction. Generalizing this property to reasoning with weak mutual implications that are not causal dependencies, we propose the rule: *reasoning in the direction of the greater strength of an m-implication is deduction, and reasoning in the direction of the weaker strength is induction (abduction, if the m-implication represents a domain knowledge). If reasoning in both directions has the same strength, there is no distinction between deduction and induction*. For example, reasoning based on tracing logical equivalence is deduction or induction both ways.

Going back to our example with Tiffany's, one may observe that α is usually significantly higher than β (unless Tiffany's is the only expensive store in the area under consideration). Thus, the forward reasoning based on (3) can be viewed as contingent deduction, and the backward reasoning as contingent abduction. The distinction between contingent deduction and contingent induction (or abduction) is in this case a matter of degree, and it depends on the assumptions underlying the m-implication used for inference.

Summarizing, conclusive deductive inference is strictly truth-preserving, and conclusive induction is strictly falsity-preserving. A conclusive deduction produces a provable (valid) consequent from a given premise in the context of BK. A conclusive induction produces a "valid" hypothesis, which logically entails the given consequent in the context of BK (though the hypothesis itself may be false). Contingent deduction is truth-preserving and contingent induction is falsity-preserving to the degree defined by the forward strength of mutual implications involved in reasoning, respectively. Contingent induction is truth-preserving to the degree defined by the backward strength of the mutual implication.

The intersection of deduction and induction, that is a truth- and falsity-preserving inference, represents an equivalence-based inference, or *reformulation* transmutation. Such an inference transforms given knowledge into logically equivalent knowledge. For example, if A is logically equivalent to A′, then the rule A ⇒ B can be transformed to A′ ⇒ B. Analogy can be viewed as an extension of equivalence-based inference, namely, as a "similarity-based" inference. For example, if A is similar to $\mathcal{A}$ in terms relevant to B (for an explanation, see section 7), then from A ⇒ B one can plausibly derive $\mathcal{A}$ ⇒ B. Analogy occupies the central area in the diagram in figure 2 because deriving new knowledge by analogy can be viewed formally as a combination of induction and deduction. Details on this idea are in section 7.

4. Knowledge transmutations

As stated earlier, transmutations are generic patterns of knowledge change, and their instantiations can be viewed as operators in knowledge spaces. A transmutation may change some aspect of the input knowledge, derive new knowledge, or perform certain manipulations on knowledge that do not change its content. Formally, a transmutation can be viewed as a transformation that takes as arguments a set of sentences (S), a set of entities (E), and background knowledge (BK), and generates a new set of sentences (S'), and/or new set of entities (E'), and/or new background knowledge (BK'):

$$T: S, E, BK \rightarrow S', E', BK' \qquad (4)$$

Transmutations can be classified into two categories. In the first category are *knowledge-generation* transmutations that change informational content of the input knowledge. Such transmutations represent patterns of inference. For example, they may derive consequences from given knowledge, suggest new hypothetical knowledge, determine relationships among knowledge components, confirm or disconfirm given knowledge, perform mathematical operations on quantitative knowledge, organize knowledge into certain structures, etc. Knowledge-generation transmutations are performed on statements that have a truth status.

In the second category are *knowledge-manipulation* transmutations that view input knowledge as data or objects to be manipulated. They can be performed on statements (well-formed logical expressions) or on terms (sets). They include inserting (deleting) knowledge components into (from) give knowledge structures, physically transmitting or copying knowledge to/from other knowledge bases, or ordering knowledge components according to some syntactic criteria.

Transmutations are typically bidirectional operations, that is, they can be grouped into pairs of opposite operators, except for derivations that span a range of transmutations; the endpoints of this range are opposites. Below is a summary of knowledge transmutations that have been identified in the theory as frequently occuring in human reasoning or machine learning algorithms. This is not an exhaustive list; further research will likely identify other transmutations. The first eight groups represent knowledge-generation transmutations, and the remaining ones represent knowledge-manipulation transmutations. It should be noted that these transmutations can be applied to all kinds of knowledge expressed in a declarative way—specific facts, general statements, metaknowledge, control knowledge, or goals.

1. *Generalization/specialization*. The generalization transmutation extends the reference set of the input, that is, it generates a description that characterizes a larger reference set than the input. Typically, the underlying inference is inductive, that is, the extended set is inductively hypothesized. Generalization can also be deductive, when the more general description is deductively derived from the more specific one using background knowledge. It can also be analogical, when the more general description is hypothesized through analogy to a generalization performed on a similar reference set. The opposite transmutation is *specialization*, which narrows the reference set. Specialization usually employs deductive inference, but there can also be an inductive or analogical specialization.

2. *Abstraction/concretion*. Abstraction reduces the amount of detail in a description of the given reference set. It may change the description language to one that uses more abstract concepts or operators, which ignore details irrelevant to the reasoner's goal. The underlying inference is typically deduction. An opposite transmutation is *concretion*, which generates additional details about the reference set.

3. *Similization/dissimilization*. *Similization* derives new knowledge about a reference set on the basis of the similarity between this set and another reference set about which the learner has more knowledge. The similization is based on analogical inference. The opposite operation is *dissimilization*, which derives new knowledge on the basis of the lack of similarity between the compared reference sets. These transmutations are based on the patterns of inference presented in the theory of plausible reasoning by Collins and Michalski (1989). For example, knowing that England grows roses and that England and Holland have similar climates, a similization transmutation is to hypothesize that Holland may also grow roses. An underlying background knowledge here is that there exists a dependency between the climate of a place and the type of plants growing in that location. A dissimilization transmutation is to infer that bougainvilleas probably do not grow in Holland, because Holland has very different climate from the Caribbean Islands where they are very popular. These transmutations are based on analogical inference, which can be characterized as a combination of inductive and deductive inference (see section 7).

4. *Association/disassociation*. The association transmutation determines a dependency between given entities or descriptions based on the observed facts and/or background knowledge. The dependency may be logical, causal, statistical, temporal, etc. Associating a concept instance with a concept name is an example of an association transmutation.

The opposite transmutation is *disassociation*, which asserts a lack of dependency. For example, determining that a given instance is not an example of some concept is a disassociation transmutation.

5. *Selection/generation*. The selection transmutation selects a subset from a set of entities (e.g., a set of knowledge components) that satisfies some criteria. For example, choosing a subset of relevant attributes from a set of candidates, or determining the most plausible hypothesis among a set of candidate hypotheses, is a selection transmutation. The opposite transmutation is *generation*, which generates entities of a given type. For example, generating an attribute to characterize a given entity, or creating an alternative hypothesis to the one already generated, is a form of generation transmutation.

6. *Agglomeration/decomposition*. The agglomeration transmutation groups entities into larger units according to some goal criterion. If it also hypotheses that the larger units represent general patterns in data, then it is called *clustering*. The grouping can be done according to a variety of principles, e.g., to maximize some mathematical notion of similarity, as in conventional clustering, or to maximize "conceptual cohesiveness," as in conceptual clustering (e.g., Stepp & Michalski, 1983). The opposite transmutation is a *decomposition*, which splits a group (or a structure) of entities into subgroups, according to some goal criterion.

7. *Characterization/discrimination*. A *characterization* transmutation determines a *characteristic* description of a given set of entities, which differentiates these entities from any other entities. A simple form of such a description is a list (or a conjunction) of all properties shared by the entities of the given set. The opposite transmutation is *discrimination*, which determines a description that discriminates the given set of entities from another set of entities (Michalski, 1983).

8. *Derivations: Reformulation/intermediate transmutations/randomization. Derivations* are transmutations that derive one piece of knowledge from another piece of knowledge (based on some dependency between them), but do not fall into the special categories described above. Because the dependency between knowledge components can range from logical equivalence to random relationship, derivations can be classified on the basis of the strength of dependency into a wide range of forms. The extreme points of this range are *reformulation* and *randomization*. Reformulation transforms a segment of knowledge (a set of conceptually related sentences) into a logically equivalent segment of knowledge. For example, mapping a geometrical object represented in a right-angled coordinate system into a radial coordinate system is a reformulation. In contrast, randomization transforms one knowledge segment to another one by making random changes. For example, the *mutation* operation in a genetic algorithm represents a randomization. Deductive derivation, abductive explanation, and prediction can be viewed as intermediate derivations. Mathematical or logical transformations of knowledge also represent forms of derivations. A weak intermediate derivation is the *crossover* operator used in genetic algorithms, which derives new knowledge by exchanging two segments of related knowledge components.

9. *Insertion/deletion*. The insertion transmutation inserts a given knowledge component (e.g., a component generated by some other transmutation) into a given knowledge structure. The opposite transmutation is *deletion*, which removes some knowledge component from a given structure. An example of deletion is forgetting.

10. *Replication/destruction*. Replication reproduces a knowledge structure residing in some knowledge base in another knowledge base. Replication is used, e.g., in *rote learning*. There is no change of the contents of the knowledge structure. The opposite transmutation is *destruction*, which removes a knowledge structure from a given knowledge base. The difference between destruction and deletion is that destruction removes a copy of a knowledge structure that resides in some knowledge base, while deletion removes a component of a knowledge structure residing in the given knowledge base.

11. *Sorting/unsorting*. The sorting transmutation changes the organization of knowledge according to some criterion. For example, ordering decision rules in a rule base from the shortest (having the smallest number of conditions) to the longest is a sorting transmutation. An opposite operation is *unsorting*, which is returning to the previous organization.

Figure 3 provides a summary of the above transmutations together with the underlying types of inference. It is postulated that, depending on the amount of available background knowledge and the way that the input and the background knowledge are employed, any knowledge-generation transmutation can be, in principle, accomplished by any type of inference, i.e., deduction, induction, or analogy. Figure 3 illustrates this by linking these transmutations with all three forms of inference. Exceptions to this rule are similization and dissimilization, which are based on analogy (analogy is viewed as deduction and induction combined). A vertical link between lines stemming from the nodes denoting similarity/dissimilarity transmutations signifies that these transmutations combine deduction with induction (for an explanation, see section 7).

Transmutations that employ induction, analogy, or contingent deduction increase the amount of *intrinsic* knowledge in the system. By intrinsic knowledge we mean knowledge that cannot be conclusively deduced from other knowledge in the system. Learning that changes the amount of the system's intrinsic knowledge is called *synthetic* (it has been also called "learning at the knowledge level" (Newell, 1981; Dietterich, 1986)). Transmutations that employ only conclusive deduction increase the amount of *derived* knowledge in the system. Such knowledge is a logical consequence of what the learner already knows. Learning that changes only the amount of derived knowledge in the system is called *analytic* (Michalski & Kodratoff, 1990).

In actual use, different transmutations are typically performed using only one type of inference. For example, generalization and agglomeration are typically done through induction, and specialization and abstraction through deduction.

Generalization can also be deductive (as, e.g., in explanation-based generalization), or analogical (when a more general description is derived by an analogy to some other generalization transformation). Specialization is typically deductive, but it can also be inductive or analogical.

Thus, the theory views transmutations as different types of change in knowledge, and inferences as different ways in which these changes can be accomplished. This is a radical departure from the traditional view of these issues. The traditional view blurs the proposed distinctions; for example, it typically equates generalization with induction, and specialization with deduction.

The proposed view stems from our efforts to provide an explanation of different operations on knowledge observed in people's reasoning and to relate this explanation to formal types of inference in a consistent way. Experiments performed with human subjects have

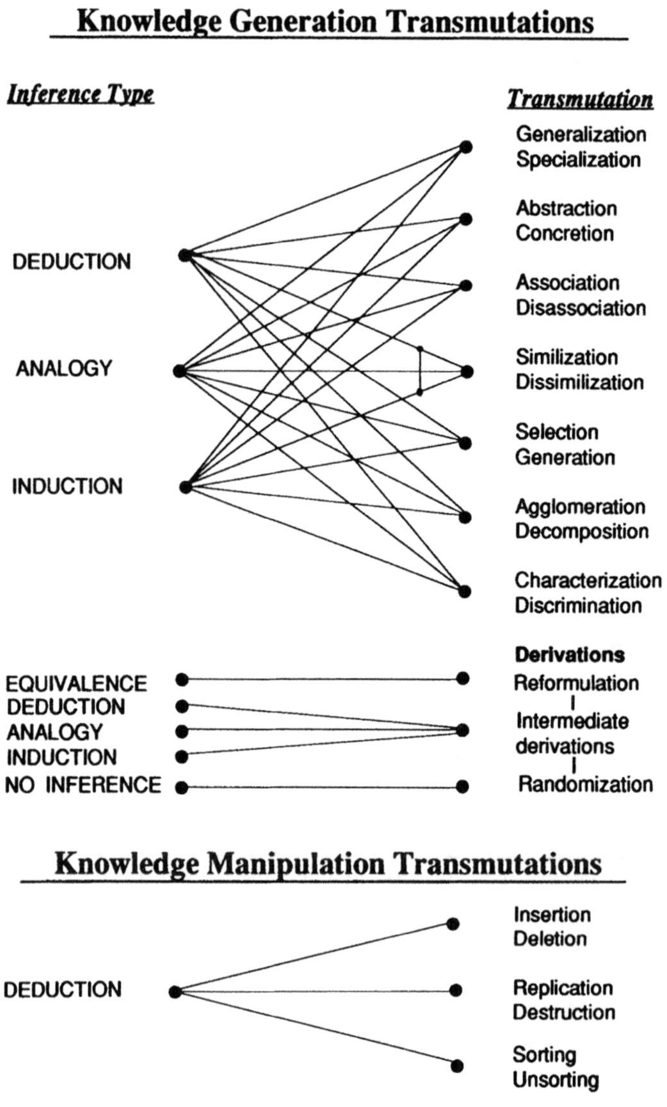

Figure 3. A summary of transmutations and the underlying types of inference.

shown that the proposed ideas agree well with typical intuitions people have about different types of transmutations. Further research is needed to formalize these ideas precisely.

The theory views learning as a sequence of goal-oriented knowledge transmutations. For example, a generation transmutation may generate a set of attributes to characterize given entities. Another generation transmutation may create examples expressed in terms of these attributes. A general description of these examples is created by a generalization transmutation. By repeating different variants of a generalization transmutation, a set of alternative general descriptions of these examples can be determined. A selection transmutation would choose the "best" candidate description according to a criterion specified by the given learning goal. If a new example contradicts the description, a specialization transmutation would produce a new description that takes care of the inconsistency. The description obtained may be added to the knowledge base by an insertion transmutation. A replication transmutation may then copy this description into another knowledge base.

The next section analyzes those transmutations that employ inductive inference, which are fundamental for the creation of instrinsically new knowledge.

5. Admissible induction and inductive transmutations

As described in section 3, induction produces a premise (a fact, a rule, a set of sentences, a theory, etc.) that together with BK entails a given consequent. In the case of inductive generalization, the entailment is guaranteed by the set–superset relationship between the input and output. In the case of abduction, the entailment is due to the implicative domain-dependent relationship that is being traced backward. For any given consequent C and non-trivial BK, one can generate a potentially infinite number of hypotheses that together with BK entail C, but only a few of them may be of any interest. One is usually interested only in "simple," "justifiable," and/or "plausible" hypotheses. Therefore, to limit the choices, an *admissible induction* is defined by adding constraints to the definition of induction in section 3.

Definition. Given a consequent C and background knowledge BK, an admissible induction hypothesizes a premise P, consistent with BK, such that

$$P \cup BK \models C \qquad (5)$$

and P satisfies the *hypothesis selection criterion.*

The selection criterion specifies how to choose a hypothesis among all candidates satisfying (5), and may be a combination of several elementary criteria. In different contexts, or for different forms of induction, the selection criterion has been called a *preference criterion* (Popper, 1972; Michalski, 1983), a *bias* (Utgoff, 1986; Grosof & Russell, 1989) and a *comparator* (Poole 1989). Ideally, the selection criterion should reflect the properties of a hypothesis that are desirable from the viewpoint of the learner's goals, rather than be influenced by the properties of a particular induction method.

In some learning programs, a part of the selection criterion may be hidden in the description language used (a "description language bias"). For example, an inductive program may use a description language that is limited to only conjunctive statements involving attributes from a predefined set. Therefore any hypothesis generated will have to be in this form. Often, the selection criterion relates to the knowledge representation used. For example, when learning decision trees, the selection criterion may seek trees with a small number of nodes (by choosing at each step the locally most informative attribute); when learning DNF descriptions, it may seek the shortest DNF descriptions.

There are three generally desirable characteristics of a hypothesis: *plausibility, utility,* and *generality.* The plausibility expresses a desire to find a "true" hypothesis. Because the problem is logically underconstrained, the "truth" of a hypothesis cannot be guaranteed in principle. To satisfy equation (5) a hypothesis has to be *complete* and *consistent* with regard to the input facts (Michalski, 1983). Experiments have shown, however, that in situations where the input contains errors or noise, an inconsistent and/or incomplete hypothesis (with regard to the input) will often lead to a better overall predictive performance than a complete and consistent one (e.g., Bergadano et al., 1992). The utility criterion requires a hypothesis to be simple to express and easy to apply to the expected set of problems. The generality criterion seeks a hypothesis that can predict a large range of new cases.

The view of induction described above is more general than the one often expressed in machine learning literature. It is also consistent with many long-standing thoughts on this subject going back to Aristotle (e.g., Adler & Gorman, 1987; Aristotle, 1987). Aristotle, and many subsequent thinkers, e.g., Bacon (1620), Whewell (1857), Cohen (1970), Popper (1972), and others, viewed induction as a fundamental inference for all processes of creating new knowledge. They did not limit it—as is sometimes done—to only inductive empirical generalization.

Induction underlies a number of knowledge transmutations, such as *inductive generalization, inductive specialization, abductive derivation,* and *concretion* (not a complete list). The first two were illustrated in section 3. The other two are illustrated below.

In principle, all knowledge-generation transmutations described in section 4 can have a form involving inductive inference. Inductive generalization is central to many learning processes. As mentioned earlier, it extends the reference set described, e.g., it extends a set of training concept examples to the set of all concept instances. Such an operation can be done with or without changing the description space.

If generalization is done without change of description space (i.e., without modifying descriptors or introducing new descriptors), then generalization is called *empirical* or *selective.* If generalization is done by changing the description space into a more problem-oriented one (e.g., some initially given descriptors are modified or removed, and new descriptors added), then generalization is called *constructive* (Michalski, 1983; Wnek & Michalski, 1991a). (See figure 4 for an example.)

Another form of inductive transmutation is inductive specialization, which decreases the reference set described in the input. Typically, a generalization is inductive and a specialization is deductive. However, depending on the way the input is transformed, a generalization transmutation may also be deductive, and a specialization transmutation may also be inductive (as shown in figure 4). Both generalization and specialization transmutations may also be analogical when the description of an extended or contracted reference set is hypothesized by analogy. Abuductive derivation derives an explanation of properties of a given reference set. Concretion is the opposite of abstraction (see the next section). It hypothesizes more specific information about a given reference set.

Figure 4 presents examples of the above transmutations. In the examples, to indicate that some m-implications are not conclusive (not logical implications) but are sufficiently strong to warrant consideration (characterize a tendency), the symbol $\leftrightarrow$ is used. The parameter α stands here for "maybe." Given an input and BK, there are usually many possible inductive transmutations of them; here we list one of each type—the one that is normally perceived as the most "natural." The first, third, and fourth example in figure 4 represent conclusive

• ***Empirical inductive generalization***
(Background knowledge-limited)

Input:	Pntng(GF, Dwski) ⇒ Btfl(GF)	(Dawski's paintings, "A girl's face" and
	Pntng(LC, Dwski) ⇒ Btfl(LC)	"Lvov's cathedral," are beautiful)
BK:	∀x,P(x) ⇒ P(a)	(The universal specialization rule: short form)
Output:	∀x,Pntng(x, Dwski) ⇒ Btfl(x): α	(*Maybe* all Dawski's paintings are beautiful)

• ***Constructive inductive generalization (generalization + deductive derivation)***
(Background knowledge-intensive)

Input:	Pntng(GF, Dwski) ⇒ Btfl(GF)	(Dawski's paintings, "A girl's face" and
	Pntng(LC, Dwski) ⇒ Btfl(LC)	"Lvov's cathedral," are beautiful)
BK:	∀x,y, Pntng(x,y)&Btfl(x) <—> Exp(x)	(Btfl pntngs tend to be expensive & opposite)
Output:	∀x,Pntng(x, Dwski) ⇒ Exp(x): α	(*Maybe* all Dawski's paintings are expensive)

• ***Inductive specialization***

Input:	Lives(John, Virginia)	(John lives in Virginia)
BK:	Fairfax ⊂ Virginia	(Fairfax is a "subset" of Virginia)
	∀x,y,z, y ⊂ z&Lives(x,y)⇒Lives(x,z)	(Living in x implies living in superset of x)
Output:	Lives(John, Fairfax): α	(*Maybe* John lives in Fairfax)

• ***Concretion***

Input:	Going-to(John, New York)	(John is going to New York)
BK:	Likes(John, driving)	(John likes driving)
	∀x,y, Driving(x,y) ⇒ Going-to(x,y)	("Driving to" is a special case of "going to.")
	∀x,y, Likes(x,driving)⇒Driving(x,y)	(Liking to drive m-implies driving to places)
Output:	Driving(John, New York): α	(*Maybe* John is driving to New York)

• ***Abductive derivation***

Input:	In(House, Smoke)	(There is smoke in the house)
BK:	In(x, Smoke) <--> In(x, Fire)	(Smoke usually indicates fire &conversely)
Output:	In(House, Fire): α	(*Maybe* there is fire in the house)

• ***Constructive inductive generalization (generalization plus abduction)***

Input:	In(John'sApt, Smoke)	(Smoke is in John's apartment)
BK:	In(x, Smoke) <--> In(x, Fire)	(Smoke usually indicates fire &conversely)
	John'sApt ⊂ GKBld	(John's apt. is in the Golden Key building)
Output:	In(GKBld, Fire): α	(*Maybe* there is fire in the Golden Key bld)

Figure 4. Examples of inductive transmutations.

induction (in which the hypothesis with BK strongly implies the input); the second and the last two examples represent contingent induction. The second example would be a conclusive induction, if the rule in BK were

$$\forall x,\ y\ (\text{Pntng}(x,\ y)\ \&\ \text{Btfl}(x)\ \Leftrightarrow\ \text{Exp}(x){:}\ \alpha\ =\ \text{usually},\ \beta\ =\ 1$$

("All beautiful paintings are usually expensive, but expensive paintings are always beautiful"), which does not reflect the facts in real life. In the examples, the subset symbol "⊂" is used under the assumption that cities, states, apartments, and buildings can be viewed as sets of space parcels.

6. Generalization vs. abstraction

This section analyzes two fundamental knowledge-generation transmutations, namely, generalization and abstraction, and their opposites, specialization and concretion, respectively. Generalization and abstraction are sometimes confused with each other; therefore we provide an analysis of the differences between them. We start with generalization and specialization.

6.1. Generalization and specialization

As stated earlier, our view of generalization is that it is a knowledge transmutation that extends the reference set of a given description. Depending on the background knowledge and the way it is used, generalization can be inductive, deductive, or analogical. Such a view of generalization is more general than the one traditionally expressed in the machine learning literature, which recognizes only one form of generalization, namely, inductive generalization.

Based on experiments with human subjects, we claim that the view presented here more adequately captures the common intuitions and the natural language usage of the term "generalization." To express the proposed view rigorously, let us provide a more precise definition of the reference set.

Suppose S is a set of statements in predicate logic calculus. Suppose further that an argument of one or more predicates in statements in S stands for a set of entities, and that S is interpreted as a description of this set.

Under this interpretation, the set of entities described by S is called the *reference set* for S. If the reference set is replaced by a set-valued variable, then the resulting expression is called a *descriptive schema*, and denoted D[R], where R stands for the reference set. For example, suppose given is a statement:

S: In(John'sApt, Smoke) (Smoke is in John's apartment.)

This statement can be interpreted as a description of the set {John'sApt}. Thus we have

D[R]: In (R, Smoke)
R: John'sApt.

For a given statement, if one ignores the context in which it is used, there could be more than one reference set and the corresponding descriptive schema. For example, consider the statement: "George Mason lived at Gunston Hall." It can be interpreted as a description of "George Mason" (a singleton set), which specifies the place where he lived. It can also be interpreted as a description of "Gunston Hall," which specifies a property of this place, namely, that George Mason lived there. The appropriate interpretation of a statement depends on the context in which it is used. For example, in the context of a discussion about George Mason, the first interpretation would apply; but if Gunston Hall is the object of a discussion, the second interpretation would apply.

Suppose two sets of statements, S1 and S2, are given that can be interpreted as having reference sets R1 and R2 and descriptive schemes D1 and D2, respectively, i.e., S1 = D1[R1] and S2 = D2[R2]

Definition. The statement set S2 is more *general* than statement set S1 if and only if

$$R2 \supset R1 \text{ and}$$

$$D2[R2] \cup BK \Rightarrow D1[R1] \qquad (5')$$

$$D1[R1] \cup BK \Rightarrow D2[R2] \qquad (5'')$$

If condition (5′) holds, S2 is an *inductive* generalization of S1; if condition (5″) holds, S2 is a *deductive* generalization of S1. By requiring that the compared statements satisfy an implicative relation in the context of given background knowledge, the definition allows one to compare the generality of statements that use different descriptive concepts or languages.

Let us illustrate the above definition using examples from section 5.

Example 1. (*Empirical inductive generalization*)

S1:	Pntng(GF, Dwski) & Btfl(GF)	(Dawski's painting, "A girl's face," is beautiful.)
D1[R1]:	Pntng(R1, Dwski) & Btfl(R1)	
R1:	GF	(GF is a singleton, {Girl's face})
S2:	$\forall$x, Pntng(x, Dwski) $\Rightarrow$ Btfl(x)	(All Dawski's paintings are beautiful.)
	Alternatively: Btfl(All_DPs)	(All_DPs denotes the set of all Dawski's paintings.)
D2[R2]:	Btfl(R2)	(Paintings from the set R2 are beautiful.)
R2:	All_DPs	(All Dawski's paintings.)
BK:	GF $\subset$ All_DPs	

The interpretation of the predicate Btfl(R) is that the property Btfl applies to every element of the set R. Since R2 $\supset$ R1, and D2[R2] $\Rightarrow$ D1[R1], then S2 is more general than S1.

Example 2. (*Deductive generalization*)

S1:	Lives(John, Fairfax)	(John lives in Fairfax.)
D1[R1]:	Lives(John, R1)	
R1:	Fairfax	
S2:	Lives(John, Virginia)	(John lives in Virginia.)
D2[R2]:	Lives(John, R2)	
R2:	Virginia	
BK:	Fairfax $\subset$ Virginia	

S2 is more general than S1 because R2 $\supset$ R1, and D1[R1] $\cup$ BK $\Rightarrow$ D2[R2].

In human reasoning, generalization is frequently combined with other types of transmutations producing various composite transmutations. Here is an example of such a composite transmutation.

Example 3. (*Inductive generalization and abduction*)

S1:	In(John'sApt, Smoke)	(There is smoke in John's apartment.)
D1[R1]:	In (R1, Smoke)	
R1:	John'sApt	
BK:	In(x, Smoke) $\leftrightarrow$ In(x, Fire)	
	John'sApt $\subset$ GKBldng	
S2:	In(GKBldng, Fire)	(There is fire in Golden Key Building.)
D2[R2]:	In(R2, Fire)	
R2:	GKBldng	

In this example, a generalization transmutation of the input produces a statement "Smoke is in the Golden Key building." An abductive derivation (also called abductive explanation) applied to the same input would produce a statement "There is fire in John's apartment." By applying abductive derivation to the outptut from generalization, one obtains a statement "There is fire in Golden Key building."

The above definition defined a generalization relation only between two sets of statements. Let us now extend this definition to the case in which the input may be a collection of sets of statements. Such a case occurs in learning rules that generalize a set of examples (each example may be described by one or more statements.).

Definition. The statement set, S, is a *generalization of a collection of statement sets* $\{S_i\}$, $i = 1, 2, .. k$, if and only if S is more general than each S_i.

Summarizing, a generalization transmutation is a mapping from one description (input) to another description (output) that extends the reference set of the input. Depending on the background knowledge, such an operation can be inductive or deductive.

A transmutation opposite to generalization is *specialization*, which reduces the reference set of a given set of statements. A typical form of specialization is deductive, but there can also be an inductive specialization. For example, a reverse of the inductive specialization in figure 4 is a deductive generalization:

Input:	Lives(John, Fairfax)	(John lives in Fairfax.)
BK:	Fairfax $\subset$ Virginia	(Fairfax is a "subset" of Virginia.)
	$\forall$x, y, z, y $\subset$ z & Lives(x,y) $\Rightarrow$ Lives(x, z)	(Living in y implies living in a superset of y.)
Output:	Lives(John, Virginia)	(John lives in Virginia.)

In the above example, Fairfax and Virginia are interpreted as reference sets (sets of land parcels). The Input states that a property of Fairfax is that "John lives there." The property "Living in a set of land parcels" means occupying some elements of this set. This is *an existential property* of a set, which is defined as a property that applies only to some unspecified elements of the set. If a set has such property, then so do its supersets. This is why the above inference is deductive.

In contrast, a *universal property* of a set applies to all elements of the set. If a set has such a property, so does its every subset, but not every superset. Thus, if in the above example a "universal property" was used, e.g., "Soil(good, Fairfax)," a generalization transmutation to "Soil(good, Virginia)" would be inductive.

Generalization/specialization transmutations are related to another type of transmutations, namely, abstraction/concretion. Transmutations of these two types often co-occur in commonsense reasoning; therefore they are easy to confuse with each other. By changing the interpretation of an input statement (i.e., by differently assigning the reference set and descriptive schema in a statement), deductive generalization can often be *reinterpreted* as abstraction. Abstraction and concretion transmutations are analyzed below.

6.2. Abstraction and concretion

Abstraction reduces the amount of information conveyed by a description of a set of entities (the reference set). The purpose of abstraction is to reduce the amount of information about the reference set in such a way that the information relevant to the learner's goal is preserved and the irrelevant information is discarded. For example, abstraction may transfer a description from one language to another language in which the properties of the reference set relevant to the reasoner's goal are preserved, but other properties are not. An opposite operation to abstraction is *concretion*, which generates additional details about a given reference set.

A simple form of abstraction is to replace a specific attribute value (e.g., the length in centimeters) in the description of an entity by a less specific value (e.g., the length stated in linguistic terms, such as short, medium, or long). A complex abstraction would be, e.g., to take a description of a computer in terms of electronic circuits and connections, and, based on background knowledge, change it into a description in terms of the functions of major components. Typically, abstraction is a form of deductive transmutation, because it preserves the important information in the input and does not hypothesize any information (this latter possibility may occur when the input or BK contain uncertain information).

Let us express this view of abstraction more formally. An early formal definition of abstraction was proposed by Plaisted (1981), who considered it as a mapping between languages that preserves instances and negation. A related but somewhat different view was presented by Giordana, Saitta, and Roverso (1991), who consider abstraction as a mapping between abstract models. In the view presented here, abstraction is a mapping between descriptions based on background knowledge. Specifically, it is a knowledge transmutation that creates a less detailed description from a more detailed description of the same set of entities (the reference set), using the same or other terms. Unlike generalization, it does not change the reference set, but only changes the description of it.

Suppose given are two sets of expressions, S1 and S2, that can be interpreted as having descriptive schemes D1 and D2, respectively, and the same reference set, R.

Definition. S2 is more *abstract* than S1 *in the context* of background knowledge BK, and with *the degree of strength* α, if and only if

$$D1[R] \cup BK \Rightarrow D2[R]: \alpha, \text{ where } \alpha \geq Th \quad (6)$$

and there is a homomorphic mapping between the set of properties specified in D1, and the set of properties specified in D2. The threshold Th denotes a limit of acceptability of transformation as abstraction.

The last condition is needed to exclude arbitrary deductive derivations. The most common form of abstraction is when (6) is a standard (conclusive) implication ($\alpha = 1$). In this case, the set of strong inferences (deductive closure) that can be derived from the output (abstract) description and BK is a proper subset of strong inferences that can be derived from the input description and BK. This case can be called a *strong* abstraction, in contrast to *weak* abstraction, which occurs when $\alpha < 1$.

An example of weak absraction is when a picture of a table seen from one side (without seeing all legs) is transformed to a sketch of this table from a somewhat different side, showing four legs. When inference goals are defined, a "good" abstraction should preserve the inferences that are important to the goals and ignore those that are not. Comparing (5) and (6), one can see that an abstraction transmutation can be a part of an inductive generalization transmutation. For that reason, these two transmutations are sometimes confused with each other.

6.3. An illustration of the difference between abstraction and generalization

Let us illustrate the difference between abstraction and generalization by a simple example. Consider a statement $d(\{r_i\}, v)$, saying that descriptor d takes value v for entities from the set $\{r_i\}$. Thus, the reference set of this statement is $R = \{r_i\}$, $i = 1, 2, \ldots$, and a descriptive schema is $D[R] = d(R, v)$. Let us write the above statement in the form that illustrates syntactically the difference between the reference set and a descriptor value:

$$d(R) = v \tag{7}$$

Changing (7) to $d(R) = v'$, where v' represents a more general concept, e.g., a parent node in a generalization hierarchy of values of the attribute d, is an abstraction transmutation. Changing (7) to a statement $d(R') = v$, in which R' is a superset of R, is a generalization operation.

For example, transferring the statement "color(my-pencil) = light-blue" into "color(my-pencil) = blue" is an abstraction operation. To see this, notice that {[color(my-pencil) = light-blue]} & (light-blue ⊂ blue) ⇒ [color(my-pencil) = blue]. Transforming the original statement into "color(all-my-pencils) = light-blue" is a generalization operation. Finally, transferring the original statement into "color(all-my-pencils) = blue" is both generalization and abstraction. In other words, associating the same property with a larger set is a generalization; associating less information with the same set is an abstraction operation. Combining the two is a composite transmutation.

An opposite transmutation to abstraction is concretion, which increases the amount of information that is conveyed by a statement about the given set of entities (reference set).

The two pairs of mutually opposite transmutations, i.e., {generalization, specialization} and {abstraction, concretion}, differ by the aspects of knowledge they change. If a transmutation changes the size of the reference set of a description, then it is *generalization* or *specialization*. If a transmutation changes the amount of information (detail) conveyed by a description of a reference set, then it is *abstraction* or *concretion*. In other words, generalization (specialization) transforms descriptions along the set-superset (set-subset) direction, and is typically falsity-preserving (truth-preserving). In contrast, abstraction (concretion) transforms descriptions along the more-to-less-detail (less-to-more-detail) direction, and is typically truth-preserving (falsity-preserving). Generalization often uses the same description space (or language) for input and output statements, whereas abstraction often involves a change in the description space (or language).

7. Similization vs. dissimilization

The similization transmutation uses analogical inference to derive new knowledge. A dissimilization transmutation derives new knowledge based on a lack of analogy. As mentioned in section 2, analogical reasoning can be considered as a combination of inductive and deductive inference. Before we demonstrate this claim, let us observe that an important part of our knowledge is dependencies among various entities in the world. These dependencies can be of different strengths or types, such as functional, monotonic, correlational, general trend, etc. For example, we know that the dimensions of a rectangle exactly determine its area (this is a unidirectional functional dependency), that smoking causes lung cancer (this is a weakly causal dependency), or that improving education of citizens is good for the country (this is an unquantified belief).

Such dependencies are often bidirectional, but the "strength" of the dependency in different directions may vary considerably. For example, from the fact that Martha is a heavy smoker one may develop an expectation that she will likely get lung cancer later in her life; from learning that Betty has lung cancer, one may hypothesize that perhaps she was a smoker. The "strength" of these conclusions, however, may be quite different. Betty may have lung cancer for other reasons, or perhaps she was only married to a smoker. The dependencies can be known at different levels of specificity. In the past, the dependency between smoking and lung cancer was only a general hypothesis; now we have a much more precise knowledge of this dependency.

Section 3 introduced the notion of mutual implication (equation (2)) to express a wide class of such relationships. In order to describe a similization transmutation, we will extend the notion of mutual implication into a more general *mutual dependency*. As defined earlier, mutual implication expresses a relationship between two predicate logic statements (well-formed formulas; closed predicate logic sentences with no free variables). A mutual dependency expresses a relationship between two *sentences* that are both either predicate logic statements or term expressions (open predicate logic sentences, in which some of the arguments are free variables).

To state that there is a mutual dependency (*m-dependency*) between two sentences S1 and S2, we write

$$S1 \Leftrightarrow S2{:}\ \alpha,\ \beta \tag{8}$$

where merit parameters α and β represent an overall *forward strength* and *backward strength* of the dependency, respectively. α and β represent the average certainty with which a value of S1 determines a value of S2, and conversely.

If S1 and S2 are statements (well-formed formulas), then m-dependency is an m-implication. If S1 and S2 are term expressions, then mutual dependency expresses a relationship between functions (since term expressions can be interpreted as functions). If terms expressions in a mutual dependency are discrete functions, then mutual dependency is logically equivalent to a set of mutual implications. A special case of m-dependency is *determination*, introduced by Russell (1989), and used for characterizing a class of analogical inferences. Determination is an m-dependency between term expressions in which α is 1, and β is unspecified, that is, a unidirectional functional m-dependency.

The concpet of m-dependency allows us to describe similization and dissimilization transmutations. These transmutations involve determining a *similarity* or *dissimilarity* between entities, and then given some knowledge about one entity, hypothesizing some new knowledge about another entity. The concept of similarity is sometimes misunderstood and viewed as an objective, context-independent property of objects. In reality, the similarity between any two entities is highly context dependent. Any two entities (objects, sets of objects, behaviors, etc.) can be viewed as boundlessly similar or boundlessly dissimilar, depending on what descriptors are used to characterize them, or, in other words, what properties are used to compare the entities. Therefore to talk meaningfully about a similarity between entities, one needs to indicate, explicitly or implicitly, the relevant descriptors. To capture this idea, we employ the concept of the *similarity in the context* introduced by Collins and Michalski (1989). To say that entities *El E2* are similar in context CTX (which defines relevant descriptors D), we write

$$\text{E1 SIM E2 in CTX(D)} \tag{9}$$

This statement says that values of the descriptors from the set D for the entity El and for the entity E2 differ no more than by some assumed tolerance threshold. For numerical descriptors, the theshold "Th" can be expressed as a percentage, relative to the larger value. For example, if Th = 10%, the values of the descriptor cannot differ more than 10%, relative to the larger value. Descriptors in D can be attributes, relations, functions, or any transformations applicable to the entities under consideration. The threshold expresses the required degree of similarity for triggering the inference.

The similization transmutation is a form of analogical inference, and is defined by the following schema:

Input: El ⇒ A
BK: El SIM E2 in CTX(D)
D ⇒ A: α > RT
———————————
Output: E2 ⇒ A (10)

where α> RT states that the strength of the forward term dependency D ⇒ A should be above a *relevance threshold*, RT, in order to trigger the inference. RT is a control parameter for the inference.

Given that entity El has property A, and knowing that there is a similarity between El and E2 in terms of descriptors defined by D, the rule hypothesizes that entity E2 may also have property A. This inference is allowed, however, only if there is a dependency between the property A and descriptors defined by D. The reason for the latter condition can be illustrated by the following example. Suppose we know that some person who is handsome and has received their Ph.D. from MIT. It would not be reasonable to hypothesize that another person who we find handsome also received their Ph.D. from MIT. The reason is that we do not expect any dependency between looks of a person and the university from which that person gets a Ph.D. degree.

A dissimilization transmutation draws an inference from the knowledge that two entities are very different in the context of some descriptors. A dissimilization transmutation follows the schema

$$\begin{array}{ll} \textit{Input:} & E1 \Rightarrow A \\ \textit{BK:} & E1 \text{ DIS } E2 \text{ in } CTX(D) \\ & D \Rightarrow A: \alpha > RT \\ \hline \textit{Output:} & E2 \Rightarrow \sim A \end{array} \qquad (11)$$

where DIS denotes a relation of dissimilarity, and other parameters are as in (10).

Given that some entity E1 has property A, and knowing that entities E1 and E2 are very different in terms of descriptors that are in mutual dependency relation to A, the transmutation hypothesizes that maybe E2 does not have the property A.

The following simple example illustrates dissimilarity transmutation. Suppose we are told that apples grow in Poland. Knowing that apples are different from oranges in a number of ways, including the climate they require in order to grow, and that the climate of the area is m-dependent on the type of fruit grown there, one may hypothesize that perhaps oranges do not grow in Poland. Other examples of dissimilization are discussed by Collins and Michalski (1989).

Let us now illustrate the similization transmutation by a real-world example, and then demonstrate that it can be viewed as a combination of inductive and deductive inference. To argue for a national, ultra-speed electronic communication network for linking industrial, governmental, and academic organizations in the U.S., its advocates used an analogy that "Building this network is an information equivalent of building national highways in the '50s and '60s," There is little physical similarity between building highways and electronic networks, but there is an end-effect similarity in that they both improve communication. Since building highways helped the country, and thus was a good decision, then by analogy, building the national network will help the country, and is also a good decision to make. Using the schema (10), we have:

$$\begin{array}{ll} \textit{Input:} & \text{Decision(Bld, NH) SIM Decision(Bld, NN) in CTX (FutCom)} \\ \textit{BK:} & \text{Decision(Bld, NH)} \Rightarrow \text{Effect-on(U.S., good)} \\ & \text{FutCom (US, x)} \Rightarrow \text{Effect-on(US, x)}: \alpha > RT \\ \hline \textit{Output:} & \text{Decision(Bld, NN)} \Rightarrow \text{Effect-on(US., good)} \end{array} \qquad (12)$$

where

NH—stands for National Highways
NN—stands for National Network
Decision(Bld, x)—a statement expressing the decision to build x
FutCom(area, state)—a descriptor expressing an evaluation of the future state of communication in the "area" that can take values: "will improve" or "will not improve"
Effect-on(US, x)—a descriptor stating that "the effect on the US is x."

We will now show how the general schema (10) can split into an inductive and deductive step.

An inductive step:

Input: E1 SIM E2 in CTX(D)
BK: D ⇔ A: α > RT

Output: E1 SIM E2 in CTX(D, A) (13)

From the similarity between two entities in terms of descriptor D, and a mutual dependency between the descriptor and some new term (descriptor) A, the schema hypothesizes a similarity between the entities in terms of D and A. The deductive step uses the hypothesized relationship of similarity to derive new knowledge.

A deductive step:

Input: E1 SIM E2 in CTX(D, A)
BK: E1 ⇒ A($\mathfrak{A}$)

Output: E2 ⇒ A($\mathfrak{A}'$) (14)

where A($\mathfrak{A}$) states that descriptor A takes value $\mathfrak{A}$, and $\mathfrak{A}$ is equal or sufficiently close (for the learner's goals) to $\mathfrak{A}'$.

Using the above schemes, we can now describe the previous example of similization in terms of an inductive and deductive step.

An inductive step:

Input: Decision(Bld, NH) SIM Decision(Bld, NN) in CTX (FutCom)
BK: FutCom(US, x) ⇒ Effect-on(US, x): α > RT

Output: Decision(Bld, NH) SIM Decision(Bld, NN) in CTX (FutCom, Effect-on) (15)

A deductive step:

Input: Decision(Bld, NH) SIM Decision(Bld, NN) in CTX (FutCom, Effect-on)
BK: Decision(Bld, NH) ⇒ Effect-on(US, good)

Output: Decision(Bld, NN) ⇒ Effect-on(US, good) (16)

From the knowledge that the decision to build national highways is similar to the decision to build national networks from the viewpoint of communication in the U.S., and that communication in the U.S. has an effect on the U.S., the inductive step hypothesizes that there may be a similarity between two decisions also in terms of their effect on the U.S. The deductive step uses this similarity to derive a conclusion that building NN will have a good effect on the U.S., because building highways had a good effect. The validity of the deductive step rests on the strength of the hypothesis generated in the inductive step.

Summarizing, a similization (dissimilization) transmutation, given knowledge about one entity, hypothesizes knowledge about another entity, if the other entity is similar (dissimilar) to the first entity. The similarity is measured in terms of properties or transformations characterizing the relationship among the entities. The above rule holds, however, only if the hypothesized properties are sufficiently related, by an m-dependency, to the properties used for defining the similarity.

8. Multistrategy task-adaptive learning

The ideas presented in previous sections provide a conceptual framework for *multistrategy task-adaptive learning* (MTL), which aims at integrating a whole range of learning strategies. A general underlying idea of MTL is that a learning system should by itself determine the learning strategy, i.e., the types of inference to be employed and/or the representational paradigm that is most suitable for the given learning task (Michalski, 1990; Tecuci & Michalski 1991a, b). As introduced in the Inferential Learning Theory, a learning task is defined by three components: what information is provided to the learner (i.e., *input* to the learning process), what the learner already knows that is relevant to the input (i.e., *background knowledge* (BK)), and what the learner wants to learn (i.e., the goal or goals of learning). Given an input, an MTL system analyzes its relationship to BK and the learning goals and on that basis determines a learning strategy or a combination of them. If an impasse occurs, a new learning task is assumed, and the learning strategy is determined accordingly.

The above characterization of MTL covers a wide range of systems, from "loosely coupled" systems that use the same representational paradigm and employ different inferential strategies as separate modules, to "tightly coupled" (or "deeply integrated") systems in which individual strategies represent instantiations of one general knowledge and inference mechanism, to *multirepresentational* multistrategy systems that can synergistically combine and adapt both the knowledge representation and inferential strategies to the learning task.

A general schema for Multistrategy Learning is presented in figure 5. The input to a learning process is supplied either by the External World through Sensors, or from a previous learning step.

The Control module directs all processes. The Actuators perform actions on the External World that are requested by the Control module, e.g., an action to get additional information. The input is filtered by the Selection module, which estimates the relevance of the input to the learning goal. Only information that is sufficiently relevant to the goal is passed through. The current learning goal is decided by the Control Module according to the information received from an external "master"' system, e.g., teacher, or from the analysis of goals residing in the learner's knowledge base. The knowledge base is called a Multitype Knowledge Base (MKB) to emphasize the fact that it may contain, in the general case, different types of knowlege (various forms of symbolic and/or numeric and/or iconic knowledge), which can be specified at different levels of abstraction.

Learning goals are organized into a *goal dependency network* (GDN), which captures the dependency between different goals. Goals are represented as nodes, and the dependency among goals by labeled links. The labels denote the type and the strength of dependency.

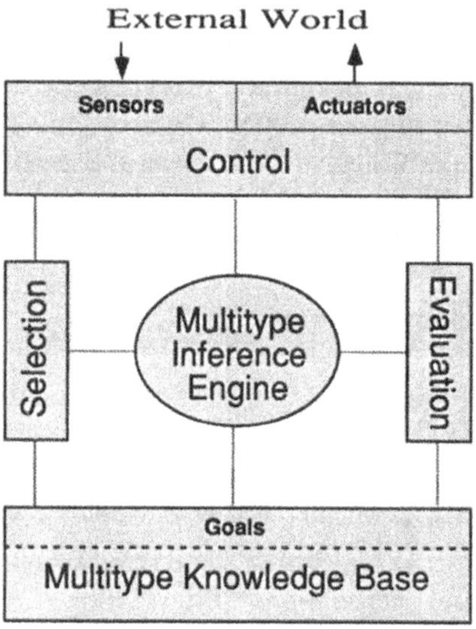

Figure 5. A general schema of a multistrategy task-adaptive learning (MTL) system.

If a goal Gl subsumes goal G2, then node Gl has an arrow pointing to node G2. For example, the goal "Learn rules characterizing concept examples" subsumes the goal "Find concept examples," and is subsumed by the goal "Use rules for recognizing unknown concept instances." The idea of a GDN network was introduced by Stepp and Michalski (1983) and was originally used for conceptual clustering.

In a general GDN for learning processes, the most general and domain-independent goal (represented by a node and no input links) is to store any given input and any plausible information that can be derived from it. More specific, though also domain-independent, goals are to learn certain types of knowledge.

For example, domain-independent goals may be to learn a general rule that characterizes facts supplied by the input, to reformulate a part of the learner's knowledge into a more efficient form, to determine knowledge needed for accomplishing some task, to develop a conceptual classification of given facts, to validate given knowledge, etc. Each of these goals is linked to some more specific subgoals. Some subgoals are domain dependent and call for determining some specific piece of knowledge, e.g., "learn basic facts about the Washington monument." Such a goal in turn subsumes a more specific goal, e.g., "learn the height of the Washington monument."

Any learning step starts with the goal either directly defined by an external source (e.g., a teacher, a failure to accomplish something, etc.) or determined by the analysis of the current learning situation. The control module dynamically activates new goals in the GDN as the learning process proceeds. The Multitype Inference Engine performs various types of inferences/transmutations required by the Control module in search for the knowledge specified by the current goal. Any knowledge generated is evaluated and critiqued by the Evaluation module from the viewpoint of the learning goal. If the knowledge satisfies the Evaluation module, it is assimilated into the MKB. It can then be used in subsequent learning processes.

Developing a learning system that would have all the features described above is a very complex problem, and thus a long-term goal. Current research explores more limited approaches to multistrategy-task adaptive learning. One such approach is based on building *plausible justification trees* (see the article by Tecuci in this issue).

Another approach, called *dynamic task analysis*, is outlined below. The learning system analyzes the dynamically changing relationship between the input, the background knowledge, and the current goal, and based on this analysis controls the learning process. The approach uses a knowledge representation that is specifically designed to facilitate all basic forms of inference. The representation consists of collections of type (or generalization) hierarchies and part hierarchies (representing part-of relationships). The nodes of the hierarchies are interconnected by "traces" that represent observed or inferred knowledge. This form of knowledge representation, called DIH ("**D**ynamically **I**nterlaced **H**ierarchies"), allows the system to conduct different types of inference by modifying the location of the nodes connected by traces. This representation stems from the theory of human plausible reasoning proposed by Collins and Michalski (1989). Details are described by Hieb and Michalski (1993).

To give a very simple illustration of the underlying idea, consider a statement "Roses grow in the Summer." Such a statement would be represented in DIH as a "trace" linking the node *Roses*, in the type hierarchy of *Plants*, with the node *grow*, in the type hierarchy of *Actions*, and with the node *Summer*, in the hierarchy of *Seasons*. By "moving" different nodes linked by the trace in different direction, different transmutations are performed. For example, moving the node *Roses* downward to Yellow *roses* would be a specialization transmutation; moving it upward to *Garden flowers* would be a generalization transmutation. Moving the node *Summer* horizontally to *Autumn* would be a similization transmutation.

In the dynamic task analysis approach, a learning step is activated when system receives some input information. The input is classified into an appropriate category. Depending on the category and the current goal, relevant segments of MKB are evoked and designated as BK. The next step determines the type of relationship that exists between the input information and BK. The method distinguishes among five basic types of relationship. The classification presented below of the types of input is only conceptual. It does not imply that a learning system needs to process each type by a separate module. To the contrary, due to the underlying knowledge representation (DIH), all these functions are integrated into one seamless system, in which they are processed in a synergistic fashion. Here are the basic types of the relationship between the input and the background knowledge.

1. *The input represents programatically new information.* An input is pragmatically new to the learner if no entailment relationship can be determined between it and BK, i.e., if it cannot be determined if it subsumes, is subsumed by, or contradicts BK, within goal-dependent time constraints. The learner tries to identify parts of BK that are siblings of the input under the same node in some hierarchy (e.g., other examples of the concept represented by the input). If this effort succeeds, the related knowledge components are generalized, so that they account now for the input and possibly for other information stored previously. The resulting generalizations and the input facts are evaluated for "importance" (to the goal) by the Evaluation module, and those that pass an *importance criterion* are stored. If the above effort does not succeed, the input is stored, and the control is passed to case 4. Generally, case 1 involves some form of inductive learning (empirical learning, constructive induction), and/or learning by instruction.

2. *The input is implied by or implies BK.* This case represents a situation when BK accounts for the input or is a special case of it. The learner creates a derivational explanatory structure that links the input with the involved part of BK. Depending on the learning task, this structure can be used to create new knowledge that is more adequate ("operational," more efficient, etc.) for future handling of such cases. If the new knowledge passes an "importance criterion," it is stored for future use. This mechanism is related to ideas about the utility of explanation-based learning (Minton, 1988). If the input represents a "useful" result of a problem-solving activity, e.g., "given state x, it was found that a useful action is y, and if such a rule is sufficiently general to be evoked sufficiently often, then storing it is cost-effective. Such a mechanism is related to chunking used in SOAR (Laird, Rosenbloom, & Newell, 1986). If the input information (e.g., a rule supplied by a teacher) implies some part of BK, then an "importance criterion" is applied to it. If the criterion is satisfied, the input is stored, and an appropriate link is made to the part of BK that is implied by it. In general, this case handles situations requiring some form of analytic learning.

3. *The input contradicts BK.* The system identifies the part of BK that is contradicted by the input information, and then attempts to specialize this part. If the specialization involves too much restructuring or the confidence in the input is low, no change to this part of BK is made, but the input is stored. When some part of BK has been restructured to accommodate the input, the input also is stored, but only if it passes an "importance criterion." If contradicted knowledge is a specific fact, this is noted, and any knowledge that was generated on the basis of the contradicted fact is to be revised. In general, this case handles situations requiring a revision of BK through some form of synthetic learning or managing inconsistency.

4. *The input evokes an analogy to a part of BK.* This case represents a situation when the input does not match any background fact or rule exactly, nor is related to any part of BK in the sense of case 1, but there is similarity between the fact and some part of BK at some level of abstraction. In this case, matching is done at this level of abstraction, using generalized attributes or relations. If the fact passes an "importance criterion," it is stored with an indication of a similarity (analogy) to a background knowledge component, and with a specification of the aspects (abstract attributes or relations) defining the analogy. For example, an input describing a lamp may evoke an analogy to the part of BK describing the sun, because both lamp and sun match in terms of an abstract attribute "produces light."

5. *The input is already known to the learner.* This case occurs when the input matches exactly some part of BK (a stored fact, a rule or a segment). In such a situation, a measure of confidence associated with this part is updated.

Summarizing, an MTL learner may employ any type of inference and transmutation during learning. A deductive inference is employed when an input fact is consistent with, implies, or is implied by the background knowledge; analogical inference is employed when the input is similar to some part of past knowledge at some level of abstraction; and inductive inference is employed when there is a need to hypothesize new and/or more general knowledge. The above cases have been distinguished for the sake of theory. By using a proper knowledge representation (such as DIH), they all can be performed in a seamless way by one integrated mechanism.

9. An illustration of MTL

To illustrate the ideas of MTL outlined above in terms of the Inferential Theory of Learning, let us use a well-known example of learning the concept of a "cup" (Mitchell, Keller & Kedar-Cabelli, 1986). The example is deliberately oversimplified, so that the ideas can be presented in a very simple way.

Figure 6 presents several inferential learning strategies as applicable to different learning tasks (as defined by a combination of the input, BK, and the desired output). For each strategy, the figure shows the input and the background knowledge required by a given learning strategy, and the output knowledge produced. The strategies are presented as independent processes only in a conceptual sense. In the actual implementation of MTL, all strategies are to be performed within one integrated inference sytem. The system specializes to any specific strategy using one general computational mechanism, based on Dynamic Interlaced Hierarchies (Hieb & Michalski, 1993). In figure 6, the name "obj" (in small letters) denotes a variable; the name "CUP1" (in capital letters) denotes a specific object. The top part of the figure presents the following:

- An *abstract concept description* (*Abstract CD*) for the concept "cup."
  Such a description characterizes a concept (or a set of entities that constitute the concept) in absract terms, i.e., in terms that are assumed not be directly observable or measurable. Here, it states that a cup is an open vessel that is stable and liftable. The relationship between individual conditions and the concept name is viewed as mutual implication.
- The *domain rules*.
  These rules (formally, m-implications) relate abstract terms to observable or measurable properties ("operational" properties). These rules can be used to derive abstract properties from operational properties or operational properties from abstract ones. For example, the abstract property "open vessel" can be derived from the observed property that the object is "up-concave," and that the object is "stable," if it has "flat bottom."
- A *specific object description* (*Specific OD*) of an example of a cup.
  Such a description characterizes a specific object (here, a cup) in terms of operational properties. By an example of a concept is meant a specific OD that is associated with the concept name.
- An *abstract object description* (*Abstract OD*).
  Such a description characterizes a specific object in abstract terms. It is not a generalization of an object, since its reference set is still the same object. Here, this description characterizes the specific cup, CUP1, in terms of abstract properties.
- An *operational concept description* (*Operational CD*).
  This description characterizes the concept in observable or measurable terms ("operational" terms). Such a description is used for recognizing the object from observable properties of the object. Notice that the argument of the predicates here is not some specific cup, but the variable "obj."

The bottom part of the figure illustrates several inferential learning strategies (corresponding to the primary knowledge transmutation involved) using the above concepts. For each strategy, the input to the process, the background knowledge (BK), and the goal description are specified.

Cup(obj)

↕

Abstract CD:

Open-vessel(obj) & Stable(obj) & Liftable(obj)

Domain rules:

Open-vessel(obj) ↕ Up-concave(obj)

Stable(obj) ↕ Has-flat-bottom(obj)

Liftable(obj) ↕ Is-light(obj) & Has-handle(obj)

Example (Specific OD):

Up-concave(CUP1) & Has-flat-bottom(CUP1) & Is-light(CUP1) & Has-handle(CUP1) & Color(CUP1) = red & Owner(CUP1) = RSM & Made-of(CUP1) = glass &.... ↔ Cup(CUP1)

Abstract OD:

Open-vessel(CUP1) & Stable(CUP1) & Liftable(CUP1) ↔ Cup(CUP1)

Operational CD:

Up-concave(obj) & Has-flat-bottom(obj) & Is-light(obj) & Has-handle(obj) ↔ Cup(obj)

Transmutation	Input + BK:		Learning Goal:
Abstraction	Example Domain rules	|>	Abstract OD
Deductive Generalization	Example Abstract CD Domain rules	|>	Operational CD
Empirical Induction	Examples BK'	|>	Operational CD
Constructive Induction (Case of Generalization)	Example(s) Domain rules	|<	Abstract CD
Constructive Induction (Case of Abduction)	Example(s) Abstract CD	|<	Domain rules
Multistrategy Task-adaptive Learning	Applies any of the above transmutation, or their combination, depending on the learning task, defined by the input, BK and the learning goal.		

Explanation: OD and CD stand for object description and concept description, respectively. CUP1 stands for a specific cup; obj denotes a variable. BK' denotes some limited background knowledge, e.g., a specification of the value sets of the attributes and their types. Symbol ↔ stands for mutual implication in which the merit parameters (the backward and the forward strength) are unspecified. Symbols |> and |< indicate deduction and induction, respectively.

Figure 6. An illustration of inferential strategies.

The input and BK are related to the goal description by a symbol indicating the type of the underlying inference: |> for deduction and |< for induction. A description of an object or of a concept is associated with a concept name by a mutual dependency relation ↔ (without defining the merit parameters). The use of mutual dependencies emphasizes a bidirectionality of the inference. If an unknown entity matches the left-hand side of the dependency, then it can be assigned the concept on the right-hand side. Conversely, if one knows that an entity represents a concept on the right-hand side, then one can derive properties stated on the left-hand side of the dependency. The sign ↔ of mutual implication also expresses the fact that the general concept description is a hypothesis rather than a proven generalization. The mutual implication used here can be viewed as a generalization of the *concept assignment operator* "::>" which is sometimes used in the machine learning literature for denoting the link between a concept description and the corresponding concept name.

10. Summary

The Inferential Theory of Learning provides a unifying theoretical framework for characterizing logical capabilities (or competence) of learning processes. It analyzes learning processes in terms of generic patterns of knowledge transformation, called transmutations. Transmutations take input information and background knowledge, and generate some new knowledge. They represent either different patterns of inference ("knowledge-generation transmutations") or different patterns of knowledge manipulation ("knowledge-manipulation transmutations"). Knowledge-generation transmutations change the logical content of input knowledge, while knowledge-manipulation transmutations perform managerial operations that do not change the knowledge content. Transmutations can be performed using any kind of inference—deduction, induction, or analogy.

Several fundamental knowledge-generation transmutations have been analyzed and illustrated by examples: generalization, abstraction, and similization. These were shown to differ in terms of the aspects of knowledge that they change. Specifically, generalization and specialization change the reference set of a description; abstraction and concretion change the level of detail of a description of the reference set; and similization and dissimilization hypothesize new knowledge about a reference set based on the similarity or lack of similarity between the source and the target reference sets.

By analyzing diverse learning strategies and methods in terms of abstract, implementation-independent transmutations, the Inferential Theory of Learning offers a very general view of learning processes. Such a view provides a clear understanding of the roles and the applicability conditions of diverse inferential learning strategies and facilitates the development of a theoretically well-founded methodology for building multistrategy learning systems.

The theory was used to outline a methodology for multistrategy task-adaptive learning (MTL). An MTL system determines by itself which strategy, or combination of strategies, is most suitable for a given learning task. A learning task is defined by the input, background knowledge, and the learning goal. MTL aims at integrating strategies such as empirical and constructive generalization, abductive derivation, deductive generalization, abstraction, and analogy.

Many ideas presented here are at a very early stage of development, and a number of topics need to be explored in future research. Much more work is needed on the formalization of the proposed transmutations, on a clarification of their interrelationships, and on the identification and analysis of other types of knowledge transmutations. Future research needs to address also the problem of the role of goal structures, their representation, and the methods for their use for guiding learning processes.

Open problems also include the development of an effective method for measuring the amount of knowledge change resulting from different transmutations, and the amount of knowledge contained in various knowledge structures in the context of a given BK. Other important research topics are to systematically analyze existing learning algorithms and paradigms using concepts of the theory, that is, to describe them in terms of knowledge transmutations employed. A research problem of great practical value is to use the theory for determining clear criteria for the most effective applicability of different learning strategies in diverse learning situations.

The proposed approach to multistrategy task-adaptive learning was only briefly sketched. It needs much more work and a proof of concept. Future research should also investigate different approaches to the implementation of multistrategy task-adaptive learning, investigate their relationships, and implement experimental systems that synergistically integrate all major learning strategies. It is hoped that the presented research, despite its early state, provides a good insight into the complexities of research in multistrategy learning and that it will stimulate the reader to undertake some of the indicated research topics.

Acknowledgments

The author thanks Thomas Arciszewski, Mike Hieb, Zenon Kulpa, Elizabeth Marchut-Michalski, Ray Money, Lorenza Saitta, David A. Schum, Anna Stein, Gheorghe Tecuci, Brad Whitehall, Janusz Wnek, and unknown reviewers for constructive suggestions and criticisms that substantially helped in the preparation of this article.

This research was done in the Center for Artificial Intelligence at George Mason University. The Center's research is supported in part by the National Science Foundation under the grant No. IRI-9020226, in part by the Defense Advanced Research Projects Agency under the grant No. N00014-91-J-1854, administrated by the Office of Naval Research, and the grant No. F49620-92-J-0549, administered by the Air Force Office of Scientific Research, in part by the Office of Naval Research under the grant No. N00014-91-J-1351.

References

Adler, M.J., & Gorman, W. (Eds.). (1987). The great ideas: A synopicon of great books of the western world. *Encyclopedia Britannica*, Vol. 1, Ch. 39 (Induction), pp 565–571.

Aristotle (1987). Posterior analytics. In R.M. Hutchins (Ed.), *The works of Aristotle*, Vol. 1. *Encyclopedia Britannica*. Inc.

Bacon, F. (1620). *Novum Organum*. In R.M. Hutchins (Ed.), *Great Books of the Western World*, Vol. 30. *Encyclopedia Britannica*, 1987.

Bergadano, F., Matwin, S., Michalski, R.S., & Zhang, J. (1992). Learning two-tiered descriptions of flexible concepts: The POSEIDON system. *Machine Learning*, 8, 5–43. (Originally published in *Machine Learning and Inference Reports, No. MLI-3*, Center for Artificial Intelligence, George Mason University, Fairfax, VA, September 1990).

Birnbaum, L., & Collins, G. (1991). *Proceedings of the 8th International Conference on Machine Learning*. Chicago.

Bloedorn, E., & Michalski, R.S. (1991). Data-driven constructive induction. *Proceedings of the Tools for Artificial Intelligence Conference*. San Jose, CA.

Cohen, L.J. (1970). *The implications of induction*. London:

Collins, A., & Michalski, R.S. (1989). The logic of plausible-reasoning: A core theory, *Cognitive Science, 13*, 1-49.

Console, L., Theseider, D., & Torasso, P. (1991). On the relationship between abduction and deduction. *Journal of Logic and Computation, 1* (5).

Danyluk, A.P. (1987). The use of explanations for similarity-based learning. *Proceedings of IJCAI-87* (pp. 274–276). Milan, Italy.

Danyluk, A.P. (1989). Recent results in the use of context for learning new rules. Technical Report No. TR-98-066. Philips Laboratories.

Danyluk, A.p. (1993). Gemini: An integration of analytical and empirical learning. In R.S. Michalski & G. Tecuci (Eds.) *Machine learning: A multistrategy approach*. Vol. *IV.*

De Raedt, L., & Bruynooghe, M. (1993). Interactive theory revision. In R.S. Michalski & G. Tecuci (Eds.), *Machine learning: A multistrategy approach*. Vol. *IV.* Morgan Kaufmann.

Dietterich, T.G., & Flann, N.S. (1988). An inductive approach to solving the imperfect theory problem. *Proceedings of 1988 Symposium on Explanation-Based Learning*, (pp. 42–46). Stanford University, 1988.

Dietterich, T.G. (1986). Learning at the knowledge level. *Machine Learning, 1* (3), 287–316. (Reprinted in J.W. Shavlik & T.G. Dietterich (Eds.), (1990). *Readings in machine learning*. San Mateo, CA: Morgan Kaufmann.)

Fulk, M., & Case, J. (1990). *Proceedings of the 3rd Annual Workshop on Computational Learning Theory.* University of Rochester, NY, August 6–8.

Giordana, A., Saitta, L., & Roverso, D. (1991). Abstracting concepts with inverse resolution. *Proceedings of the 8th International Workshop on Machine Learning* (pp. 142–146). Evanston, IL:

Goldberg, D.E. (1989). *Genetic algorithms in search, optimization, and machine learning*. Reading, MA: Addison-Wesley.

Goodman, L.A., & Kruskal, W.H. (1979). *Measures of association for cross classifications*. New York: Springer-Verlag.

Grosof, B.N., & Russell (1989). Declarative bias for structural domains. *Proceedings of the Sixth International Workshop on Machine Learning*, Cornell Univesity. Ithaca, NY: Morgan Kaufmann.

Hieb, M., & Michalski, R.S. (1993). A knowledge representation system based on dynamically interlaced hierarchies: Basic ideas and examples. *Reports of Machine Learning and Inference Laboratory MLI 93-5*, Fairfax, VA: Center for Artificial Intelligence, George Mason University.

Hunter, L. (1990). Planning to learn. *Proceedings of the Twelfth Annual Conference of the Cognitive Science Society*. (pp. 26–34). Hillsdale, NJ: Lawrence Erlbaum Associates.

Kodratoff, Y., & Michalski, R.S. (Eds.) (1990). *Machine learning: An artificial intelligence approach* (Vol. 3). Morgan Kaufmann.

Kodratoff, Y., & Tecuci, G. (1987). DISCIPLE-1: Interactive apprentice system in weak theory fields. *Proceedings of IJCAI-87* (pp. 271–273). Milan, Italy.

Laird, J.E. (Ed.). (1988). *Proceedings of the Fifth International Conference on Machine Learning*, University of Michigan, Ann Arbor, June 12–14.

Laird, J.E., Rosenbloom, P.S., & Newell, A. (1986). Chunking in SOAR: the anatomy of a general learning mechanism. *Machine Learning, 1*(*1*), 11–46.

Lebowitz, M. (1986). Integrated learning: Controlling explanation. *Cognitive Science, 10* (2), 219–240.

Michalski, R.S. (1983). Theory and methodology of inductive learning. In R.S. Michalski, J.G. Carbonell, and T.M. Mitchell (Eds.), *Machine learning: An artificial intelligence approach*. Tioga.

Michalski, R.S. (1990). Learning flexible concepts: Fundamental ideas and a method based on two-tiered representation. In Y. Kodratoff and R.S. Michalski (Eds.), *Machine learning: An artificial intelligence approach*, vol. III. Morgan Kaufmann.

Michalski, R.S. (1990a). Toward unified theory of learning: Multistrategy task-adaptive learning. *Reports of Machine Learning and Inference Laboratory MLI-90-1*. (Subsequently published in B.G. Buchanan and D.C. Wilkins (Eds.), *Readings in knowledge acquisition and learning*. Morgan Kaufmann.

Michalski, R.S. (1991b). A methodological framework for multistrategy task-adaptive learning. *Proceedings of the Fifth International Symposium on Methodologies for intelligent Systems*. Knoxville, TN: Elsevier.

Michalski, R.S. (1991). Toward unified theory of learning: An outline of basic ideas. In M. De Glas & D. Gabbay (Eds.), *Proceedings of the First World Conference on the Fundamentals of Artificial Intelligence*, Paris, France, July 1–5.

Michalski, R.S., & Kodratoff, Y. (1990). Research in machine learning: Recent progress, classification of methods and future directions. In Y. Kodratoff and R.S. Michalski (Eds.), *Machine learning: An artificial intelligence approach* (Vol. 3). Morgan Kaufmann.

Minton, S. (1988). Quantitative results concerning the utility of explanation-based learning. *Proceedings of AAAI-88* (pp. 564–569). Saint Paul, MN.

Minton, S., Carbonell, J.G., Etzioni, O., Knoblock, C.A., & Kuokka, D.R. (1987). Acquiring effective search control rules: Explanation-based learning in the PRODIGY system. *Proceedings of the 4th International Machine Learning Workshop* (pp. 122–133). University of California, Irvine.

Mitchell, T.M., Keller, T., & Kedar-Cabelli, S. (1986). Explanation-based generalization: A unifying view. *Machine learning. 1* (1), 47–80.

Mooney, R.J., & Ourston, D. (1993). A multistrategy approach to theory refinement. In R.S. Michalski & G. Tecuci (Eds.), *Machine learning: A multistrategy approach*, Vol. *IV.* Morgan Kaufmann.

Newell, (1981). The Knowledge Level. *AI Magazine, 2*, 1–20.

Muggleton, S. (1988). A strategy for constructing new predicates in first-order logic. *Proceedings of EWSL-88* (pp. 123–130). Glasgow, Scotland.

Pazzani, M.J. (1988). Integrating explanation-based and empirical learning methods in OCCAM. *Proceedings of EWSL-88* (pp. 147–166). Glasgow, Scotland.

Pierce, C.S. (1965). Elements of logic. In Ch. Hartshorne & P. Weiss (Eds.), *Collected papers of Charles Sanders Peirce* (1839–1914). Cambridge, MA: The Belknap Press, Harvard University Press.

Pearl, J. (1988). *Probabilistic reasoning in intelligent systems: Networks of plausible inference.* Morgan Kaufmann.

Piatetsky-Shapiro, G. (1992). Probabilistic data dependencies. In I.M. Zytkow (Ed.), *Proceedings of the ML92 Workshop on Machine Discovery*, Aberdeen, Scotland, July 4.

Plaisted, D. (1981). Theorem proving with abstraction. *Artificial Intelligence, 16*, 47–108.

Polya, G. (1968). *Mathematics and plausible reasoning*, Vol. I and II. Princeton, NJ: Princeton University Press.

Poole, D. (1989). Explanation and prediction: An architecture for default and abductive reasoning. *Computational Intelligence, 5*, 97–110.

Popper, K.R. (1972). *Objective knowledge: An evolutionary approach.* Oxford: Clarendon Press.

Porter, B.W., & Mooney, R.J. (Eds.). (1990). *Proceedings of the 7th International Machine Learning Conference*, Austin, TX.

Ram, A. (1991). A theory of questions and question asking. *The Journal of the Learning Sciences, 1(3&4)*, 273–318.

Ram, A., & Hunter, L. (in press). The use of explicit goals for knowledge to guide inference and learning. *Applied Intelligence.* (Also available as Technical Report GIT-CC-92/04, College of Computing, Georgia Institute of Technology, Atlanta, Georgia, January, 1992.)

Rivest, R., Haussler D., & Warmuth, M. (1989). *Proceedings of the Second Annual Workshop on Computational Learning Theory*, University of Santa Cruz, July 31–August 2.

Russell, S. (1989). *The use of knowledge in analogy and induction.* San Mateo, CA: Morgan Kaufmann.

Schafer, D. (Ed.). (1989). *Proceedings of the 3rd International Conference on Genertic Algorithms.* Fairfax, VA: George Mason University.

Schultz, T.R., & Kestenbaum, N.R. (1985). Causal reasoning in children. In G.J. Whitehurst (Ed.), *Annals of Child development*, vol. 2, pp. 195–249. JAI Press.

Segre, A.M. (Ed.). (1989). *Proceedings of the Sixth International Workshop on Machine Learning*, Cornell University. Ithaca, NY: Morgan Kaufmann.

Sleeman, D., & Edwards, P. (1992). *Proceedings of the Ninth International Workshop.* Great Britain: Aberdeen, Morgan Kaufmann.

Stepp, R.S., & Michalski, R.S. (1993). How to structure structured objects. *Proceedings of the International Machine Learning Workshop.* (pp. 156–160). Urbana, IL: University of Illinois Allerton House.

Tecuci, G., & Michalski, R.S. (1991a). A method for multistrategy task-adaptive learning based on plausible justifications. In L. Birnbaum & G. Collins (Eds.). *Machine Learning: Proceedings of the eighth international workshop.* San Matteo, CA: Morgan Kaufmann.

Tecuci, G., & Michalski, R.S. (1991b). Input 'understanding' as a basis for multistrategy task-adaptive learning. In Z. Ras & M. Zemankova (Eds.), *Proceedings of the 6th International Symposium on Methodologies for Intelligent Systems.* Lecture Notes on Artificial Intelligence. Berlin: Springer Verlag.

Tecuci, G. (in press). Plausible justification trees: A framework for deep and dynamic integration of learning strategies. *Machine Learning Journal* (Special Issue on Multistrategy Learning).

Touretzky, D., Hinton, G., & Sejnowski, T. (Eds.). (1988). *Proceedings of the 1988 Connectionist Models Summer School*, Carnegie Mellon University, June 17–26.

Utgoff, P. (1986). Shift of bias for inductive concept learning. In R.S. Michalski, J.G. Carbonell, & T.M. Mitchell (Eds.), *Machine learning: An artificial intelligence approach* (Vol. 2). Morgan Kaufmann.

Warmuth, M., & Valiant, L. (Eds.). (1991). *Proceedings of the 4th Annual Workshop on Computational Learning Theory*, Santa Cruz, CA: Morgan Kaufmann.

Whewell, W. (1857). *History of the inductive sciences*, 3rd edition. London.

Whitehall, B.L. (1990). Knowledge-based learning: Integration and deductive and inductive learning for knowledge base completion. Ph.D. Thesis, Computer Science Department, University of Illinois.

Whitehall, B.L., & Lu, S. C-Y. Theory Completion using Knowledge-Based Learning, In R.S. Michalski & G. Tecuci (Eds.), *Machine learning: A multistrategy approach*, Vol. IV. Morgan Kaufmann.

Wilkins, D.C., Clancey, W.J., & Buchanan, B.G. (1986). *An overview of the odysseus learning apprentice*. New York: Kluwer Academic.

Wnek, J., & Michalski, R.S. (1991a). Hypothesis-driven constructive induction in AQ17: A method and experiments. In K. Morik, F. Bergadano, and W. Buntine (Eds.), In *Proceedings of the IJCAI-91 Workshop on Evaluating and Changing Representation in Machine Learning*, (pp. 13–22). Sydney, Australia, August 24–30.

Wnek, J., & Michalski, R.S. (1991b). An experimental comparison of symbolic and subsymbolic learning paradigms: Phase I–Learning logic-style concepts. In R.S. Michalski & G. Tecuci (Eds.), *Proceedings of the First International Workshop on Multistrategy Learning*. GMU Center for Artificial Intelligence, Harpers Ferry, Nov. 7–9.

Wnek, J., & Michalski, R.S. (1993). Comparing Symbolic and Subsymbolic Learning: Three Studies. In R.S. Michalski & G. Tecuci (Eds.), *Machine learning: A multistrategy approach*, Vol. IV. Los Altos, CA: Morgan Kaufmann.

Zadrozny, W. (1990). The logic of abduction (preliminary report). *First International Workshop on Principles of Diagnosis*, Stanford, CA.

Received September 30, 1991
Accepted January 20, 1992
Final Manuscript February 28, 1992

Machine Learning, 11, 153-172 (1993)

Multistrategy Learning and Theory Revision

LORENZA SAITTA SAITTA@DI.UNITO.IT
MARCO BOTTA BOTTA@DI.UNITO.IT
FILIPPO NERI NERI@DI.UNITO.IT
Dipartimento di Informatica, Università di Torino, Corso Svizzera 185, 10149—Torino, Italy

Abstract. This article presents the system WHY, which learns and updates a diagnostic knowledge base using domain knowledge and a set of examples. The a priori knowledge consists of a causal model of the domain that states the relationships among basic phenomena, and a body of phenomenological theory that describes the links between abstract concepts and their possible manifestations in the world. The phenomenological knowledge is used deductively, the causal model is used abductively, and the examples are used inductively. The problems of imperfection and intractability of the theory are handled by allowing the system to make assumptions during its reasoning. In this way, robust knowledge can be learned with limited complexity and a small number of examples. The system works in a first-order logic environment and has been applied in a real domain.

Keywords: Multistrategy learning, causal models, abduction, diagnostic expert systems

1. Introduction

Several authors have advocated the necessity of using deep models of the structure and behavior of the entities involved in a given domain, for instance, in diagnostic systems (Davis, 1984; Genesereth, 1984; Reiter, 1984; de Kleer & Seely Brown, 1986). On the other hand, everyday experience suggests that, in order to achieve high performance in reasonable time, the integrated use of expertise and reasoning from underlying principles should provide the best results (Chandrasekaran & Mittal, 1983; Kahn, 1984).

A shift of attention toward methodologies more focused in a deeper understanding of the world is even more appropriate in learning. And, in fact, this shift is actually going on. Early systems relied on purely inductive techniques (Mitchell, 1982; Michalski, 1983; Quinlan, 1986). Induction can detect regularities in large amount of data, but it can neither explain why these regularities occur nor guarantee their meaningfulness. Nevertheless, inductive systems have been proved viable tools for solving some real-world problems (Michalski & Chilausky, 1980; Quinlan, 1986; Cestnik, Kononenko, & Bratko, 1987; Bergadano, Giordana, & Saitta, 1988, 1990).

The papers by Mitchell, Keller, and Kedar-Cabelli (1986) and DeJong and Mooney (1986) proposed a new, deductive approach to learning that had the great merit of focusing attention on the fundamental role a priori knowledge can play in this process. Deductive learning offers grounds for the knowledge it derives, at the cost of supplying a complete and consistent theory of the domain. Since this last requirement cannot be met in real applications, attempts have been made to take the best of the inductive and deductive approaches by integrating them into a single framework (Lebowitz, 1986; Bergadano & Giordana, 1988; Pazzani, 1988; Danyluk, 1991).

On the other hand, other authors proposed to use deep models of the domain also in learning and to integrate different reasoning schemes (Morris & O'Rorke, 1990; Michalski,

1991 (see also this issue); Tecuci, 1991 (see also this issue); Saitta et al., 1991; Kodratoff, 1991; Mooney & Ourston, 1991; Matwin & Plante, 1991; De Raedt & Bruynooghe, 1991). In this article we are concerned with a particular type of deep models, namely, *causal* models. The notion of causal relation has been widely debated, and different definitions have emerged in various disciplines. AI scientists have also contributed to the discussion (de Kleer & Seely Brown, 1986; Cox & Pietrzykowski, 1987; Poole, 1988; Torasso & Console, 1989; Console et al., 1990). We shall rely, here, on the following intuitive interpretation of causal relation: A is the cause of B if a physical mechanism can be specified that shows how the occurrence of A brings about B. In order to exploit the information embedded in the causal model, we make use of an *abductive* reasoning scheme. Abduction is meant as the process of regressing, through chains of cause–effect relations, from observations to a set of axioms, the first *causes*, which are the ultimate hypotheses we are disposed to accept. Obviously, the definition of the first causes is task dependent and can be suggested by an expert in the domain on pragmatic grounds.

In order to reduce the computational complexity of this type of reasoning, *assumptions* about the state of the world can be made. In this way, the causal model focuses the search for a problem solution toward fundamental phenomena, producing a "deep skeleton" in which "surface" details can be added later. A more extensive analysis of the motivations for using causal models in learning can be found in Saitta et al. (1991).

A causal model $\mathcal{C}$ of a domain does not exhaust all the information needed for learning. In fact, $\mathcal{C}$ might be too abstract to allow practical rules to be learned on its basis alone. Therefore, we shall consider, besides $\mathcal{C}$, a *phenomenological* theory $\mathcal{P}$, stating how abstract concepts can be instantiated in the world. $\mathcal{P}$ contains structural information about objects and definitions of relevant categories and their taxonomic organization; but, more importantly, $\mathcal{P}$ contains a set of rules aimed at describing the manifestations of abstractly defined concepts, i.e., re-expressing them in terms of "operational" predicates (Keller, 1988). The knowledge $\mathcal{P}$, even if necessary in order to fill the gap between abstract entities and their possible manifestations, can only explain *how* things happen, but not *why*. Then, pragmatically, a phenomenon will be considered *justified* only if it is explained by $\mathcal{C}$, i.e., if it is "covered" by a first cause. The distinction between $\mathcal{C}$ and $\mathcal{P}$ is also reflected in the different representation formalisms and in the associated reasoning mechanisms (abductive for $\mathcal{C}$ and deductive for $\mathcal{P}$). In support of the usefulness of keeping $\mathcal{P}$ and $\mathcal{C}$ apart, we notice that in diagnostic problems, for instance, the same malfunction (recognizable from the symptoms specified by $\mathcal{P}$) may often have different causes (specified by $\mathcal{C}$) and that only the knowledge of the true cause allows an effective repair.

We shall now describe how the above-mentioned ideas have been implemented in the system WHY, developed as an extension of the learning system ML-SMART (Bergadano, Giordana, & Saitta, 1988), in which inductive and deductive techniques have already been integrated (Bergadano & Giordana, 1988). WHY has been applied to a real-world problem of mechanical troubleshooting (Saitta et al., 1991). However, a simpler example of a heat transfer problem will be used in this article, for the sake of comprehensibility.

Several aspects differentiate the system WHY from others devoted to similar learning tasks. First of all, WHY is able to deal with first-order logic languages, representing both the domain theory and the target knowledge, by keeping track of the (possibly multiple) bindings between variables in the formulas and components of the instances. Second, the system can be used for acquiring and refining a target knowledge base as well as for revising the a priori knowledge supplied to it. In this last task, the system works in a semi-automated way, allowing a direct interaction with the expert, who can suggest modifications to the background or to the target knowledge; the expert will receive an immediate feedback to his/her suggestions, because WHY evaluates the effects of the modifications and presents them back to the expert for validation. In order to ease this interactive aspect, WHY is provided with a friendly interface toward the user, based on a frame system supporting a menu-like interaction protocol. Another innovative aspect of WHY is the integration of the performance element into the learner, so that they both use the same knowledge structures and the same reasoning process can serve both classification and learning.

This article is organized as follows. Section 2 describes the representation formalisms used for the various types of knowledge used by WHY. Section 3 describes the basic reasoning mechanisms in isolation, whereas section 4 illustrates how these reasoning schemes can be combined to build up justifications. In section 5, one-step learning and the refinement of the target knowledge are described, whereas section 6 is devoted to the interactive theory revision phase. Section 7 contains some conclusions.

2. Knowledge representation

WHY handles four bodies of knowledge: the causal model, $\mathcal{C}$, the phenomenological knowledge, $\mathcal{P}$, the target knowledge base, $\mathcal{KB}$, and the control knowledge.

The representation schemes for all the kinds of knowledge share a first-order logic language $\mathcal{L}$ in Horn clause form. In the following, a double arrow $\Rightarrow$ will denote material implication, whereas the simple arrow $\rightarrow$ a causal link. Moreover, lower-case letter predicates are operational (i.e., directly observable on the data), whereas capital letter predicates are non-operational. These two types of predicates belong to the sets $P^{(o)}$ and $P^{(n)}$, respectively.

2.1. *Target knowledge base*

As a first approximation, the target knowledge base can be viewed as an unordered set of decision rules:

$$\mathbf{r} \equiv \forall e \; [\exists \; \mathbf{x} \mid \varphi(e, \mathbf{x}) \Rightarrow \mathrm{h}(e)] \qquad (1)$$

where $\mathbf{x}$ denotes a set of variables, e an event to be interpreted, h a concept belonging to a set H_0, and φ a formula of $\mathcal{L}$. Actually, the target knowledge base has a more complex representation, as will be explained in section 5.

The set S(h) of rules, whose conclusion is h, is an *intensional* description of the concept h. During the learning process, each $\varphi(e, \mathbf{x})$ has also an *extensional* representation, consisting of all the training examples satisfying φ; the extension of φ is stored as a relation in a relational data base (Bergadano, Giordana, & Saitta, 1988). More precisely, let F be a set of (structured) events and $\varphi^{(o)}(x_1, x_2, \ldots, x_k)$ an operational formula. Given an event $e \in F$, every possible binding, satisfying $\varphi^{(o)}$, between k-tuples of components of e and the k-tuple of variables $x_1, x_2, \ldots, x_k$ is represented in a (k + 2)-ary relation $\varphi^* = \langle F, H, X_1, X_2, \ldots, X_k \rangle$. The field F contains the identifier of the example and H its correct classification (the concepts, which e is an instance of); moreover, $X_1, X_2, \ldots, X_k$ are the names of the constants (components of e) bound to the variables $x_1, x_2, \ldots, x_k$. Notice that several (k + 2)-tuples, belonging to the same event, may occur in φ^*.

2.2. Causal model

The logical representation of the causal model $\mathfrak{C}$ consists of an acyclic graph. In figure 1 a very simple model of heat transfer phenomena is reported. Nodes in the network are either *primary* (ellipses) or *accessory* (rectangles and clouds). Primary nodes correspond to processes or system states, and a subset of these nodes contains the *first causes* (shaded nodes), which do not have entering edges. Effects of the same cause are AND-ed; causes of the same effect are OR-ed.

Accessory nodes represent two types of additional information: *constraints* (rectangles) and *contexts* (clouds). Constraints are attached to edges and correspond to conditions that are to be necessarily verified in order to be able to instantiate the corresponding cause–effect relation. Contexts are attached to primary nodes and represent the environmental conditions allowing the instantiation of the related phenomenon. One of the differences between constraints and contexts is the following: constraints describe physical properties of the involved bodies or structural information, i.e., properties that do not depend on time.

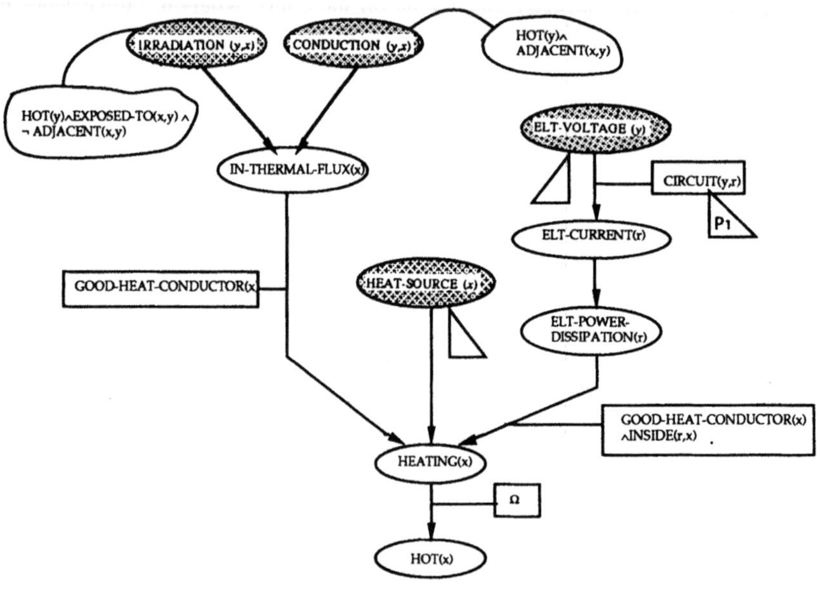

Figure 1. Simplified model of heat transfer phenomena.

Contexts state conditions that are possibly only temporarily true, and usually involve parts of the considered system larger than the one currently under analysis; for example, conditions may refer to system components different from the one for which the causal network has currently been activated. In figure 1, the explanation of why a body x is hot may involve the presence of a hot body y, adjacent to it, from which heat can flow toward x through heat conduction.

Primary nodes of the network may or may not be observables, i.e., evaluable either directly on the data (if their description involves operational predicates only) or indirectly, using the phenomenological theory $\mathcal{P}$. Constraints and contexts must be observable; as an exception, contexts may also be described in terms of primary causal nodes, introducing recursion in the net. This is the case of HOT(y) in the contexts of IRRADIATION(y, x) and CONDUCTION(y, x) in figure 1.

Finally, a triangle associated to a node contains that part of the phenomenological theory $\mathcal{P}$ that describes the manifestations associated to the node. As an example, triangle P_1 contains the following set of rules, allowing the predicate CIRCUIT(y, r) to be evaluated:

TERMINALS(y) ∧ RESISTANCE(r) ∧ connected-to(y, r) ⇒ CIRCUIT(y, r)
plug(y) ⇒ TERMINALS(y)
terminals(y) ⇒ TERMINALS(y)
ELT-CABLE(x, y) ⇒ TERMINALS(y)
cord(z) ∧ plug(y) ∧ connected-to(y, z) ⇒ ELT-CABLE(z, y)
resistance(r) ⇒ RESISTANCE(r)

Operationalizing predicates occurring in nodes of $\mathcal{C}$ is not the unique link between $\mathcal{P}$ and $\mathcal{C}$; in fact, the name of a node of $\mathcal{C}$ can occur in the body of some clauses defining non-operational predicates in $\mathcal{P}$. This is also the way the links between $\mathcal{C}$ and the concepts in H_0 are established; as a matter of fact, concepts are non-operational predicates defined in $\mathcal{P}$. Suppose, for instance, that we want to use the network of figure 1 to characterize objects that are dangerous to be touched because they burn. We define the class UNSAFE-TO-TOUCH(x) as follows (names of nodes occurring in $\mathcal{C}$ are underlined in $\mathcal{P}$):

<u>HOT</u>(x) ⇒ UNSAFE-TO-TOUCH(x)
<u>HOT</u>(y) ∧ obj(x) ∧ part-of(y, x) ⇒ UNSAFE-TO-TOUCH(x)

2.3. Phenomenological theory

The phenomenological theory $\mathcal{P}$ consists of a set of Horn clauses describing taxonomies, structural information, general knowledge, and links between abstract concepts and manifestations. For instance:

table(x) ⇒ FURNITURE(x)
(*taxonomic knowledge*)
NEAR(z, y) ∧ part-of(x, z) ⇒ NEAR(x, y)
(*general knowledge*)

cord(x) ∧ plug(y) ∧ connected-to(y, x) ⇒ ELT-CABLE(x, y)
(*structural knowledge*)
bright(x) ⇒ INCANDESCENT(x)
(*manifestation*)

Another example of $\mathcal{P}$ is the rule set P_1 reported before. Notice that the causal network $\mathcal{C}$ subdivides $\mathcal{P}$ into subsets, allowing the reasoner to consider only limited parts of $\mathcal{P}$ at any given time.

2.4. Theory incompleteness

When encoding a domain theory, incompleteness may affect almost any part of it (DeJong, 1990), and we may not be aware of where and what knowledge is missing. On the other hand, there are cases in which either we know exactly where some information is missing, but we do not know what information, or we want to hide information on purpose (for instance, for tractability reasons). In these cases we would like to warn the system about this lack of information. To this aim, the special predicate Ω (unknown) is introduced. For example, the rule

$$\text{elt-plate}(x) \wedge \Omega \Rightarrow \text{HEAT-SOURCE}(x) \tag{2}$$

means that an electric plate *may* be a heat source, if some other unspecified condition is verified (for instance, if it is plugged in). As an extreme case, Ω may coincide with the whole body of a clause, as in the following:

$$\Omega \Rightarrow Q(x) \tag{3}$$

Rule (3) denotes that we are unable (or do not want) to specify how the predicate Q(x) can be operationalized. Sometimes, we are in an intermediate situation: the expert can tell that the predicate Q(x) is expressible in terms of a combination of other predicates $\{R_1, R_2, \ldots, R_n\}$, either operational or non-operational, but he/she does not know exactly which ones. Then, we associate the set $\{R_1, R_2, \ldots, R_n\}$ to Ω in a *dependency* rule (Bergadano, Giordana, & Ponsero, 1989):

$$\{R_1, R_2, \ldots, R_n\} \Rightarrow \Omega \Rightarrow Q(x) \tag{4}$$

which can be used by the inductive reasoner as a reduced search space.

2.5. Control knowledge

The system WHY, as well as its parent ML-SMART, is a knowledge-intensive learner, which has a body of declarative knowledge to control its behavior. The control acts at two main levels: the high-level control chooses among the available reasoning schemes (abduction, induction, deduction) the most suitable one for each learning step. The low-level control determines the behavior of a single learning strategy. The control knowledge is implemented as a set of frames, containing the description of a situation and the action(s) suitable to handle that situation.

3. Basic reasoning mechanisms

Three basic reasoning schemes are integrated in the system WHY: induction, deduction, and abduction. Each of these is briefly illustrated in the following.

3.1. Induction

Induction is used to fill the possible gaps in the domain theory and is performed by invoking the inductive module of the ML-SMART system. This module searches, using a general-to-specific strategy, in a space of first-order logical formulas and outputs a network of decision rules, whose left-hand sides are the selected formulas. A body of control knowledge, in declarative form, is used to guide the search toward the most promising paths and to evaluate candidate formulas for inclusion in the final rule set. Criteria for evaluating formulas include (but are not limited to) their completeness and consistency.

ML-SMART is also responsible for maintaining the relational data base, in which the examples and the extensions of the rules are stored. Multiple bindings between variables in the formulas and parts in the examples are allowed: this feature proved to be very useful during the justification process, as explained in the next sections. An extensive description of ML-SMART can be found in Bergadano, Giordana, and Saitta (1988).

3.2. Deduction

Deduction is also performed using ML-SMART's deductive module, as described in Bergadano and Giordana (1988). The module handles a first-order theory expressed in Horn clause form and is based on Robinson and Siebert's (1982) LOGLISP. The deductive mechanism deals with many examples at the same time, exploiting the existing data base in ML-SMART. A novelty introduced by WHY is the possibility of also performing a forward deduction, i.e., of building the operationalization tree starting from the operational predicates true of the considered examples.

3.3. Abduction

Abductive reasoning is needed to exploit the causal model. In figure 2 a typical part of the causal network is reported, for the sake of illustration of the basic reasoning steps.

Reasoning with the causal model can be performed by moving from effects to causes (search for an explanation via abduction) or from causes to effects (prediction via deduction) in order to assert the truth status of each node:

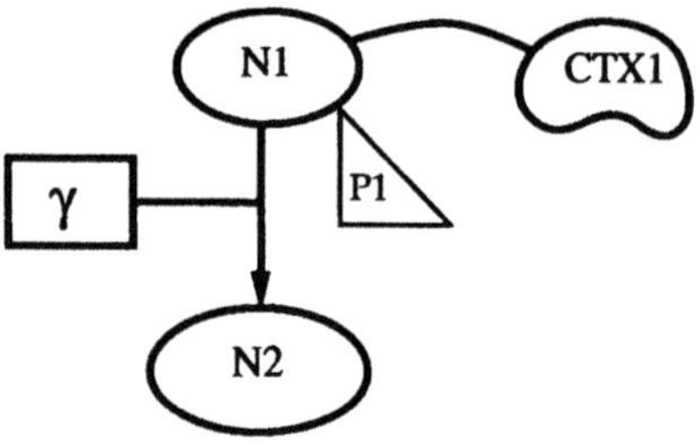

Figure 2. Scheme of the relations among nodes in the causal network. Two basic reasoning steps are defined: deduction from causes to effects and abduction from effects to causes.

- Deduction from causes to effects:

$$N_1 \wedge CTX_1 \wedge \gamma \rightarrow N_2$$

If node N_1 is true in the context CTX_1 and the constraints γ are verified, then node N_2 deterministically (if Ω does not occur in γ) or plausibly (if Ω occurs in γ) follows.

- Abduction from effects to causes:

$$N_2 \wedge \gamma \rightarrow N_1 \wedge CTX_1$$

If effect N_2 has been observed (or hypothesized) and the constraints γ are verified, then we can hypothesize that N_2 was originated by N_1 in the context CTX_1. In this abductive step, Ω does not have any influence.

Notice that the truth status of a node can also be determined by its observability, i.e., by its evaluation on the data (rules P_1, for instance), independently of the presence of its causes and/or effects. This fact constitutes another connection between phenomenological and causal reasoning.

The above reasoning steps, as simple as they appear, are quite complex to be implemented in a first-order logic environment, because of the variable bindings. How to maintain these bindings and the truth status of each node (possibly different for each binding of each instance) will be described in section 4.

The "context" nodes play a particular role in the causal reasoning. Suppose that we are trying to explain why a given object x is hot. The causal network tells us that there are a number of causes justifying this phenomenon; however, some of these are acceptable only if the environment supplies the conditions to support them. For instance, heat conduction requires that there is an object y, different from x, which is, in turn, hot and adjacent to x. When the causal reasoning is invoked on a given part of the system (in the example, the object x), contexts act as defaults and are always assumed true. Then, each of the first causes, hypothesized to explain the phenomenon, has its context hypothesized at the same time. It is up to the general control strategy to decide whether accepting the assumed context by default or to verify it, possibly re-entering the causal network. This strategy closely matches the one often used by human experts and has also the advantage of breaking recursion in the causal reasoning.

3.4. Handling assumptions

Making assumptions is a fundamental aspect of the reasoning process in uncertain environments and, in particular, when only an incomplete theory is available. In WHY, assumptions can be made during both the phenomenological and the causal reasoning, but the ways they are handled in the two cases differ.

Let us consider a set of clauses in $\mathcal{P}$, sharing the same head:

$$\varphi_k(x) \Rightarrow P(x) \qquad (1 \leq k \leq n)$$

According to Clark's completion (Clark, 1978), we can assume that

$$P(x) \Leftrightarrow \varphi_1(x) \vee \ldots\ldots \vee \varphi_n(x) \tag{5}$$

If the predicate Ω does not occur in any of the $\varphi_k(x)$'s, then using rule (5), predicate P(x) can be proved false if and only if all the $\varphi_k(x)$ $(1 \leq k \leq n)$ are false. Things are different if Ω does occur. If the predicate occurs in the body of a clause, as, for instance, in (2), the effect of Ω is that *P*(x) will never be true, but can only be *assumed* true if the other predicates in the body of the rule are true. If a clause like (3) occurs, then Clark's completion of P will contain it as a disjunct:

$$P(x) \Leftrightarrow \varphi_1(x) \vee \ldots\ldots \vee \varphi_n(x) \vee \Omega \tag{6}$$

According to (6), P(x) is never false, because Ω is, by default, assumed true. The number of assumptions made during reasoning is an important strategic parameter.

In the causal network, the symbol Ω may only occur in constraints and contexts. Predicates occurring in constraints and different from Ω are *necessary*, in the sense that they are assumed false if they cannot be proved true. The presence of Ω in a constraint denotes a weakening in the causal relation associated with the corresponding edge: in this case, the cause *may* produce the effect, but not necessarily. For example, in figure 1, an object x can become hot upon heating only if a sufficient time has elapsed or if it is not melting. Effects generated by a cause in a possibilistic way have a status of assumed true even if the cause is true.

4. Integrating multiple strategies

An abstract description of the overall learning process can be given by outlining its main phases:

ELICITATION:

Elicit from the expert a body of background knowledge, partitioned into a causal network and a phenomenological theory $\mathcal{T} = \mathcal{C} \cup \mathcal{P}$, using the USER INTERFACE. Moreover, let F_0 be a set of training examples.

JUSTIFICATION:

Phase 1 — Build up an AND/OR forest $\mathcal{G}$, called the *justification forest*, by applying the forward deduction algorithm FORW-DED to the phenomenological theory $\mathcal{P}$. Insert in the data base the extension, evaluated on the set F_0, of each node in $\mathcal{G}$. Activate some nodes of the causal network $\mathcal{C}$.

Phase 2 — Apply the abductive algorithm CAUSAL to find paths in the causal network, regressing from the activated nodes toward first causes.
Insert in the data base the extension, evaluated on the set F_0, of each node in each causal path activated in $\mathcal{C}$.

Phase 3 — Verify hypothesized contexts, possibly recursively re-entering the causal network.

ONE-STEP LEARNING:

Generate decision rules for the concepts in H_0, by collecting the predicates which are true (or assumed true) along the activated causal paths, and insert the rules in $\mathcal{KB}$.

If The rules have an "acceptable" degree of completeness and consistency
Then Stop
Else Go to KNOWLEDGE REFINEMENT
If Some contradiction arises
Then Go to THEORY REVISION

KNOWLEDGE REFINEMENT:

Given an unknown example f
Classify f using $\mathcal{KB}$.
If The classification is correct
Then Update the data base.
Update the justification forest.
Else Locate on $\mathcal{G}$ the node(s) responsible for the error.
If There is an omission error
Then Generalize $\mathcal{KB}$, possibly by invoking induction and/or interacting with the expert.
If There is a commission error
Then Specialize $\mathcal{KB}$, possibly by invoking induction and/or interacting with the expert.
Update the data base.
Update the justification forest.

THEORY REVISION:

If A justification should have been found and was not
Then Invoke induction for filling a gap in $\mathcal{P}$ or ask the expert to generalize $\mathcal{P}$ and/or extend $\mathcal{C}$.
If A justification was found and should not have been found
Then Ask the expert to specialize $\mathcal{P}$ and/or modify $\mathcal{C}$.
Evaluate the consequences of the suggested modifications.
Ask the expert to choose his/her preferred modifications and add them to $\mathcal{T}$.
Update all data structures.

In the following, the justification process will be described, as well as the relations between the justification forest and the target knowledge base. For the sake of exemplification, we shall use the task, mentioned in section 3, of characterizing possibly UNSAFE-TO-TOUCH objects, given a set of 14 examples and 18 counterexamples of this concept, taken from everyday life (irons, pots, lamps, knives, etc.).

4.1. Construction of the justification forest

In order to describe how the system works, some definitions have to be introduced first. Let $\mathfrak{J} = \mathcal{C} \cup \mathcal{P}$ be the domain theory. Let, moreover, Σ be the set of primary nodes in the causal network $\mathcal{C}$ and Σ_0 the subset of nodes corresponding to the first causes. Two kinds of justifications will be considered: the first one (analogous to the one introduced in EBL) refers to *instances* and is an explanation, in terms of cause/effect relations, of why an example f is an instance of a concept h.

Definition 1 — Given a theory $\mathfrak{J} = \mathcal{C} \cup \mathcal{P}$ and an instance f of a concept h (denoted by h(f)), we call *explanation* E(h, f) of f w.r.t. h the pair $\{\sigma_o(f), A\}$ such that:

$$\mathfrak{J} \cup \sigma_0(f) \cup A \vdash h(f)$$

where $\sigma_0(f)$ is a first cause, true of f, and A is a set of assumptions, i.e., a set of predicates belonging to P, which have to be assumed true in order to derive h(f). □

The second type of justification refers to *rules* and *instances* and explains why a given rule is correctly verified by an instance f of a concept h.

Definition 2 — Given a rule $r \equiv (\varphi(z, x) \Rightarrow h(z)) \in \mathcal{KB}$, and an instance f of h, let $\varphi^{(o)}(f)$ be the operationalization of φ true of f. Then, a *justification* J(r, f) of r w.r.t. f is a 4-tuple $\{\sigma_0(f), A, \psi^{(o)}, \rho)$ such that:

a) $\mathfrak{J} \cup \sigma_0(f) \cup A \vdash (\psi^{(o)}(f) \Rightarrow h(f))$
b) $\psi^{(o)} = \rho \wedge \xi_1$ and $\varphi^{(o)} = \rho \wedge \xi_2$ (i.e., $\psi^{(o)}$ and $\varphi^{(o)}$ have a subformula ρ in common)
c) $\sigma_0(f)$ is a first cause, true of f, and A is a set of assumptions □

We distinguish between *total justification*, in which $\rho \equiv \varphi^{(o)}$ and *partial justification*, in which $\xi_2 \neq \emptyset$. Definitions 1 and 2 can be generalized to the case of a set of examples F, obtaining E(h, F) and J(r, F), respectively.

The justification forest $\mathcal{G}$ is an extension of the classical explanation tree used in EBL to the case of simultaneous operationalization of several predicates on many examples. The construction of $\mathcal{G}$ is performed by the algorithm *FORW-DED*, which starts from the set of operational predicates $P^{(o)}$ and applies forward the rules in $\mathcal{P}$ until either no more rules are applicable or some primary node of the causal network has been reached.

Algorithm FORW-DED

Let Stimuli be a set of activated rules in $\mathcal{P}$ and let $P^{(o)}$ be the set of operational predicates. (A rule is *activated* when at least one conjunct in its left-hand side is true of at least one example).

$\mathcal{G} = \emptyset$.
Initialize Stimuli with the rules activated by the predicates in $P^{(o)}$.
Add all the predicates in $P^{(o)}$, true on some example, to $\mathcal{G}$ as leaves.
Create in the data base the relation associated to each leaf.
Repeat
(1) Select a rule $r \equiv \varphi \rightarrow P$ from Stimuli.
    Operationalize P through r by completely unfolding φ.
    If $P \in \mathcal{G}$ **Then** Add to $\mathcal{G}$ the new operationalization as an OR-son of P.
        Update relation P^* by merging the old with the new one.
    Else Create a new node P in $\mathcal{G}$ and associate to it P^*.
        If $P \in \Sigma$ (primary nodes in $\mathcal{C}$)
            Then Remove r from Stimuli and Go To (1).
    Remove r from Stimuli.
    Add to Stimuli all the rules in whose body P occurs.
Until Stimuli $= \emptyset$.

In figure 3, a part of the justification forest built up for the 32 examples of unsafe and safe objects is reported.

The set of numbers associated with each node in figure 3 represents the set of examples satisfying the formula associated to the node. Notice that, for each example, more than one binding is possible. A major source of complexity in the construction of $\mathcal{G}$ is the need

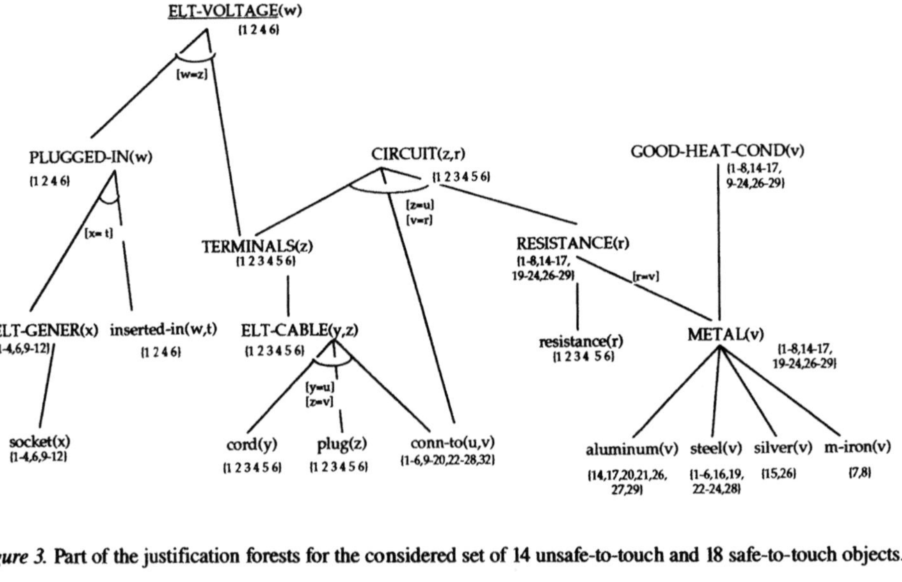

Figure 3. Part of the justification forests for the considered set of 14 unsafe-to-touch and 18 safe-to-touch objects.

to maintain identity constraints among variables in AND nodes. In fact, the bindings between variables and components in the examples are performed independently from one another in the son nodes (being the forest built up bottom-up). As an example, all the pairs of objects connected each other are stored in the extension of the node conn-to(u, v); however, only those pairs of connected objects that are a cord and a plug, respectively, are to be selected to form an electric cable. Therefore, it may happen that an AND node is false, but their son nodes are true, in isolation. This detailed information about bindings is fundamental for the tasks of knowledge refinement and theory revision, because it allows the location where an explanation fails to be exactly individuated.

Additional pieces of information are also added to each node: one is its possible connection with primary or secondary nodes of $\mathcal{C}$, and another is a *truth status*, which can assume one among the set {True, Assumed True, Assumed False, False} of values. An "Assumed True" status may derive from the presence of an Ω within an operationalization or from the assumption of some predicate that was not specified in the data, but could not be proved false. Obviously, the status is not a global property of the node, because different assumptions might have been made for different examples. Then, the status is evaluated for every binding of each example and stored, as an additional field in each tuple, in the relation associated to the node.

4.2. Finding causal paths

During the preceding phase, a subset of the nodes in Σ have been activated. Now, we want to use abduction to hypothesize first causes, moving back from the activated nodes. The abductive process is performed by the following algorithm *ABDUCTION*. For the sake of simplicity, the parts of the algorithm handling the extensional representation of the causal nodes and the assumptions have been omitted.

Algorithm ABDUCTION
Let σ be an activated node from which a causal path starts, and let CAUSES be the set of immediate causes of σ.

Let SUCCESS be the set of paths successfully arrived to a first cause from σ and FAIL the set of failed paths.

SUCCESS = FAIL = $\emptyset$
CAUSES = {Immediate causes of σ}
For each node $\sigma_i \in$ CAUSES do
  Let $path_i$ be a sequence of causal nodes, starting from σ
  Let γ_i be the (possibly empty) constraint on the edge connecting σ_i to σ in $\mathcal{C}$
  Evaluate the formula $path_i = \sigma \wedge \gamma_i \wedge \sigma_i$
  If No example verifies $path_i$ or (σ_i has a subset P_i of $\mathcal{P}$ associated to it and No example verifies P_i)
    Then FAIL = FAIL $\cup$ {$path_i$}
    Else Hypothesize σ_i with its associated context CTX_i (if any)
      SUCCESS = SUCCESS $\cup$ {$path_i$}
  Remove σ_i from CAUSES.

The above algorithm describes how a single step of abduction is performed. Sequences of abduction steps belonging to the same path are kept together in a single global description. When an exhaustive search for causal paths is too expensive, paths that currently have fewer assumptions are followed first. In the example of figure 3, the following causal paths have been successfully completed (among others):

Path_1 = ⟨HOT(x), HEATING(x), GOOD-HEAT-CONDUCTOR(x), IN-THERMAL-FLUX(x), CONDUCTION(y, x), *HOT*(y), *ADJACENT*(x, y)⟩ for the set of examples {1, 2, 4, 6, 16, 17, 19, 23}

Path_2 = ⟨HOT(x), HEATING(x), GOOD-HEAT-CONDUCTOR(x), INSIDE(r, x), ELT-POWER-DISSIPATION(r), ELT-CURRENT(r), CIRCUIT(y, r), ELT-VOLTAGE(y)⟩ for the set of examples {1, 2, 4, 6}

In the paths, underlined predicates are primary nodes in $\mathcal{C}$, whereas italic predicates belong to contexts. The examples involved are four electric irons {1, 2, 4, 6}, which are hot because of the Joule effect produced by the electric current flow, and different types of pots {16, 17, 19, 23}, which are hot because of the heat conduction from some heat source. During causal justification, the context *HOT*(y) ∧ *ADJACENT*(x, y), associated with the first cause CONDUCTION(y, x) is hypothesized at the same time as the first cause. Then, CONDUCTION(y, x) is a potential explanation also for the four irons. Due to this ambiguity, the hypothesized context is checked, and turns out to be false for {1, 2, 4, 6} and true for the remaining objects. Notice that, during verification of the context, the predicate ADJACENT(y, x) is tested first, because it does not involve recursion. In this way, for the three irons {1, 2, 4} this verification fails immediately and the re-activation of the causal reasoning on HOT(y) is necessary only for {6}. However, this also fails, because the iron is adjacent to an object that is cold. Then, the first cause CONDUCTION(y, x) only covers examples {16, 17, 19, 23}, whereas ELT-VOLTAGE(y) only covers {1, 2, 4, 6}.

5. Acquisition and refinement of the target knowledge

After the process of building up, for the training examples, the justification forest and the set of causal paths, learning can start. In particular, an initial $\mathcal{KB}$ is extracted and afterwards can be refined, if it is the case.

5.1. One-step learning

From the causal paths, an initial set of decision rules is generated, one rule for each set of explained examples. For the sake of exemplification, let us consider the two sets of examples {1, 2, 4, 6} and {16, 17, 19, 23} for which the final causal explanations are the following:

Cause_1 = ⟨HOT(x), HEATING(x), GOOD-HEAT-CONDUCTOR(x), IN-THERMAL-FLUX(x), CONDUCTION(y, x), *HOT*(y), *ADJACENT*(x, y)⟩ for the set of examples {16, 17, 19, 23}

Cause_2 = ⟨HOT(x), HEATING(x), GOOD-HEAT-CONDUCTOR(x), INSIDE(r, x), ELT-POWER-DISSIPATION(r), ELT-CURRENT(r), CIRCUIT(y, r), ELT-VOLTAGE(y)⟩ for the set of examples {1, 2, 4, 6}

In order to complete a causal path, several predicates, not denoting primary causal nodes, have been verified and associated with the path. In particular, let ∂ be the conjunction of the necessary conditions (constraints) and ψ the conjunction of the remaining ones. For Cause_1 the two sets are

∂ {16, 17, 19, 23} = GOOD-HEAT-CONDUCTOR(x)

ψ {16, 17, 19, 23} = HOT(y) $\wedge$ ADJACENT(x, y),

whereas, for Cause_2, we obtain (by operationalizing ELT-VOLTAGE(y) by means of PLUGGED-IN(y)):

∂ {1, 2, 4, 6} = GOOD-HEAT-CONDUCTOR(x) $\wedge$ INSIDE(r, x) $\wedge$ CIRCUIT(y, r)

ψ {1, 2, 4, 6} = PLUGGED-IN(y)

As a first approximation, we shall consider the following heuristic decisions rules:

r_1 ≡ *GOOD-HEAT-CONDUCTOR(x)* $\wedge$ HOT(y) $\wedge$ ADJACENT(x, y) ⇒

⇒ UNSAFE-TO-TOUCH(x) (7)

r_2 ≡ *GOOD-HEAT-CONDUCTOR(x)* $\wedge$ *INSIDE(r, x)* $\wedge$ *CIRCUIT(y, r)* $\wedge$

PLUGGED-IN(y) ⇒ UNSAFE-TO-TOUCH(x) (8)

The distinction between the necessary conditions (in italics) and the others is kept as such in the heuristic rules, because we want the performance system to manage them in different ways: necessary conditions are assumed false if they cannot be proved true, whereas the other conditions are assumed true if they cannot be proved false, during classification, as well.

As we can notice, rules (7) and (8) contain non-operational predicates. This is allowed, not only for making assumptions in classification, but also for obtaining a more compact $\mathcal{KB}$. Let us consider, for instance, the predicate GOOD-HEAT-CONDUCTOR(x); we know that metals are good heat conductors, so rule (7) may correspond to a possibly large number of operational rules, each one obtained by substituting steel(x), aluminum(x), silver(x), etc., in place of GOOD-HEAT-CONDUCTOR(x). These rules are essentially the same rule. It is, then, more convenient to allow non-operational predicates to occur in the left-hand sides of the rules (Segre, 1987; Hirsh, 1988). Another advantage can be obtained with this choice: we do not need to write a $\mathcal{KB}$ separate from the justification structure. It is sufficient to link, in $\mathcal{G}$, the non-operational predicate UNSAFE-TO-TOUCH(x) to an

AND node corresponding to the left-hand side of each rule. In this way, the process of classifying a new instance coincides with that of justifying it and also of locating the failure point when an error occurs.

In the example given above, rules (7) and (8) are consistent (they do not cover any counterexample), but they are not complete (only eight examples are covered by them). It turns out that one more consistent rule can be obtained in this phase, covering a hot pan inside an oven. For the remaining objects (three types of bulbs and two cups filled with hot coffee), no explanation can be obtained (all paths are cut because of the failure of necessary conditions), and, hence, no rule. This case requires a session of theory revision. Even if in the example presented this is not the case, it may also happen that explanations can be found by making some assumptions. Then, the obtained rules may not be consistent. This case requires a session of rule refinement.

5.2. *Knowledge refinement*

Knowledge refinement will only be briefly outlined here, because it has already been discussed elsewhere (Botta, Giordana, & Saitta, 1990; Baroglio, Botta & Saitta, 1992). It is not necessary that knowledge refinement is invoked on a $\mathcal{KB}$ acquired as described in the previous subsection. On the contrary, the $\mathcal{KB}$ may come from a different source, for instance, from an expert. Hence, let us suppose that someone suggested the following rule:

$$r \equiv \text{OBJ}(x) \wedge \text{body}(y) \wedge \text{part-of}(y, x) \wedge \text{closed}(y) \wedge \text{METAL}(y) \wedge \text{CABLE}(z) \wedge$$
$$\text{part of}(z, x) \wedge \text{medium-size}(x) \Rightarrow \text{UNSAFE-TO-TOUCH}(x) \quad (9)$$

By considering that CABLE(x) can be operationalized by thread(x) and by ELT-CABLE (x, y), rule (9) has two alternative operationalizations on the set of 32 training examples:

$$r_1 \equiv \text{OBJ}(x) \wedge \text{body}(y) \wedge \text{part-of}(y, x) \wedge \text{closed}(y) \wedge \text{aluminum}(y) \wedge \text{thread}(z) \wedge$$
$$\text{part-of}(z, x) \wedge \text{medium-size}(x) \Rightarrow \text{UNSAFE-TO-TOUCH}(x) \quad (10)$$

$$r_2 \equiv \text{OBJ}(x) \wedge \text{body}(y) \wedge \text{part-of}(y, x) \wedge \text{closed}(y) \wedge \text{steel}(y) \wedge \text{cord}(z) \wedge \text{plug}(w) \wedge$$
$$\text{connected-to}(w, z) \wedge \text{part-of}(z, x) \wedge \text{medium-size}(x) \Rightarrow$$
$$\Rightarrow \text{UNSAFE-TO-TOUCH}(x) \quad (11)$$

Rule r_1 correctly covers a hot electric iron, but incorrectly covers a windowshade handle, which is safe to touch. On the other hand, r_2 correctly covers three plugged-in irons and incorrectly covers two unplugged irons. If we try to justify rule r_1, we notice that the windowshade handle belongs to the extension of CABLE(x), but not to that of ELT-CABLE (x, y). Therefore, CABLE(x) is too general, and the counterexample can be cut by specializing (9) as follows:

$$\text{OBJ}(x) \land \text{body}(y) \land \text{part-of}(y, x) \land \text{closed}(y) \land \text{METAL}(y) \land \text{ELT-CABLE}(z, w) \land \text{part of}(z, x) \land \text{medium-size}(x) \Rightarrow \text{UNSAFE-TO-TOUCH}(x) \quad (12)$$

Rule (12) still covers two unplugged irons. Using the algorithm for finding causal paths, described in section 4, we can prove that, for the set of hot irons,

$$\mathfrak{T} \vdash [\text{OBJ}(x) \land \text{body}(y) \land \text{part-of}(y, x) \land \text{METAL}(y) \land \text{cord}(z) \land \text{plug}(w) \land \text{connected-to}(w, z) \land \text{resistance}(u) \land \text{socket}(v) \land \text{connected-to}(z, u) \land \text{inside}(u, y) \land \text{inserted-in}(w, v) \Rightarrow \text{UNSAFE-TO-TOUCH}(x)] \quad (13)$$

Comparing rule (13) and rule (12), we notice that there is an overlapping part:

$$\rho \equiv \text{OBJ}(x) \land \text{body}(y) \land \text{part-of}(y, x) \land \text{METAL}(y) \land \text{ELT-CABLE}(z, w) \land \text{part of}(z, x)$$

which constitutes the justified part of rule (12). Notice that the predicates closed(y), referring to the body, and medium-size(x) are not justified by the theory. In order to cut the two unplugged irons, rule (13) suggests a set of predicates to be possibly added to rule (12): {resistance(u), socket(v), connected-to(z, u), inside(u, y), inserted-in(w, v)}. By analyzing the extensions of these predicates, we notice that inserted-in(w, v) covers exactly the four irons that we want to cover and nothing else. However, by climbing the justification forest, we find the node PLUGGED-IN(w), which is more general (hence potentially covering more examples) and does not cover any counterexamples, so this last node is chosen to be added. Finally, we obtain the consistent rule:

$$\text{OBJ}(x) \land \text{body}(y) \land \text{part-of}(y, x) \land \text{METAL}(y) \land \text{ELT-CABLE}(z, w) \land \text{part of}(z, x) \land \text{PLUGGED-IN}(z) \Rightarrow \text{UNSAFE-TO-TOUCH}(x) \quad (14)$$

6. Interaction with the expert and theory revision

An interesting aspect of the system WHY is its ability to work in an interactive manner during several phases of its behavior. In order to facilitate this interaction, a friendly, menu-driven user interface has been implemented.

Interaction with the expert occurs at the beginning, when he/she is required to give an initial bulk of phenomenological theory and an abstract causal model. Since this knowledge can be easily revised later, it is not very critical that it is as complete and consistent as possible from the beginning. Owing to the deep integration of the performance element into the learning process, the expert can let WHY run on his/her suggested modifications, analyze the results, and modify the theory accordingly. This is a two-way interaction: the feedback from WHY helps the expert focalize his/her attention on defective parts of the theory, whereas the expert can direct the system to explore the consequences of a subset of the current theory, saving computational efforts.

Human expertise can also be exploited in knowledge refinement, since the expert can directly suggest heuristic rules or parts of them, or can guide the system toward more promising rule specializations or generalizations, telling explicitly which predicates to try to remove or add. For instance, in this case, the expert is presented with the following menu:

REFINE MENU
The expert selects a rule r to be refined. Rule r exists in the knowledge base or can be a hint from the expert.

Current rule:	r
Rule syntax:	$\varphi \rightarrow$ h
Rule assumptions:	{set of conjuncts in φ that have been assumed}
Dependency rules:	{if φ contains an Ω, a dependency rule may be associated to it, in order to limit induction to a subspace of formulas}
Extension:	{set of bindings for each example covered, containing the identifier of the instance, the correct classes, the sets of instance parts satisfying φ, and the number of assumptions made for each binding}
General:	{set of rules, more general than r, existing in $\mathcal{KB}$}
Specific:	{set of rules, more specific than r, existing in $\mathcal{KB}$}

The expert can select among the following choices:

Delete	= Disactivate r
Forest	= Show the justification forest for r
Save	= Save r
Spec	= Activate a rule in **Specific**, instead of r
Gen	= Activate a rule in **General**, instead of r
Ref-pred	= Modify **r** by refining a predicate {climbing a taxonomy or choosing an operationalization}
Ref-ind	= Specialize **r** by invoking induction

The intervention of the expert during theory revision can be spontaneous or requested by WHY, when some contradiction arises. As an example, let us consider the case of the three hot bulbs, which cannot be justified even by making assumptions. The reason is that there is not mention, in $\mathcal{T}$, of how electric current can flow into the bulb filament. Since we know that the bulbs are positive instances of the concept UNSAFE-TO-TOUCH, and no explanation could be found, we are in presence of incompleteness in the theory. Then, WHY signals the problem and presents the expert with the part of the justification forest instantiated on the bulbs and with the set FAIL of failed causal paths. At the same time, it asks the expert if he/she wants to modify the causal model or the phenomenological theory. According to the expert's answer, an appropriate menu appears (not reported here because its structure matches that of the REFINE MENU).

In the case considered, the expert chooses to revise $\mathcal{P}$, because he knows that the problem is in the incomplete definition of what TERMINALS is. Then, he adds a new operationalization of TERMINALS, stating that there can be an electric contact between a part of the bulb and a part of the supporting lamp. It is interesting to note that a first trial to refine an incomplete explanation for the bulbs by induction succeeded: in fact, WHY covered the three bulbs and no counterexamples by adding to the partial rule (which had been extracted from the justification forest) the predicate bright(x), true for all the three objects. However, this modification is doubtful, because of the number of considered examples, whereas the same predicate, added after completing the theory, can be trusted.

7. Conclusions

The system WHY, which learns diagnostic rules from a set of examples (by induction), from a phenomenological theory (by deduction), and from a causal model (by abduction), has been presented. The system can work both automatically and in an interactive mode. The system has been tested on an artificial domain of heat transfer and then has been applied to a real domain of mechanical troubleshooting (Giordana et al., 1993). In the troubleshooting application, the rules learned from only 30 examples (5 for each class) showed, on a test set of 170 examples, performances comparable with those of the rule base learned without causal model (but with domain theory) from 140 examples and tested on 60 examples (Saitta et al., 1991). Moreover, the rules obtained from the causal model (several of which coincided with the previous ones) were perfectly understandable to the expert, in terms of his knowledge of the domain. The suggested conclusion is that a causal model allows robust and meaningful knowledge to be learned with acceptable computational complexity.

References

Baroglio, C., Botta, M. & Saitta, L. (1992). WHY: A system that learns using causal models and examples. In R. Michalski & G. Tecuci (Eds.), Machine learning: A multistrategy approach. Morgan Kaufmann.

Bergadano, F., Giordana, A. & Saitta, L. (1988). Automated concept acquisition in noisy environment. *IEEE Transactions PAMI, PAMI-10,* 555–575.

Bergadano, F. & Giordana, A. (1988). A knowledge intensive approach to concept induction. *Proceedings of the Machine Learning Conference* (pp. 305–317). Ann Arbor, MI.

Bergadano, F., Giordana, A. & Ponsero, S. (1989). Deduction in top-down inductive learning. *Proceedings of the Machine Learning Conference* (pp. 23–25). Ithaca, NY.

Bergadano, F., Giordana, A. & Saitta, L. (1990). Automated versus manual knowledge acquisition: a comparison in a real domain. *Proceedings of the First Japanese Knowledge Acquisition for Knowledge-Based Systems Workshop* (pp. 301–314). Tokyo, Japan.

Botta, M. & Saitta, L. (1988). Improving knowledge base system performances by experience. *Proceedings of the EWSL-88* (pp. 15–23). Glasgow, UK.

Botta, M., Giordana, A. & Saitta, L. (1990). Knowledge base refinement using a causal model. In Z. Ras & M. Zemankova (Eds.), *Intelligent systems: State of the art and future trends*, Ellis-Horwood, Chichester, U.K.

Cestnik, B. & Bratko, I. (1988). Learning redundant rules in noisy domains. *Proceedings of the ECAI-88* (pp. 348–350). Munich, Germany.

Chandrasekaran, B. & Mittal, S. (1983). Deep versus compiled knowledge approaches to diagnostic problem-solving. *International Journal of Man-Machine Studies, 19,* 425–436.

Clark, K. (1978). Negation as failure. In H. Gallaire & J. Minker (Eds.), *Logic and data bases.* Plenum Press, New York, NY.

Console, L., Torasso, P. & Theseider Dupré, D. (1990). A completion semantics for object-level abduction. *Proceedings of the AAAI Symposium on Automated Abduction* (pp. 72–75). Stanford, CA.

Cox, P.T. & Pietrzykowski, T. (1987). General diagnosis by abductive inference. *Proceedings of the IEEE Symposium on Logic Programming* (pp. 183–189).

Danyluk, A. (1991). Gemini: An integration of analytical and empirical learning. *Proceedings of the First International Workshop on Multistrategy Learning* (pp. 191–206). Harpers Ferry, WV.

Davis, R. (1984). Diagnostic reasoning based on structure and behavior. *Artificial Intelligence, 24,* 347–410.

DeJong, G. & Mooney, R. (1986). Explanation based learning: An alternative view. *Machine Learning, 1*, 47–80.
DeJong, G. (1990). Plausible inference vs. abduction. *Proceedings of the AAAI Symposium on Automated Abduction* (pp. 48–51). Stanford, CA.
de Kleer, J. & Seely Brown, J. (1986). Theories of causal ordering. *Artificial Intelligence, 29*, 33–61.
De Raedt, L. & Bruynooghe, M. (1991). CLINT: a multistrategy interactive concept learner and theory revision system. *Proceedings of the First International Workshop on Multistrategy Learning* (pp. 175-190). Harpers Ferry, WV.
Genesereth, M. (1984). The use of design descriptions in automated diagnosis. *Artificial Intelligence, 24*, 411–436.
Giordana, A., Saitta, L., Bergadano, F., Brancadori, F. & DeMarchi, D. (1993). ENIGMA: A system that learns diagnostic knowledge. *IEEE Trans. on Knowledge and Data Engineering, 5 (1)*.
Hirsh, H. (1988). Reasoning about operationality for explanation-based learning. *Proceedings of the Machine Learning Conference* (pp. 214–220). Ann Arbor, MI.
Kahn, G. (1984). On when diagnostic systems want to do without causal knowledge. *Advances in Artificial Intelligence*, (pp. 21–30).
Keller, R. (1988). Defining operationality for EBL. *Artificial Intelligence, 35*, 227–242.
Kodratoff, Y. (1991). Induction and the organization of knowledge. *Proceedings of the First International Workshop on Multistrategy Learning* (pp. 34–48). Harpers Ferry, WV. (See also this issue.)
Lebowitz, M. (1986). Integrated learning: Controlling explanation. *Cognitive Science, 10*, 219–240.
Matwin, S. & Plante, B. (1991). A deductive-inductive method for theory revision. *Proceedings of the International Workshop on Multistrategy Learning* (pp. 160–174). Harpers Ferry, WV. (See also this issue.)
Michalski, R. (1983). A theory and methodology of inductive learning. *Artificial Intelligence, 20*, 111–161.
Michalski, R. (1991). Inferential learning theory as a basis for multistrategy task-adaptive learning. *Proceedings of the First International Workshop on Multistrategy Learning* (pp. 3–18). Harpers Ferry, WV.
Michalski, R.S. & Chilausky, R.L. (1991). Learning by being told and learning from examples: an experimental comparison of the two methods of knowledge acquisition in the context of developing an expert system for soybean disease diagnosis. *International Journal of Policy Analysis and Information Systems, 4*, 125–126.
Mitchell, T. (1982). Generalization as search. *Artificial Intelligence, 18*, 203–226.
Mitchell, T., Keller, R. & Kedar-Cabelli, S. (1986). Explanation based generalization. *Machine Learning, 1*, 47–80.
Mooney, R.J. & Ourston, D. (1991). A multistrategy approach to theory refinement. *Proceedings of the First International Workshop on Multistrategy Learning* (pp. 115–131). Harpers Ferry, WV.
Morris, S. & O'Rorke, P. (1990). An approach to theory revision using abduction. *Proceedings of the AAAI Symposium on Automated Abduction* (pp. 33–37). Stanford, CA.
Pazzani, M.J. (1988). Integrating explanation-based and empirical learning methods in OCCAM. *Proceedings of the European Working Session on Learning* (pp. 147–165). Glasgow, UK.
Poole, D. (1988. Representing knowledge for logic-based diagnosis. *Proceedings of the International Conference on Fifth Generation Computer Systems* (pp. 1282–1290). Tokyo, Japan.
Quinlan, R. (1986). Induction of decision trees. *Machine Learning, 1*, 81–106.
Reiter, R. (1984). A theory of diagnosis from first principles. *Artificial Intelligence, 32*, 57–95.
Robinson, J.A. & Siebert, E.E. (1982). LOGLISP: An alternative to Prolog. *Machine Intelligence, 10*, 399–419.
Saitta, L., Botta, M., Ravotto, S. & Sperotto, S.B. (1991). Improving learning by using deep models. *Proceedings of the First International Workshop on Multistrategy Learning* (pp. 131–143). Harpers Ferry, WV.
Segre, A.M. (1987). On the operationality/generality trade-off in explanation-based learning. *Proceedings of the IJCAI-87* (pp. 242–248). Milan, Italy.
Tecuci, G. (1991). Learning as understanding the external world. *Proceedings of the First International Workshop on Multistrategy Learning* (pp. 49–64). Harpers Ferry, WV.
Torasso, P. & Console, L. (1989). *Diagnostic problem solving*. Van Nostrand Reinhold, New York, NY.

Received September 30, 1991
Accepted September 30, 1991
Final Manuscript February 28, 1992.

Machine Learning, 11, 173–194 (1993)

Learning Causal Patterns: Making a Transition from Data-Driven to Theory-Driven Learning

MICHAEL PAZZANI PAZZANI@ICS.UCI.EDU
Department of Information and Computer Science, University of California, Irvine, CA 92717

Abstract. We describe an incremental learning algorithm, called theory-driven learning, that creates rules to predict the effect of actions. Theory-driven learning exploits knowledge of regularities among rules to constrain learning. We demonstrate that this knowledge enables the learning system to rapidly converge on accurate predictive rules and to tolerate more complex training data. An algorithm for incrementally learning these regularities is described and we provide evidence that the resulting regularities are sufficiently generally to facilitate learning in new domains. The results demonstrate that transfer from one domain to another can be achieved by deliberately overgeneralizing rules in one domain and biasing the learning algorithm to create new rules that specialize these overgeneralizations in other domains.

Keywords. Causality, theory-driven learning, multistrategy learning

1. Introduction

In order to understand the environment, people must learn to predict the effects of their own actions and the actions of others. This prediction process requires the learner to associate state changes with actions. Many researchers have shown that, even in very young children, this learning process is constrained by general knowledge of the actions that are likely to be responsible for state changes. Bullock, Gelman, and Baillargeon (1982) and Schultz and Kestenbaum (1985) provide excellent overviews of the types of general constraints that are exploited during the learning of specific causal rules.

In Pazzani (1991), we propose a computational learning model that is intended to explain why learning some predictive relationships is more difficult than learning others for human learners. Here, we report on experiments that show that this learning model provides an advantage over a purely data-driven learner under a variety of circumstances. The learning model relies on an explicit representation of general knowledge of causality. Here, we also propose an algorithm for learning this general knowledge of causality. We computationally explore the hypothesis that much of the general knowledge of causality (with some simple specific causal rules) can be learned by simple correlational processes. Once this general knowledge of causality is acquired, the later acquisition of more complex, specific causal rules is constrained and facilitated by the general knowledge of causality that has been acquired. As general knowledge of causality is acquired, the learner shifts learning strategies from a data-driven strategy that attempts to find regularities in a set of examples to a theory-driven strategy that looks for instantiations of its general knowledge.

In particular, a learner will be described that starts with only temporal knowledge of causality (i.e., temporal contiguity and temporal priority). This knowledge is sufficient to

Table 1. An example of the output produced by Talespin, divided into 14 time intervals.

(0) Karen was thirsty. (1) She pushed the door away from the cupboard. The cupboard was open. (2) She took a small red plastic cup from the cupboard. Mike pushed the light switch. She had the cup. The cup was not in the cupboard. The light was on. (3)She pushed the door to the cupboard. The cupboard wasn't open. (4) The auburn cat pushed a large clear glass vase to the tile floor. Karen pushed the handle away from the cold faucet. The cold water was flowing. The vase was broken. (5) She moved the cup to the faucet. The cup was filled with the water. (6) She pushed the handle to the faucet. The cold water wasn't flowing. (7) Karen dropped the cup to the tile floor. The cup wasn't filled with the water. (8) She pushed the door away from the cupboard. The cupboard was open. (9) She took a small clear glass cup from the cupboard. She had the cup. The cup was not in the cupboard. (10) Karen pushed the handle away from the cold faucet. The cold water was flowing. The phone was ringing. (11) She moved the cup to the faucet. Lynn picked up the phone reciever. The cup was filled with the water. The phone wasn't ringing. (12)Karen pushed the handle to the faucet. The cold water wasn't flowing. (13) She drank the water. The cup wasn't filled with the water. Karen wasn't thirsty.

induce simple causal rules. We hypothesize that more general causal knowledge is acquired by finding common patterns in the simple causal rules. This more general knowledge represents additional spatial and configural patterns that are present in causal rules.

To make the problem more concrete, consider the sequence of events in table 1. This is the output of Talespin (Meehan, 1981), a program designed to generate short stories describing actors attempting to achieve goals. We will use Talespin to simulate a world in which the learner must observe actions and predict their results.

The output is divided into a number of discrete time intervals. In each time interval, some actions may be observed and the state of the world may change. Although this simulated input is necessarily a simplification of the complex world in which a child learns causal rules, we have added a number of complexities to Talespin to make it more realistic while still allowing systematic experimentation by varying parameters such as the amount of noise in the data. For example, two actions may occur in the same time interval (e.g., time 4). Therefore, the agent must be able to determine which effect is associated with which action. This problem is complicted by the fact that some actions may have more than one effect (e.g., time 9) and some actions may have no effect. In addition, the same action may have different effects (e.g., dropping an object in times 4 and 7). Finally, some state changes may be observed, although the action that caused the state change may not be observed (e.g., the phone ringing during time 10).

This learning problem can be summarized as follows:

Given: A sequence of time interval where each time interval consists of a set of actions and a set of state changes.

Create: A set of rules that predict when a state change will occur.

In this article, we first discuss the representation of examples, causal rules, and general knowledge of causality. Next, we review a learning method called theory-driven learning (TDL) that makes use of general knowledge of causality to constrain the search for causal rules. Finally, we discuss an extension to theory-driven learning that allows the general knowledge of causality to be learned from initial observations and demonstrate that the induced knowledge facilitates learning in new domains.

1.1. Representation of examples

To avoid problems of natural language understanding, we will assume that the training examples are in some internal representation. Our learning model will make use of Conceptual Dependency (CD) (Schank & Abelson, 1977), the internal representation used by the Talespin program. A role-filler notation is used to represent CD structures. CD structures have a head and a set of roles and fillers. The filler for a role is a CD structure that must have a head and may have zero or more roles. Common heads are ACT (for actions), STATE (for unary predicates), RELATION (for binary predicates), and PP (for physical objects). For ACTS, the roles used are type, actor, object, from, and to. STATES have type, actor, and mode roles. RELATIONs have type, actor, val, and mode roles.[1] PP's have a wide variety of roles, such as type, subtype, size, color, etc. Every individual PP has a special role, unique-id, used to indicate the referent in Talespin's world.

In Talespin, each change of the world is indicated by the assertion of a new STATE or RELATION (indicated by a mode of POS) or the retraction of a STATE or RELATION (indicated by a mode of NEG). STATEs and RELATIONs are assumed to hold for all future time intervals until explicitly retracted (cf. Elkan, 1990).

1.2. Representation of causal rules

The task required by the learner is to predict the state changes that will occur when an action is observed. In order to achieve this task, a set of causal rules is learned. Each rule contains a general description of a class of actions, and a description of a state change. Table 2 illustrates the representation of a simple rule that indicates that a phone stops ringing after the phone receiver is picked up.[2] A question mark before a symbol (e.g., ?X) indicates that the symbol is a variable. In this rule, the variable is needed to indicate that the phone whose receiver is lifted is the phone that stops ringing. The CD structure after a variable in the antecedent (i.e., PP type PHONE) indicates that the object bound to the variable is constrained to match that structure also.

A variety of tasks could be achieved using rules such as that in table 2. The rule can be used for planning (specifying an action to perform to achieve the goal of stopping the telephone from ringing) or for abductive inference (infer what action may have occurred to account for a phone that stopped ringing). Here, we will consider only a prediction task.

Table 2. A rule indicating that picking up a phone receiver results in the phone not ringing.

```
IF    ACT type GRASP
          object PP type RECEIVER
                    component-of ?X
                    (PP type PHONE)
THEN      STATE     type RING
                    actor ?X
                    mode NEG
```

When an action is observed, all state changes that are the consequent of rules whose antecedents match that action will be predicted. There are two types of prediction errors that can be made. Errors of omission occur when a state change is observed but not predicted. Errors of commission occur when a state change is predicted but is not observed.

The learner needs to monitor the accuracy of the causal rules that are acquired. This is implemented by associating a confidence that is the ratio of two counters with each rule. One counter is incremented each time the rule makes a prediction; the other is incremented whenever the rule makes an incorrect prediction. In addition, any exceptions to a rule (i.e., actions on which the rule made an incorrect prediction) are stored in memory indexed by the rule.[3] The exceptions are used only for learning, and are not used during prediction.

In order to generate a story, Talespin contains a simulator that determines the effects of actions. This simulator is essentially a large Lisp conditional expression that asserts state changes when an action occurs. The causal rules learned can be viewed as a declarative representation of Talespin's simulator.

1.3. A data-driven learning process for acquiring causal rules

A variety of data-driven (i.e., associative) learning theories have been proposed that can address the problem. For example, DIDO (Scott & Markovitch, 1989), performs a similar task (i.e., determining the effects of its own operators rather than observed actions). With a suitable change of representation, neural network systems (e.g., Sutton, 1988) could also be applied to this problem. Here, we briefly describe a data-driven learning method based upon UNIMEM (Lebowitz, 1987). In our learning model, data-driven learning will be used to form initial causal rules. More general principles of causality will be derived from these rules (as described in section 3) and used by the theory-driven learning process (described in section 2).

Each time interval is represented by a set of actions and a set of state changes. The learner must acquire rules to indicate which actions are predictive of each state change. An unsupervised learning task is performed at each time interval. First, the observed actions are compared to existing causal rules, and a set of state changes are predicted. Next, the predicted state changes are compared to the observed state changes. The confidence and exceptions are updated for those state changes that were correctly predicted and for those state changes that were predicted but not observed. If there are any unpredicted state changes, the learner is run on all pairings of observed actions with unpredicted state changes.

The learner processes each time interval as it is observed. Since this is an unsupervised learning task, the learner must perform two subtasks (Fisher, 1987). First, due to the variety of training examples, the examples must be aggregated into clusters of similar examples. In this work, we rely on a UNIMEM-like approach to clustering and concentrate on the second subtask: creating a general description of the aggregated examples. This general description is the rule used to make predictions about new examples.

The first example in a new cluster becomes the initial rule. The rule is constructed by using the action as the antecedent, and the state as the consequent. If the same object (as indicated by its `unique-id`) fills more than one role in the action or the state, a variable is introduced. Variables represent equality constraints. For example, the varible `?X` in table 2 indicates the phone that stops ringing must be identical to the phone whose receiver is picked up. Whenever a new example is added to a cluster, the rule is generalized by dropping any roles that differ between the rule and the example. In addition, if the example does not conform to an equality constraint, the equality constraint is dropped.

2. Background

Theory-driven learning brings additional knowledge to the learning process. Data-driven learners exploit inter-example relationships (i.e., regularities among several training examples). Theory-driven learning has knowledge of intra-example relationships (i.e., constraints between the role fillers of an action and state change). We call these constraints *causal patterns*. The causal patterns warrant the theory-driven learning program to ignore certain regularities between examples. As a consequence, TDL searches a smaller hypothesis space and would be expected to learn accurate rules from fewer examples (provided that the smaller hypothesis space contains an accurate hypothesis). At least two learning systems have been developed that make use of general causal knowledge to constrain learning. LUCK (Schultz, 1987) makes use of a general theory of causality to identify the cause responsible for an effect. TDL (Pazzani, 1987) learns causal rules that are consistent with a general theory of causality. Pazzani (1991) discusses how *causal patterns* can be used to encode humans' general knowledge of causal relationships. In particular, the causal patterns represent spatial and temporal conditions under which human observers report that an action appears to result in a state change.

2.1. Representation of causal patterns

The theory-driven learning procedure can only learn causal rules that conform to one of the causal patterns. Here, we discuss two types of causal patterns:

Exceptionless: An exceptionless causal pattern applies when all of the examples in a cluster are followed by the same state change (or when there is only one example).

Dispositional: A dispositional causal pattern applies when some examples in a cluster are followed by a state change, while others are not. It postulates that a difference in a particular role filler is responsible for the different results.

Table 3 displays one exceptionless causal pattern: an action performed on a component of an object may result in a state change to that object. The causal rule in table 2 (picking up a phone results in the phone not ringing) conforms to this pattern.

For each exceptionless pattern, there may be a dispositional pattern. A dispositional pattern limits the search for differences between positive and negative examples to one or more roles of the action. Table 4 displays a dispositional causal pattern. In this pattern,

Table 3. An exceptionless causal pattern: An action performed on a component of an object may result in a state change to that object.

CAUSE	ACT object PP component-of ?O
EFFECT	STATE actor ?O

Table 4. A dispositional causal pattern.

CAUSE	ACT object ?O
EFFECT	STATE actor ?O
DISPOSITION	object

there is a single dispositional role: object. This pattern indicates that when similar actions performed on an object have different results, and they are performed on different objects, the differing roles of the object are responsible for the different result. This pattern would be useful in creating a rule that describes the difference between the result of a cat knocking over a large clear glass vase during time 4 in table 1 and Karen dropping a small red plastic cup in time 7. Such a rule would indicate that glass objects break when they fall while plastic objects do not. Note that correlation between examples is needed to determine that the composition rather than the color of the object is important. However, this correlation is constrained to the object role. Therefore, TDL will not entertain a hypothesis that indicates that objects break when dropped by cats, but not humans.

2.2. The process of theory-driven learning

Pazzani (1990) describes the theory-driven learning process in detail. Here we only provide an overview that is needed to understand how TDL uses a new causal patterns acquired through the process described in section 3. Both the data-driven and theory-driven learning strategies use the same clustering process. Theory-driven learning occurs whenever a new example is added to a cluster, and the current rule did not make a correct prediction. If a causal pattern matches the situation, TDL will form a causal rule that is consistent with both the data and the causal pattern.

2.3. Experiments with TDL

In this section, experiments with TDL in OCCAM are reported. OCCAM is a multistrategy learning system that includes an explanation-based, a theory-driven, and a data-driven learning component. We compare TDL to the data-driven learning algorithm in OCCAM. For consistency with previous descriptions of OCCAM, we will call this data-driven learning algorithm SBL for "similarity-based learning." We test the following hypotheses:

1. TDL will tolerate more complex training data than SBL. In this experiment, multiple actions (and state changes) will occur at the same time.

2. The TDL and SBL algorithms will degrade gracefully with noisy training data. Here, we consider one type of noise that was created by making the operators in Talespin's world nondeterministic. With a certain probability, an action may have no effect. For example, glass objects may break only 75% of the time they are knocked off a counter onto the floor.
3. A combination of TDL and SBL will tolerate incomplete and incorrect sets of causal patterns. Here we will compare the performance of TDL and SBL combined to the performance of SBL alone. In this combination SBL is run only if TDL fails to find a rule (i.e., no causal pattern matches the experiences).

We will use Talespin to generate test and training examples for these learning algorithms. In this world, actors may have one of three goals (thirsty, hungry, or bored) and perform actions to achieve these goals. The thirsty goal is satisfied by drinking a glass of milk or water from the refrigerator, or water from the faucet. Table 1 shows a typical thirsty story. The hungry goal is satisfied by eating a piece of fruit from either the counter or the refrigerator. The bored goal is satisfied by playing catch with either a ball or a balloon. Random actions may occur during any story (cats knocking objects over, phones or door bells ringing, etc.) and actors may have accidents (dropping objects, throwing balls into windows, throwing a balloon into a rose bush). A total of approximately 60 rules are needed to predict the state changes in all of these domains. The fact that 10 causal patterns can facilitate learning indicates that there is a structure in Talespin's world that can be exploited to constrain the learning process.

2.3.1. *Simultaneous actions*

In most realistic situations, more than one action is occurring at the same time. In order to run this experiment, we modified Talespin so that with a certain probability, P, two contiguous time intervals are merged into one. This merging is done recursively so that, for example, there is a P^2 probability that three contiguous time intervals are merged. Ten runs were made of SBL and TDL on the same randomly generated sequences of Talespin output of 500 time intervals (corresponding to roughly 25 stories). The errors of omission and commission of each algorithm are measured by testing on 600 action-state change pairs after every 20 time intervals for the first 100 examples and every 50 time intervals for the remaining 400 training time intervals.

SBL takes a conservative approach and learns one rule for each action that occurs in the same time interval as a state change. When an error of commission later occurs, the "confidence" in each rule is lowered (by incrementing an exception counter), but the rule is not deleted. Such rules are not deleted, since some actions do not always have the same effect (e.g., sometimes a glass cup does not break when it is dropped). In this experiment, to be more fair to SBL, we will measure errors of commission in two manners. With the first measure, errors of commission will be reported as the percent of total predicted state changes that were not observed. A second measure takes the confidence in the prediction into account by multiplying the total number of predictions and the total number of unsubstantiated predictions by the confidence of the rule that made the prediction.

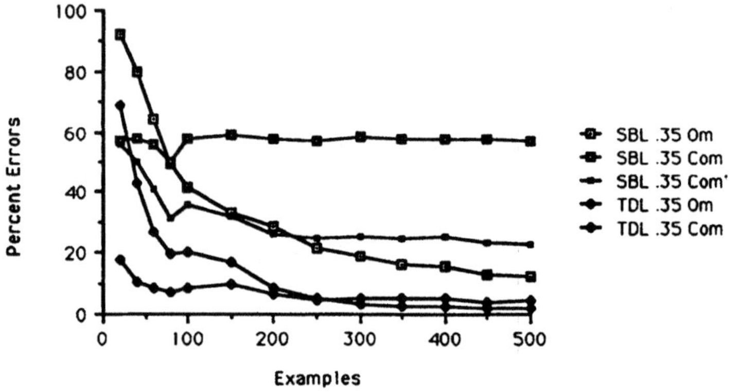

Figure 1. A comparison of TDL and SBL when there is a 0.35 probability that two actions occur simultaneously. Errors of omission and commission are plotted as a function of the number of training examples. Com′ indicates that the errors of commission calculation take account of the confidence of the prediction.

TDL will not learn a rule if a training exampled does not conform to a known causal pattern. As a consequence, TDL is predicted to be less sensitive to a complex learning environment in which multiple actions occur simultaneously. Figure 1 shows the mean percentage of errors for SBL and TDL as a function of the number of training examples when $P = 0.35$. The graph in figure 1 demonstrates that TDL converges on an accurate set of rules more rapidly than SBL.

With this complex training data, TDL has fewer errors of omission and commission than SBL. Taking the confidence of the prediction into account (the line labeled SBL .35 Com′ in the figure) lessens the difference between the SBL and TDL. This indicates that the predictions of SBL made with greater confidence are more likely to be correct. To simplify the graph, TDL errors of commission weighted by the confidence are not displayed. TDL typically has higher confidence values, so the two measures of errors of commission are very close in value. The results of this experiment confirm the prediction that TDL will be less sensitive than SBL when multiple actions occur at the same time.

2.3.2. Learning from noisy data

In learning causal rules, we consider one type of noise. With a certain probability, an action will not have any effect. In Talespin's world, this is a natural type of noise. For example, glass objects do not always break when struck and balloons don't always pop when they fall onto a grass lawn. The TDL and SBL algorithms were designed to tolerate training data with this type of noise. In particular, SBL only finds commonalities between examples in which there is a state change. When there is noise in the training data, there are fewer positive examples, so more errors of omission would be expected as the amount of noise increases. Exceptionless causal patterns in TDL operate similarly. However, dispositional patterns attempt to find a role filler (or conjunction of role fillers) that differentiate the actions accompanied by state changes from those that are not. In this case, noise in the training data may cause TDL to blame an incorrect role filler. Since the algorithm attempts

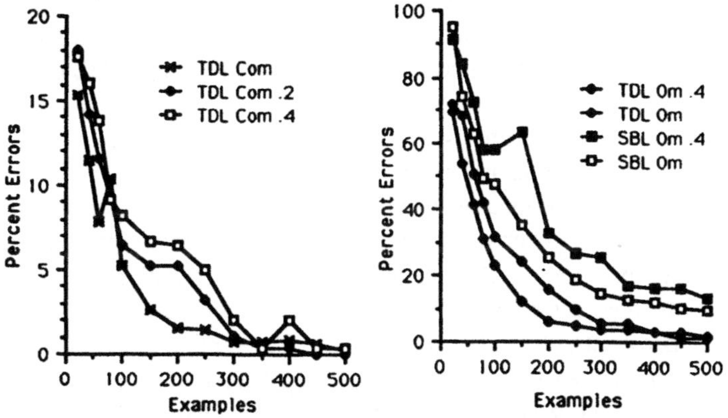

Figure 2. Errors of omission and commission when learning from noisy data as a function of the number of training examples. SBL does not make errors of commission on this data.

to find a role filler that appears in the fewest stored negative examples (rather than a role filler that appears in no negative examples), it is expected to tolerate some amount of noise. Nonetheless, one would predict a greater percentage of errors of commission with increased noise.

In order to test these predictions, an experiment was run in which 20% and 40% of the state changes were deleted randomly from the training data. We measured the accuracy (on noise-free test data) in the same manner as the first experiment. Figure 2 displays the results of these experiments. To avoid clutter, SBL and TDL with 20% noise are not shown for errors of omission. The values typically fell between the algorithm with no noise and the algorithm with 40% noise.

The graphs show that, as expected, the algorithms degrade gracefully with this type of noise. The algorithms were not intended to deal with other forms of noise (e.g., noise in the role fillers, or state changes sometimes occurring without a cause). We expect that the algorithms would require modification before tolerating other types of noise. However, this noise does not arise naturally in this domain.

2.3.3. *Incorrect causal patterns*

TDL is one of the learning components of OCCAM (Pazzani, 1990). When a new time interval is observed, if the state change was already expected (i.e., the observed outcome could be predicted by an existing rule), then no learning is necessary. Otherwise, OCCAM first tries EBL, then TDL, and finally SBL. The rationale here is that EBL is expected to produce accurate rules from fewer training examples than TDL, and TDL produces more accurate rules than SBL. Thus, this particular combination of learning methods is intended to maximize the learning rate. In addition, the learning system is intended to be widely applicable, since it can fall back on a data-driven learning algorithm in novel domains. Furthermore, the data-driven and theory-driven learning methods create rules that can be used by the explanation-based methods. Therefore, as OCCAM learns, it can switch from a knowledge-free to a knowledge-intensive learner. In section 3, we describe how the empirical learning algorithm can learn causal patterns to be used by TDL. Here, we describe an experiment that demonstrates that a combination of TDL and SBL can be used when the causal patterns are incomplete and incorrect. This is particularly important because newly created causal patterns are likely to be incorrect and the system will initially have an incomplete collection of causal patterns.

There are 10 causal patterns used by OCCAM. Six of these patterns were replaced by incorrect versions. Incorrect versions of three patterns were formed by replacing the dispositional roles with other (i.e., irrelevant) roles. Such a change might cause TDL to search for differences beween actors while a correct rule has a difference in the object role. If no such difference exists, then SBL will be used. Three other patterns were modified by changing the location of a variable. For example, a pattern requiring the object of an action to be the actor of a state was changed so that the actor of the action was required to be the actor of a state. Such a change would make the pattern match situations that are not causally related and not match sequences that are causally related. In the latter case, SBL will be tried immediately. In the former case, TDL will initially create a rule that makes inaccurate predictions. When further examples are seen, the pattern will no longer be matched (e.g., the equality constraints that were coincidentally true in the initial few examples do not hold in later examples), and SBL will be used to form a new rule.

We ran 10 trials of TDL with these incorrect causal patterns combined with SBL and measured the percentage errors. All time intervals always had exactly one action, and there was no noise in the training data. Runs were made of SBL and TDL on 10 randomly generated sequences of Talespin output of 500 time intervals (corresponding to roughly 25 stories). The errors of omission and commission of each algorithm are measured by testing on 600 action-state change pairs after every 20 examples for the first 100 examples and every 50 examples for the remaining 400 training examples. Figure 3 shows the mean percentage of errors for SBL alone, TDL alone (with correct causal patterns), and TDL with incorrect and incomplete patterns combined with SBL (labeled Bad TDL in the legend)

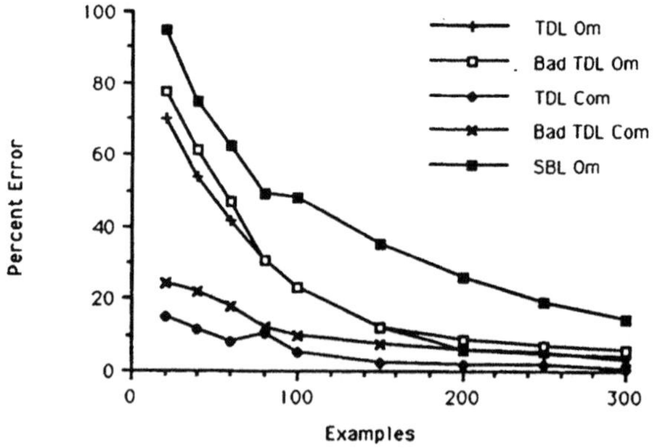

Figure 3. Errors of TDL with incorrect causal patterns (Bad TDL), TDL, and SBL as a function of the number of training examples.

as a function of the number of training examples. In the combined system, approximately 45% of the final rules were learned with TDL and the remainder were learned with SBL. The fact that the combined method has fewer errors of omisson than SBL indicates that TDL is able to determine when it is not applicable and allows SBL to learn accurate rules. However, the fact that the percentage of errors of commission of the combined methods is higher than that of TDL (with a correct theory) indicates that it takes TDL several examples to determine that an accurate rule cannot be formed that conforms to a causal pattern. This also indicates that the changes made to create the incorrect patterns were not so random that the patterns did not match any training examples.

Whether TDL should always be preferred to SBL in a simple noise-free learning environment depends upon the relative cost of errors of omission and errors of commission. However, in more complex learning environments, TDL exhibits both fewer errors of omission and commission. Furthermore, using the methods in combination, but preferring TDL, yields faster learning rates than just SBL. This combination can be applied even when the causal patterns are incomplete and incorrect.

3. Learning causal patterns

The previous section has shown how causal patterns can be represented and used to constrain the hypothesis space. Here, we discuss how causal patterns can be learned from examples. The motivation for this work is to enable TDL to be more easily adapted to new domains. An initial subset of the data is used to acquire general information to apply to the acquistion of specific knowledge in the remainder of the data.

SBL implicitly makes use of a single causal pattern, "If a state change occurs in the same time interval as an action, then the action caused the state change." This simple causal pattern does not contain any constraints between causes and effects. This allows the system to create rules without any more specific causal patterns. By noticing common patterns in established rules, new causal patterns can be created. In the future, hypotheses that conform to one of these patterns are preferred.

3.1. An algorithm for creating causal patterns

We have explored a variety of algorithms for inducing new causal patterns. A number of approaches based upon aggregating rules into clusters of similar rules and forming generalizing among the rules failed. The weak link here was the aggregation algorithm. Although UNIMEM's clustering algorithm produces reasonable clusters of events to generalize to form rules, it did not seem to produce reasonable clusters of rules to generalize to form causal patterns. The rules in such clusters were typically so dissimilar that there was not a generalization in the hypothesis language (conjunctions of role fillers with equality constraints). We also experimented with adapting other clustering algorithms (e.g., COBWEB (Fisher, 1987)) to this task without success (since COBWEB cannot represent equality constraints, and since COBWEB deals with data represented as attribute-value pairs).

The goal of creating causal patterns is to form a general pattern that can be instantiated (by the TDL algorithm) to form a new rule. Here, we describe an "eager" approach to creating new causal patterns. In effect, whenever a rule is created with SBL, the approach determines the most specific causal pattern that could be instantiated to create the same rule with TDL. If the rule learned by SBL is revised, then the pattern is revised.

After forming a rule, an exceptionless causal pattern can be formed by retaining only the equality constraints of the rule (and the heads of the CD structures to make a syntactically correct causal pattern).[4] In addition, a dispositional pattern can be created by adding dispositionial roles for every role filler in the rule. Roles explicitly encoding a type hierarchy are not used as dispositional roles, because these hierarchical roles are treated specially by the TDL algorithm. Causal patterns formed in this manner are a deliberate overgeneralization of the training data. Future causal rules that have the same equality constraints as a causal pattern are preferred to those that do not.

An incremental algorithm was implemented to create new causal patterns whenever a rule is created by SBL. If a pattern with the same equality constraints already exists, a new pattern is formed by finding the union of the dispositional roles. A dependency is recorded between each causal pattern and the rule (or rules) that resulted in the formation of the pattern. Whenever a rule is revised, the causal pattern that was formed from the rule is also revised. For example, if a role is dropped from a rule (and no other rule with the same causal pattern uses that role), then a dispositional role is removed from the causal pattern. If an equality constraint is dropped from a rule, and the rule is the only support of a causal pattern, the causal pattern is deleted, and a new causal pattern is formed from the rule (or merged into an existing pattern with the same equality constraints).

An example of creating and revising a causal pattern will help to illustrate the algorithm. Assume the first example seen is "Lynn (age 6, blond hair) took a banana from the counter. Lynn has the banana." The rule and causal pattern in table 5 is created. The equality constraints of the rule are preserved in the causal pattern. Every role that has a filler in the rule becomes a dispositional role. For example, the actor's age is present in the rule. Therefore, a disposition role is created to indicate that the age of the actor may be used to distinguish actions that result in a state change from those that do not.

A second similar example, "Mom (brown hair, age 29) gave Karen (age 4, blond hair) a balloon. Karen has the balloon." causes the rule and pattern to be revised. In the rule, the constraint that the `actor` of the `act` be the same as the `to` of the `act` and the `val` of the `relation` is dropped. This occurs because in the first example, Lynn is both the actor and the destination, while in the second example, the actor and destination of the action differ. In addition, a number of role-filler constraints are dropped such as the hair color of the `actor` (but not the `to`) and the age of the actor. The revisions to the rule also force revisions to the causal pattern. For example, the variable in the actor role of the cause is removed. In addition, dispositional roles corresponding to constants in the original rule (e.g., the actor's age) are dropped.

The goal of the above algorithm is to create causal patterns by data-driven means from an initial subset of the training data so that theory-driven learning may be used on later parts of the training data. Due to the combination of TDL and SBL, the combined system gradually shifts from using SBL to using TDL to learn new rules. As a result, when the system is trained on one domain, it learns a new domain more quickly, provided that the rules in the new domain conform to the same general patterns as the rules in the old domain.

Table 5. The initial rule and causal pattern formed from a single example. Those parts that are underlined are deleted when the second example is seen.

Rule		Pattern	
IF	ACT type ATRANS	**CAUSE**	ACT actor ?a
	actor ?A: PP type PERSON		object ?b
	age 6		to ?a
	gender FEMALE	**EFFECT**	RELATION actor ?b
	hair BLOND		val ?a
	object ?B: PP type FRUIT	**DISPOSITION:**	actor age
	subtype BANANA		actor gender
	color YELLOW		actor hair
	to ?A: PP type PERSON		object color
	age 6		to age
	gender FEMALE		to gender
	hair BLOND		to hair
	from PP type COUNTER		from color
	color WHITE		from composition
	composition TILE		
THEN	RELATION type POSES		
	actor ?B		
	val ?A		
	mode POS		

3.2. Experimental results

We ran an experiment to test whether causal patterns applied in one domain can facilitate learning in a new domain. We ran 10 trials of training the system of 15 randomly generated stories of actor's satisfying the bored goal, followed by 15 randomly generated stories about the hungry goal. Appendix 1 contains a typical hungry and a typical bored story. The combined system was using TDL and SBL and creating new causal patterns. Next, all of the rules (but not the causal patterns) were deleted. We then measured the percentage error on 400 training examples of TDL using the induced causal patterns, TDL using the hand-coded causal patterns, and SBL from stories about achieving thirsty goals. This particular training sequence was selected because the thirsty stories are the most complex and varied. The error was measured by testing on 200 randomly generated examples taken from thirsty stories.

Figure 4 shows the percentage error of the three learning systems. TDL with learned rules is called LTDL in this graph LTDL does not perform as well as TDL. An examination of the patterns learned indicates that some patterns were more specific than hand-coded patterns. In particular, some learned patterns included more equality constraints than the hand-coded ones. If these spurious equality constraints were deleted, several specific rules could be merged into a more general pattern identical to the hand-coded ones. As a consequence, fewer situations will match these specific patterns, resulting in more errors of omission for LTDL. In addition, the examination of the learned causal patterns indicates that they contain more dispositions than the hand-coded rules. As a result, the LTDL relies more on correlation and less on the knowledge encoded in the causal pattern to find differences between positive and negative examples.

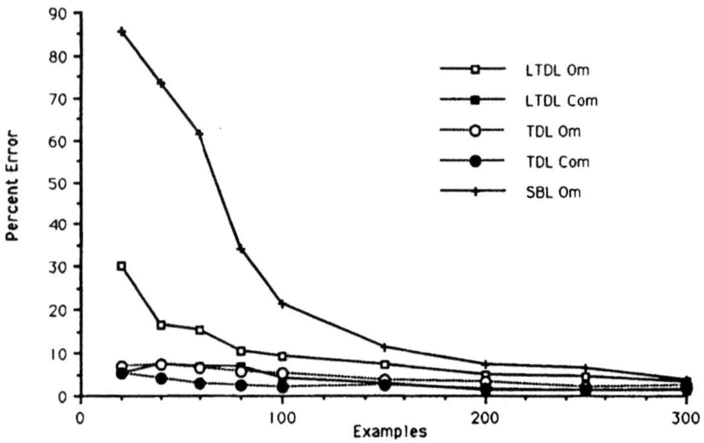

Figure 4. A comparison of SBL, TDL, and LTDL (TDL with learned causal patterns).

The graph does indicate that LTDL has fewer errors of omission than SBL. This demonstrates that the induced rules, like the hand-coded rules, capture regularities between rules that can be used to constrain future learning. Learning causal patterns in one domain accelerates learning in a new domain by enabling OCCAM to use TDL rather than SBL in the new domain.

3.3. The role of Conceptual Dependency in TDL

Theory-driven learning is intended to be independent of the representation of causal patterns and training data. For example, the causal pattern "If an action on an object is accompanied by a state change for the object, then the action results in the state change" might be represented as follows:

$$\forall a,s,t_a,t_s,l_s(Act(a)\&State(s)\&\text{Time}(a,t_a)$$
$$\&Time(s,t_s)\&(t_s-\epsilon<t_a<t_s)\&Loc(a,l_a)$$
$$\&Loc(s,l_s)\&Near(l_a,l_s))$$
$$\Rightarrow Result\ (a,s)$$

However, it is well known that the representation of the training data can have a major impact on the speed and accuracy of learning programs. OCCAM makes use of Conceptual Dependency to represent its training examples. Conceptual Dependency was designed primarily to facilitate inference for natural language understanding. The Talespin program was implemented without any thought that a learning program would attempt to learn rules that describe the effects of actions in its world. Therefore, in this research, we have not engineered the representation to suit the needs of the learning program. Nonetheless, there are several important properties of CD that simplify the learning task. Here, we identify some of these properties.

First, CD attempts to be explicit and canonical. For example, the representation of "punch" would be to apply a force, and the object applying the force is the hand of the actor. The representation of kick is to apply a force with the foot. Therefore, if one sees an example in which someone punches something and breaks his hand, and an example where someone kicks something, and breaks his foot, a regularity can be detected easily. However, if instead the training examples were not explicit (e.g., kick did not refer to foot), and canonical (kick and punch were not represented in terms of applying a force), then detecting this regularity is greatly complicated. For example, a poor choice of representation for learning might be:

```
1. kick(john1,wall) & twisted(foot4) & foot_of(john1, foot4, left)
2. punch(bob7,wall) & sprained(hand3) & hand(hand3) & right(hand3)
   part_of(bob7,hand3)
```

Note that the learning task is not impossible. with suitable axioms, sprained and twisted could be related, and the relationship between the actors and the body parts could be identified. However, these tasks will require inference. Furthermore, the clustering process would be complicated greatly. By attempting to be explicit and canonical, CD allows these regularities to be detected and generalized by a straightforward matching process. Learning with such a representation succeeds only when the designer of the representation has foreseen which items need to be explicitly represented so that meaningful generalizations can be made by deleting role fillers and introducing equality constraints.

A second useful property of CD is that a syntactic regularity between two representations implies that there is a semantic relationship between the objects being represented. The roles in CD are intended to have a constrained meaning. In representations without explicit role names, the same effect might be achieved by having a systematic interpretation of the position of arguments to predicates. Without such a system interpretation, there is no reason to believe that there would be regularities between rules, and TDL would have one pattern for each rule. For example, a poor choice of representation for learning would be:

```
1. kick(john1,wall,foot4) &
   injured(foot4)
2. punch(wall,hand3,bill1) &
   injured(hand3)
3. butt(head6,goat3,wall) &
   injured(head6)
```

Note that, once again, additional knowledge could be supplied to relate these actions via an inference process (e.g., `instrument(head6)`, `instrument(hand3)`, etc.). However, CD allows regularities between rules to be discovered by a simple matching process that finds equality constraints between roles.

3.4. Limitations

Theory-driven learning is intended to be applicable to learning causal rules between simple, overt, physical actions and their immediate effects. In these cases, there are constraints on the possible sorts of predictive relationships between actions and state changes. Indeed, we deal with only a limited form of causality in which the effect of an action is immediately apparent (cf. Shoham, 1990). In this class of relationships, the conceptual dependency, link, result (Schank & Abelson, 1977) is appropriate. More complex causal relationships, involving feedback or many intermediate states (e.g., the relationships between the tax rate and the rate of unemployment) are beyond the scope of TDL. In such a domain, a suitable system of representation for monetary actions has not been worked out, so that it is not possible to express constraints on the relationships between possible monetary actions and their effect. Furthermore, TDL does not capture the sense of "cause" that means "make more likely to occur" as in snow causes automobile accidents.

The algorithm that we have implemented for learning causal patterns has some additional limitations. In particular, it only creates exceptionless and dispositional causal patterns. OCCAM also contains "historical" patterns[5] in which a sequence of events is necessary to achieve a state change (e.g., shaking a can of soda, followed by opening the can results in the soda squirting out). The reason for this limitation is that the data-driven learning algorithm that creates causal rules does not attempt correlations between pairs of actions in different time interval and state changes. A more general instance of this same problem is that TDL is not capable of making predictions about objects with unobservable internal states.[6] In such a case, there may be an arbitrary time interval between an action that changes the internal state of an object and a subsequent action whose effect is dependent on the internal state. Unfortunately, this implies that TDL is limited in its ability to reason about the goals and plans of agents.

4. Related work

Theory-driven learning is in some ways similar to a variety of previous work. In particular, the exceptionless causal patterns of TDL are similar to determinations (Davies & Russell, 1987) and rule models (Davis, 1978). The theory-driven learning procedure is similar to SPARC (Dietterich, 1980) in that both procedures create rules by instantiation of skeletal rules (called causal patterns in TDL). Finally, TDL is related to other systems that learn with background knowledge, such as META-DENDRAL (Buchanan & Feigenbaum, 1978) and explanation-based learning (EBL) (DeJong & Mooney, 1986; Mitchell, Keller, & Kedar-Cabelli, 1986) with overly general domain theories (e.g., Cohen, 1990; Mooney & Ourston, 1989).

4.1. Determinations

Determination rules have been proposed as a form of knowledge that supports analogical reasoning and justifies why one generalization may be given a great deal of credence and another generalization may be viewed suspiciously, although both generalizations may have the same number of positive examples and negative examples. For example, one determination rule states that nationality determines language. This determination allows the generalization that all Americans speak English to be created after encountering a single example of an American speaking English. The generalization that all Americans smoke cigarettes would not be created after encountering a single example of an American smoking a cigarette because there is no determination rule that states that nationality determines smoking behavor. For creating new rules from a single training example, the following form of determinaion rule is most useful (Russell & Grosof, 1989):

$$\forall yz.\,\{\exists x.\mathrm{P}(x,y) \wedge Q(x,y)\} \Rightarrow \{\forall w.P(w,y) \Rightarrow Q(w,z)\}$$

For example, the determination rule that nationality determines language would be repreented as

$$\forall yz.\,\{\exists x.\mathit{Nationality}(x,y) \wedge \mathit{Language}(x,y)\} \Rightarrow \{\forall w.\mathit{Nationality}(w,y) \Rightarrow \mathit{Language}(w,z)\}$$

Causal patterns, like determination rules, are a weak form of background knowledge than the domain theory of EBL. In particular, the rules learned by EBL follow deductively from the domain theory. With causal patterns and determinations, the rules learned follow from the background knowledge *and* the training examples. However, unlike learning from determinations, TDL does not require that the new rule *deductively* follow from the causal patterns and the examples. Rather, the causal patterns are heuristics that suggest rules that are subject to empirical validation and refinement. Furthermore, a rule learned by TDL may tolerate exceptions, provided that no refinement of the rule has fewer exceptions.

A procedure for inducing determination rules for binary predicates from training data is described in Russell (1989). In effect, it operates by instantiating P and Q to binary predicates, finding pairs from the joint domain of P and Q, and calculating how often the determination rule holds. A determination factor from 0 to 1 is computed, rather than requiring that the determination rule be universally true. This algorithm has been used to demonstrate that interesting and potentially useful determinations exist. However, because the learning algorithm is not incremental, it has not been demonstrated that the acquisition of such determinations from an initial subset of the data facilitate the acquisition of accurate rules in the remaining data.

4.2. TIERESIAS

TIERESIAS (Davis, 1978) is a system designed to help an expert formulate rules for a rule-based expert system. One way that it assists an expert is by having rule models. A rule model encodes the type of preconditions typically associated with a rule that makes a particular type of conclusion. For example, rules that identify the category of an organism typically have preconditions describing the site of a culture, an infection, and a portal of entry of an organism. When a new rule is entered, TIERESIAS suggests that it mentions preconditions typically associated with the rule's conclusion. The rule models in TIERESIAS can be created by finding commonalities among rules with similar conclusions. Although it has not been demonstrated, these rule models should be able to provide constraints that facilitate automated learning of new rules.

4.3. SPARC

In some respects, TDL is similar to SPARC (Dietterich, 1980; Dietterich & Michalski, 1986), a system that learns rules that describe patterns in sequential data. SPARC approaches this problem by having abstract, parameterized skeletal rules that can be instantiated to form specific rules. For example, one skeletal rule represents periodic sequences of length *N*. This schema can be instantiated if commonalities are found between examples that are *N* items apart in a sequence. Once a rule is created, it is tested to determine how well it fits the data. TDL also can be viewed as creating new rules by instantiating skeletal rules (i.e., causal patterns). In addition, like SPARC, TDL instantiates a template with values obtained by constrained correlation among training instances. A primary difference between TDL and SPARC is that TDL is accompanied by an algorithm that induces rule templates from training data.

4.4. META-DENDRAL

META-DENDRAL (Buchanan & Feigenbaum, 1978; Buchanan & Mitchell, 1978) is a program that learns cleavage rules to predict which bonds in a molecule will be broken in a mass spectrometer. It starts with a half-order theory that is overly general (i.e., it predicts more bonds will break than actually occur). A program called RULEGEN uses the half-order theory to propose rules that are then tested to see if they are true in many positive examples. Next, a program called RULEMOD refines and revises the rules to insure that few negative examples are covered by a rule. In addition, RULEMOD removes redundant rules.

In TDL, like SPARC, the prior knowledge is abstract knowledge that can be instantiated to form specific rules. In contrast, RULEGEN uses its knowledge in a generate-and-test fashion. It would be possible to use the causal patterns of TDL in a generate-and-test manner. The patterns could generate rules for all combinations of action and state types. These rules would then be tested against the data and incorrect rules deleted. However, by making use of at least one example, the number of rules generated and then tested is considerably reduced.

4.5. EBL with overly general theories

The causal patterns may be viewed as an overly general domain theory. In fact, the algorithm for creating causal patterns deliberately overgeneralizes the data by only including equality constraints. It might be possible to use the overly general domain theory to explain why a particular action resulted in a state change. Then some explanation-based algorithm designed to deal with overly general domain theories could be used to create rules. Here, we discuss how IOU (Mooney & Ourston, 1989) and A-EBL (Cohen, 1990) might approach this problem. IOU (Mooney & Ourston, 1989) operates by first forming a definition via m-EBG (Flann & Dietterich, 1989) for the positive examples. Next, IOU removes any negative examples from the training set that are correctly classified by the results of m-EBG. Finally, IOU deletes those features from the remaining negative and all positive examples, and runs an induction algorithm on the features. The final concept is formed by conjoining the result of induction over the unexplained features with the result of m-EBG. The explanations produced by causal patterns would be overly general explanations. Therefore, the result of m-EBG would typically result in errors of commission. This result is specialized by an induction process that would eliminate (most of) the errors of commission. The primary difference between IOU and TDL is that TDL uses dispositional causal patterns to focus the search for a difference between the positive and negative examples. Since TDL searches a more restricted hypothesis space, one would expect that it would converge on an accurate rule from fewer examples than IOU.

The A-EBL system (Cohen, 1990) is also designed to handle overly general domain theories. It operates by finding all proofs of all positive examples, and uses a greedy set covering algorithm to find a set of operational definitions that cover all positive examples and no negative examples. Unlike IOU, A-EBL will not specialize an operationalized proof to avoid covering any negative examples. A-EBL would not be able to address the problem of learning accurate rules from causal patterns. A-EBL is best suited to those theories that are overly general because the theory has superfluous, incorrect disjunctions. In contrast, causal patterns are overly general because they contain too few preconditions. As a result, no disjunction of the operationalized proofs will exclude the negative examples. Instead, the operationalized proofs need to be specialized by some induction process.

4.6. Multistrategy learning

There are a variety of approaches to combining multiple learning strategies in an integrated learning system. For example, in Gemini (Danyluk, 1991), an empirical and an analytical learning method have predefined, specific tasks. The result is an integrated strategy in which each learning method has a separate and distinct role. Other systems, such as Meta-AQUA (Cox & Ram, 1991) treat the selection of learning strategies as an additional problem to be solved by the learner. That is, the system reasons about what learning strategy is appropriate for each learning problem.

In OCCAM, there are three learning strategies and each learning strategy can perform the same task (acquiring a predictive relationship). The strategies differe according to the amount of knowledge that they acquire. EBL requires the most detailed, specific knowledge (i.e., a set of causal rules capable of explaining how an action produces a state change). TDL requires more general knowledge of causality and finds causal rules that are instantiations of this more general knowledge. SBL places no such restrictions on the causal rules that are learned. The control strategy of OCCAM is quite simple. It uses the most knowledge-intensive learning strategy that is capable of finding a causal rule to account for an unexpected state change. However, when the less knowledge-intensive strategies are successful, they acquire knowledge that can be used in the future by the more knowledge-intensive strategies. As a consequence, as OCCAM learns, it shifts from data-driven learning methods to knowledge-intensive methods.

In more recent work (Pazzani & Kibler, 1992), a tighter integration of learning methods is proposed in which an explanation-based band data-driven learning algorithm both attempt to produce rules. An information-based evaluation function (Quinlan, 1990), uniformly applied to the hypotheses produced by each method determines which hypothesis to accept. Furthermore, the hypothesis produced by one method may be further refined by either method.

5. Conclusions

We have shown how intra-example contraints may be represented and used to constrain the problem of learning a collection of predictive rules. The resulting system converges on accurate concepts more rapidly than a similar system that does not make use of these constraints. Finally, we have shown how these constraints may be discovered in an initial subset of the data and used to facilitate later learning.

Early work on children's understanding of causality (Piaget, 1930) pointed out differences in causal explanations among various age groups. In spite of more recent evidence (Leslie & Keeble, 1987) that very young infants are able to perceive causal relationships, there is no question that older children are better at attributing causality than younger children. A current research topic in developmental psychology addresses the question of how much of this causal knowledge is innate and how much is learned empirically (Bullock, Gelman, & Baillargeon, 1982; Carey, 1984; Schultz, et al., 1986 Siegler, 1975). The amount of initial knowledge required to induce causal patterns provides additional evidence in support of the view that much of the general knowledge of causality is learned empirically. In particular, in addition to representational biases, the only initial knowledge of causality required by this computational model is temporal contiguity. From this knowledge, it is possible to learn simple predictive rules. The additional knowledge of causality (e.g., spatial contiguity) is derived from common patterns in the predictive rules. Once learned empirically, this knowledge is available to constrain future learning.

Appendix 1. Typical stories involving hunger and boredom

Karen was hungry. She asked Mom, "Would you give me the yellow long banana?" Mom picked up it. She had it. The phone was ringing. Dad picked up the receiver. The phone wasn't ringing. He had the receiver. He pushed the light switch. The light was on. The black cat pushed a large red plastic vase to the tile floor. Mom gave Karen the banana. Karen had it. Mom didn't have it. Karen peeled it. She ate it. She wasn't hungry. Karen threw the peel to the basket. She didn't have the peel. Mom pushed the light switch. The light wasn't on.

Lynn was bored. Lynn asked Karen, "Would you throw me the balloon?" She asked Mom, "Would you give me the balloon?" Mom pushed the door away from the cupboard. The cupboard was open. The auburn cat pushed a large clear glass vase to the tile floor. The vase was broken. She took the balloon from the cupboard. She had the balloon. The cupboard didn't have the balloon. She pushed the door to the cupboard. The cupboard wasn't open. She exhaled into the balloon. It was inflated. Mom picked up the balloon. She had it. She exhaled into it. It was inflated. She let go of it. She didn't have it. It was flying. It wasn't inflated. She picked up it. She had it. She exhaled into the balloon. It was inflated. She tied it. It was sealed. She gave Lynn the balloon. Lynn had it. Mom didn't have it. Lynn went to the outside. Karen went to the outside. Lynn threw Karen the balloon. Karen had it. Lynn didn't have it. Karen threw Lynn the balloon. Lynn had it. Karen didn't have it. Lynn threw Karen the balloon. Karen had it. Lynn didn't have it. Karen dropped the balloon to the green pointed grass. The balloon burst. She didn't have it.

Acknowledgments

This research is supported by a National Science Foundation Grant IRI-8908260 and by the University of California, Irvine through an allocation of computer time. Comments by Kamal Ali and Caroline Ehrlich on an earlier draft of this article were helpful in improving the presentation.

Notes

1. The `actor` role of `STATES` and `actor` and `val` roles of `RELATIONS` may be misnomers. This is terminology used by Talespin. A better name for these roles might be `argument1` and `argument2`.
2. Note that this rule is true in Talespin's world. In the real world, the situation is more complex.
3. There is a maximum number of exceptions that can be indexed by each rule. In this article, each rule maintains the five most recent exceptions.
4. If there are no equality constraints between the action and a state change, no causal pattern is created. In effect, this algorithm assumes that some object must be involved somehow in both an action and a state change. The algorithm learns additional constraints in terms of which roles of the action can be associated with roles of the state change. TDL takes advantage of these constraints to search a reduced hypothesis space.
5. This is not a problem in our experiments, because historical patterns are not needed to make predictions in Talespin.
6. Pearl and Verma (1991) discuss an approach to discovering hidden variables. However, it only takes advantage of temporal constraints on causal relationships.

References

Buchanan B., & Feigenbaum, E. (1978). Dendral and Meta-Dendral: Their applications dimension. *Artificial Intelligence, 11*, 5-25.

Buchanan, B., & Mitchell, T. (1978). Model-directed learning of production rules. In D. Waterman & F. Hayes-Roth (Eds.), *Pattern-directed inference systems*. New York: Academic Press.

Bullock, M., Gelman, R., & Baillargeon, R. (1982). The development of causal reasoning. In W. Friedman (Ed.), *The developmental psychology of time*. New York: Academic Press.

Carey, S. (1984). *Conceptual change in childhood*. Cambridge, MA: MIT Press.

Cohen, W. (1990). Learning from textbook knowledge: A case study. *Proceedings of the Eighth National Conference on Artificial Intelligence* (pp. 743–748). Boston, MA: Morgan Kaufmann.

Cox, M., & Ram, A. (1991). Using introspective reasoning to select learning strategies. *Multi-strategy Learning Workshop* (pp 217–230). Harpers Ferry, VA.

Danyluk, A. (1991). Gemini: An integration of analytical and empirical learning. *Multistrategy Learning Workshop* (pp. 191–206). Harpers Ferry, VA

Davies, T., & Russell S. (1987). A logical approach to reasoning by analogy. *Proceedings of the Tenth International Joint Conference on Artificial Intelligence* (pp. 264–270). Milan, Italy: Morgan Kaufmann.

Davis, R. (1978). Knowledge acquisition in rule-based systems: Knowledge about representation as a basis for system construction and maintenance. In D. Waterman & F. Hayes-Roth (Eds.), *Pattern-directed inference systems*. New York: Academic Press.

DeJong, G., & Mooney, R. (1986). Explanation-based learning: An alternate view. *Machine Learning, 1*, 47-80.

Dietterich, T. (1980). Applying general induction methods to the card game Eleusis. *Proceedings of the First National Conference on Artificial Intelligence* (pp. 218-220). Stanford, CA: Morgan Kaufmann.

Dietterich, T., London, B., Clarkson, K., & Dromey, G. (1982). Learning and inductive inference. In P. Cohen & E. Fiegenbaum (Eds.), *The handbook of artificial intelligence* (Vol. 3). San Mateo, CA: Morgan Kaufmann.

Dietterich, T., & Michalski, R. (1986). Learning to predict sequences. In R.S. Michalski, J. G. Carbonell, & T.M. Mitchell (Eds.), *Machine Learning: An artificial intelligence approach* (Vol. 2). San Mateo, CA: Morgan Kaufmann.

Elkan, C. (1990). Incremental, approximate planning. *Proceedings of the Eighth National Conference on Artificial Intelligence* (pp. 145-150). Boston, MA: Morgan Kaufmann.

Fisher, D. (1987). Knowledge acquisition via incremental conceptual clustering. *Machine Learning, 2*, 139-172.

Flann, N., & Dietterich, T. (1989). A study of inductive methods for explanation-based learning. *Machine Learning, 4*, 187-226.

Lebowitz, M. (1987). Experiments with incremental concept formation: UNIMEM. *Machine Learning, 2*, 103-138.

Leslie, A., & Keeble, S. (1987). Do six-month-old infants perceive causality? *Cognition, 25*, 265-288.

Meehan, J. (1981). Talespin. In R. Schank & C. Riesbeck (Eds.), *Inside computer understanding: Five programs plus miniatures*. Hillsdale, NJ: Lawrence Erlbaum Associates.

Mitchell, T., Keller, R., & Kedar-Cabelli, S. (1986). Explanation-based learning: A unifying view. *Machine Learning, 1*, 47-80.

Mooney, R., & Ourston, D. (1989). Induction over the unexplained: Integrated learning of concepts with both explainable and conventional aspects. *Proceedings of the Sixth International Workshop on Machine Learning* (pp. 5-7). Ithaca, NY: Morgan Kaufmann.

Pazzani, M. (1990). *Creating a memory of causal relationships: An integration of empirical and explanation-based learning methods*. Hillsdale, NJ: Lawrence Erlbaum Associates.

Pazzani, M. (1991). A computational theory of learning causal relationships. *Cognitive Science, 15*, 401-424.

Pazzani, M., & Kibler, D. (1992). The utility of knowledge in inductive learning. *Machine Learning, 9*, 57-94.

Pearl, J., & Verma, T. (1991). A theory of inferred causation. *In Proceedings of the Second International Conference on Principles of Knowledge Representation and Reasoning* (pp. 441-452). San Mateo, CA: Morgan Kaufmann

Piaget, J. (1930). *The child's conception of physical causality*. London: Kegan Paul.

Quinlan, R. (1990). Learning logical definitions from relations. *Machine Learning, 5*, 239-266.

Russell, S. (1989). *Analogical and inductive reasoning*. London: Pitman Press.

Russell, S., & Grosof, B. (1989). Declarative bias: An overview. In P. Benjamin (Ed.), *Change of representation and inductive bias*. Norwell, MA: Kluwer Academic Press.

Schank, R., & Albelson, R. (1977). *Scripts, plans, goals, and understanding*. Hillsdale, NJ: Lawrence Erlbaum Associates.

Scott, P., & Markovitch, S. (1989). Learning novel domains through curiosity and conjecture. *Proceedings of the Eleventh International Joint Conference on Artificial Intelligence* (pp. 669-674). Detroit, MI: Morgan Kaufmann.

Shohan, Y. (1990). Nonmonotonic reasoning and causality. *Cognitive Science, 4*, 213-252.

Shultz, T., Fisher, G., Pratt, C., & Rulf, S. (1986). Selection of causal rules. *Child Development, 57*, 143-152.

Shultz, T., (1987). *Learning and using causal knowledge*. Paper Presentation at the Meeting for Research in Child Development. Baltimore, MD.

Siegler, R.S. (1975). Defining the locus of developmental differences in children's causal reasoning. *Journal of Experimental Child Psychology, 20*, 512-525.

Sutton, R. (1988). Learning to predict by the methods of temporal differences. *Machine Learning 3*, 9-44.

Received September 30, 1991
Accepted September 30, 1991
Final Manuscript February 28, 1992

Machine Learning, 11, 195-215 (1993)

Using Knowledge-Based Neural Networks to Improve Algorithms: Refining the Chou-Fasman Algorithm for Protein Folding

RICHARD MACLIN MACLIN@CS.WISC.EDU
JUDE W. SHAVLIK SHAVLIK@CS.WISC.EDU
Computer Sciences Department, University of Wisconsin, 1210 W. Dayton St., Madison, WI 53706

Abstract. This article describes a connectionist method for refining algorithms represented as generalized finite-state automata. The method translates the rule-like knowledge in an automaton into a corresponding artificial neural network, and then refines the reformulated automaton by applying backpropagation to a set of examples. This technique for translating an automaton into a network extends the KBANN algorithm, a system that translates a set of propositional rules into a corresponding neural network. The extended system, FSKBANN, allows one to refine the large class of algorithms that can be represented as state-based processes. As a test, FSKBANN is used to improve the Chou-Fasman algorithm, a method for predicting how globular proteins fold. Empirical evidence shows that the multistrategy approach of FSKBANN leads to a statistically-significantly, more accurate solution than both the original Chou-Fasman algorithm and a neural network trained using the standard approach. Extensive statistics report the types of errors made by the Chou-Fasman algorithm, the standard neural network, and the FSKBANN network.

Keywords. Multistrategy learning, theory refinement, neural networks, finite-state automata, protein folding, Chou-Fasman algorithm

1. Introduction

As machine learning has been applied to complex real-world problems, many researchers have found themselves turning to systems that combine knowledge from multiple sources. A standard approach is to incorporate existing knowledge about a domain into an empirical learning system, so as to produce a more accurate solution. Artificial neural networks (ANNs) have been shown to be a powerful technique for empirical learning, but until recently ANNs were largely unable to take advantage of existing problem-specific knowledge. This article describes an extension to the KBANN system (Towell, Shavlik, & Noordewier, 1990), a connectionist system that refines symbolic domain knowledge. The extended system, called Finite-State KBANN (FSKBANN), translates domain theories that use state information, represented as generalized finite-state automata (FSAs) (Hopcroft & Ullman, 1979), into neural networks. The system then refines these networks using backpropagation (Rumelhart, Hinton, & Williams, 1986) with a set of examples.

The application of KBANN to the domain of gene recognition (Towell et al., 1990; Noordeweir, Towell, & Shavlik, 1991) showed that domain theories refined by neural networks can be more accurate than both the unrefined domain knowledge and neural networks trained in the standard manner. That work demonstrates the promise of a multistrategy approach based on the combination of a symbolic representation of rules with the numeric representation inherent in neural networks. By allowing domain theories to express *state* information, FSKBANN greatly extends the applicability of the KBANN approach. Researchers outside of machine learning generally publish algorithms rather than the sets of rules that machine learning researchers refer to as domain theories. Many of these algorithms maintain some sense of state, so this extension makes it easier to use machine learning to refine existing "real-world" knowledge. We test our extended system by refining the Chou–Fasman algorithm (Chou & Fasman, 1978) for predicting (an aspect of) how globular proteins fold, an important and particularly difficult problem in molecular biology.

State in a domain theory represents the context of the problem. For example, if the problem is to find a path across a room, the state variables may include whether or not the light is on. The rules introduced to solve this problem can therefore take into account the state of the problem—rules to turn on the light would only be considered when the state indicated that the light was off. In this style of problem solving, the problem is not solved in one step, but instead as a series of actions, each leading to a new state, that leads to the goal state (turning on the light, navigating to the couch, etc.).

The protein-folding problem is an open problem that is becoming increasingly critical as the Human Genome Project (Watson, 1990) proceeds. The Chou–Fasman algorithm is the focus of this article because it is one of the best-known and widely used algorithms in the field. The protein-folding problem is also of interest because a number of machine learning techniques are currently being applied to this problem, including neural networks (Holley & Karplus, 1989; Qian & Sejnowski, 1988), inductive logic programming (Muggleton & Feng, 1991), case-based reasoning (Cost & Salzberg, 1993), and multistrategy learning (Zhang, Mesirov & Waltz, 1992). Our work shows that a multistrategy approach combining the Chou–Fasman algorithm with a neural network produces a more accurate result than either method alone.

This article presents and empirically analyzes the FSKBANN approach for problem solving in domains where prior state-based knowledge exists. Section 2 presents the basic KBANN algorithm and discusses the extension of the algorithm to handle state information. Section 3 defines the protein-folding problem and reviews previous approaches taken. Experiments that investigate the utility of FSKBANN for this problem follow section 3.

2. Finite-state KBANN

Before describing FSKBANN, we review the basic KBANN (for Knowledge-Based Artificial Neural Networks) algorithm (Towell et al., 1990). KBANN translates a domain theory represented as simple rules into a promising initial neural network. This technique allows neural networks to take advantage of pre-existing knowledge about a problem.

KBANN takes as input a set of propositional, non-recursive rules, such as those shown in figure 1a. Figure 1b shows the dependencies among the rules. A dependency is indicated by a link between two propositions—arcs show conjunctive dependencies. From the set of dependencies, it is easy to map the rules to a network by replacing each proposition with a corresponding unit (and adding units where conjunctions are combined into disjunctions). Figure 1c displays the resulting network. This network has the same behavior as

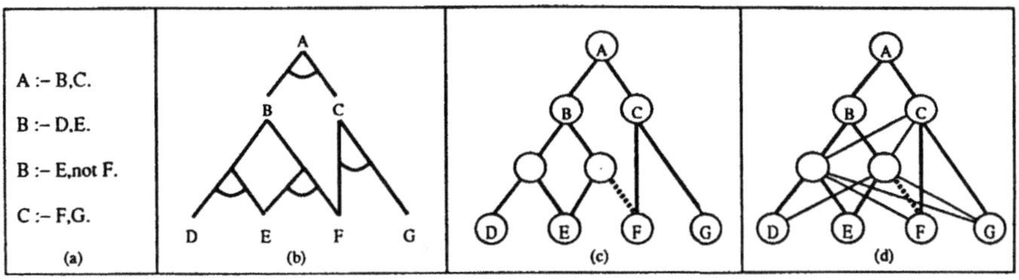

Figure 1. Sample of KBANN: (a) a set of rules; (b) dependencies among the rules; (c) the corresponding neural network; and (d) elaborated network after KBANN connects each unit to unconnected units at the next lower level.

the rules for each possible input vector. After setting the weights and biases of the units in the network, KBANN connects each unit to any unconnected units at the next lower level in the network using a small-weight link (the resulting network appears in figure 1d). KBANN adds these connections so that it can learn new dependencies during backpropagation learning. For further details, see Towell (1991).

To handle a wider class of problems, the present article extends KBANN to translate domain theories represented as *generalized* FSA.[1] The main extension for FSKBANN is the type of network onto which the domain theory is mapped. FSKBANN maps domain theories onto a variant of simple recurrent networks (Jordan, 1986; Elman, 1990), where a subset of the network output is copied back as input to the network in the next step. This copied output represents the current state calculated by the network and can be used in calculating the succeeding state.

Table 1 describes the class of problem solvers to which FSKBANN is applicable. Consider a problem solver that determines the next state on the basis of both externally provided input and its internal representation of the current state of the problem solution. The externally provided input may involve a description of the initial state or the changing measurements of sensors (as in a reactive planner). The task of the problem solver is to produce the appropriate output for this step in the problem solution (e.g., the operator to apply), as well as to choose its internal representation of the next state of the problem solution. This process repeats until a termination condition is met (e.g., a goal state is reached).

The description in table 1 is essentially a definition of state-based problem solving. The contribution of FSKBANN is a mechanism for using neural networks to improve a state-

Table 1. The type of problem solving to which FSKBANN is applicable.

Given:	a *state-dependent domain theory* and a *goal description*.			
Repeat				
	Set	*input*	=	*externally-provided information*
				+
				current internal representation of the problem-solving state
	Produce, using the domain theory and goal description,			
		output	=	*results specific to this problem solving step*
				+
				next internal representation of the problem-solving state
Until a *Termination Criterion* is met.				

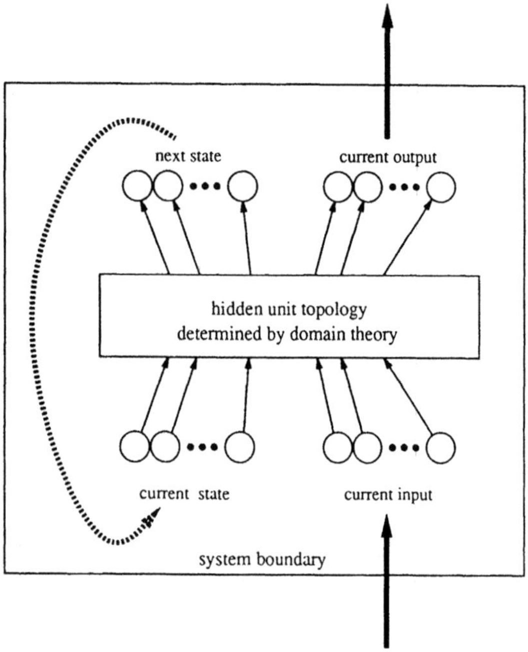

Figure 2. A schematic view of an FSKBANN network.

dependent domain theory. The inputs and outputs in table 1 directly map to input and output units in a neural network, and the basic KBANN algorithm uses the domain theory to determine the number and connectivity of the hidden units. Figure 2 shows a diagram of the type of network produced by FSKBANN.

The FSKBANN approach requires that the user provide sample input/output pairs that can be used to train the network with backpropagation. It also requires that the inputs and the outputs be of bounded size, which means the domain theory can only store a finite amount of state information. Finally, FSKBANN requires the domain theory to be propositional, since no good mechanism exists for dealing with predicate calculus variables in neural networks. Despite these current limitations, it is likely that many "real-world" algorithms can be adequately represented in this finite-state framework. It is an open empirical question whether and where our neural-based approach generalizes better than inductive logic programming approaches (Muggleton, 1992; Quinlan, 1990), which learn a larger class of languages.

3. The protein-folding problem

This section describes the protein-folding problem, an open problem in the field of molecular biology that is being examined by researchers in both the biological and machine learning communities. Following this description is an outline of a standard algorithm used by the biological community to solve this problem, along with a description of how this algorithm can be mapped into section 2's framework.

Proteins are long strings of amino acids, several hundred elements long on average. There are 20 amino acids in all (represented by different capital letters). The string of amino acids making up a given protein constitutes the *primary* structure of the protein. Once a protein forms, it folds into a three-dimensional shape known as the protein's *tertiary* structure. Tertiary structure is important because the form of the protein strongly influences its function.

At present, determining the tertiary structure of a protein in the laboratory is costly and time consuming. An alternative solution is to predict the *secondary* structure of a protein as an approximation. The secondary structure of a protein is a description of the local structure surrounding each amino acid. One prevalent system of determining secondary structure divides a protein into three different types of structures: (1) α-helix regions, (2) β-strand regions, and (3) random coils (all other regions). Figure 3 shows the tertiary structure of a protein and how the shape is divided into regions of secondary structure. For our purposes, the secondary structure of a protein is simply a sequence corresponding to the primary sequence. Table 2 shows a sample mapping between a protein's primary and secondary structures.

Table 3 contains predictive accuracies of some standard algorithms from the biological literature for solving the secondary-structure problem (Chou & Fasman, 1978; Garnier & Robson, 1989; Lim, 1974). In the data sets used to test the algorithms, 54%–55% of the amino acids in the proteins are part of coil structures, so 54% accuracy can be achieved trivially by always predicting coil. It is important to note that many biological researchers believe that algorithms that only take into account local information can only achieve limited accuracy (Wilson et al., 1985), generally believed to be at most 80%–90% (Cohen & Presnell, personal communication).

Another approach to the secondary-structure problem is to use a learning method such as neural networks (Holley & Karplus, 1989; Qian & Sejnowski, 1988). The neural networks

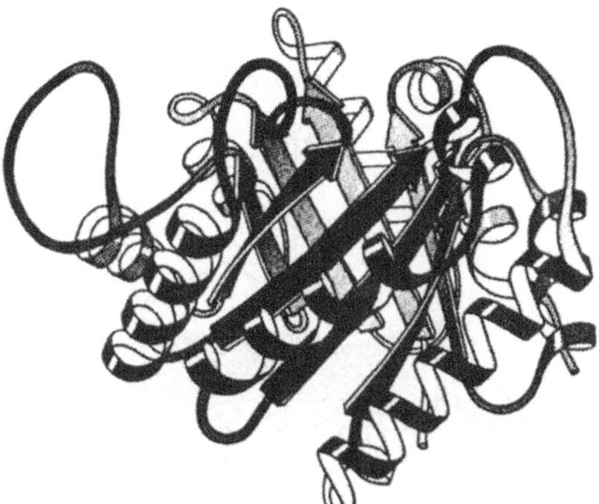

Figure 3. ***Ribbon*** drawing of the three-dimensional structure of a protein (reprinted from Richardson & Richardson, 1989). The areas resembling springs are α-helix structures, the flat arrows represent β-strands, and the remaining regions are random coils.

Table 2. Primary and secondary structures of a sample protein.

Primary (20 possible amino acids)	P	S	V	F	L	F	P	P	K	P	...
Secondary (three possible local structures)	c	c	β	β	β	β	c	c	c	α	...

Table 3. Accuracies of various (non-learning) prediction algorithms.

Method	Accuracy	Comments
Chou & Fasman (1978)	58%	Data from Qian & Sejnowski (1988)
Lim (1974)	50%	From Nishikawa (1983)
Garnier & Robson (1989)	58%	Data from Qian & Sejnowski (1988)

in these efforts have as input a *window* of amino acids consisting of the central amino acid being predicted, plus some number of the amino acids before and after it in the sequence (similar to NETTALK networks; see Sejnowski & Rosenberg, 1987). The output of the network is the secondary structure for the central amino acid. Figure 4 shows the general structure of this type of network; table 4 presents results from these studies.

Our approach is to combine the knowledge from biological methods with a neural learning method in the hopes of achieving a better solution. We chose the Chou–Fasman algorithm (1978) as our domain theory because it is widely used. The Chou–Fasman approach is to find amino acids that are likely to be part of α-helix and β-strand regions, and then to extend these predictions to neighboring amino acids. Figure 5 provides a schematic overview of the algorithm. The first step of the process is to find *nucleation sites*. Nucleation sites are amino acids that are likely to be part of α-helix or β-strand structures, based on their neighbors and according to the conformation probabilities and rules reported by Chou and Fasman. From these sites, their algorithm extends the structure both forward and

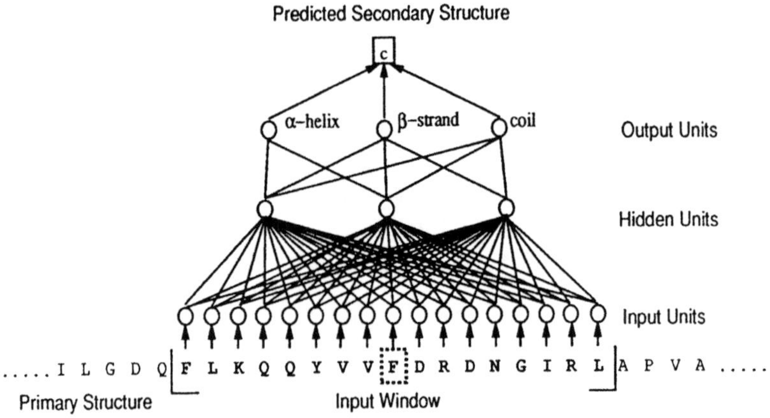

Figure 4. Neural network architecture used by Qian and Sejnowski (1988).

Table 4. Neural network results for the secondary-structure prediction task.

Method	Testset Accuracy	Number of hidden units	Window size
Holley & Karplus (1989)	63.2%	2	17
Qian & Sejnowski (1988)	62.7%	40	13

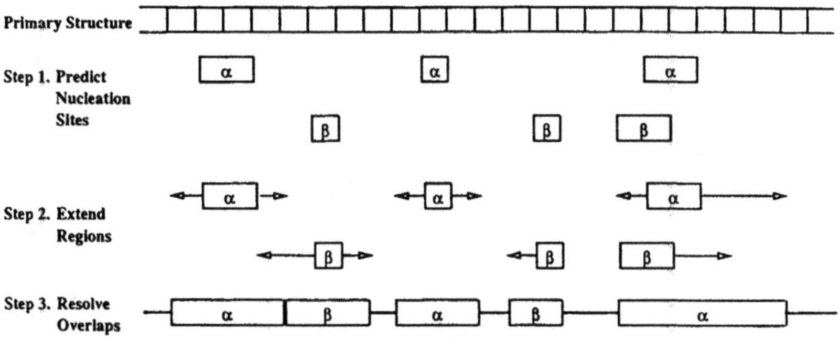

Figure 5. Steps of the Chou-Fasman algorithm.

backward along the protein, as long as the probability of being part of a α-helix structure remains sufficiently high. After predicting both α-helix and β-strand regions, the Chou-Fasman algorithm compares the relative probabilities of regions to resolve predictions that overlap.

This algorithm cannot be easily represented using propositional rules, since the prediction for an amino acid may depend on the predictions for its neighbors. However, one can represent the algorithm with a generalized FSA (see figure 6). The start state of the FSA is *coil*. To make predictions for a protein, the protein is scanned[2]; the input at each step

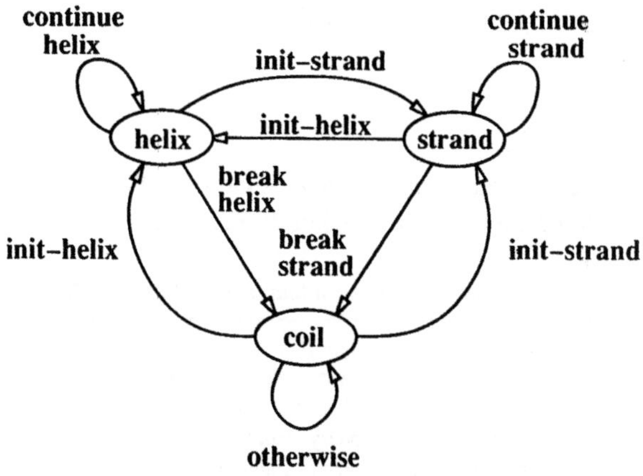

Figure 6. The finite-state automaton interpretation of the Chou-Fasman algorithm.

is the amino acid being classified plus its neighbors (a window). Each prediction is based on the last prediction (or state) and depends on which "transitions" are valid for the current input window. The notion of transition in figure 6's automata is complex. Each transition is actually a set of rules dependent on the input window and the current state. For example, in the FSA there is transition from state *helix* to state *coil* on *break-helix*. This is represented by the rule:

$$coil_i \leftarrow helix_{i-1} \wedge break\text{-}helix.$$

The term *break-helix* is not an input to the network, but is instead itself a predicate derived from the input. *Break-helix* is defined in terms of two other rules:

break-helix ← *helix-break@0* ∧ *helix-break@1*.
break-helix ← *helix-break@0* ∧ *helix-indiff@1*.

The terms *helix-break@0, helix-break@1*, and *helix-indiff@1* are further defined by other rules (see the appendix for the full set of rules defining the FSA).

Table 5 shows how this algorithm fits into the FSKBANN framework of table 1. The resulting network appears in figure 7 (although not shown, recall that the network also contains low-weighted links into hidden units). This network is similar to the one in figure 4, but with two major differences. First, the input to the network includes a copy of the past prediction made by the network—this represents the state of the network. Second, the topology of the hidden units is determined by the rules implementing the Chou-Fasman algorithm.

4. Experimental study

This section reports several experiments on the protein-folding problem that evaluate FSKBANN. They demonstrate that FSKBANN has a small, but statistically significant, gain in accuracy over both standard artificial neural networks (ANNs) and over the non-learning Chou–Fasman algorithm. This section also contains an in-depth empirical analysis of the strengths and weaknesses of the different methods.

4.1. Experimental details

The experiments use the data set from Qian and Sejnowski (1988). Their data set consists of 128 segments from 106 proteins with a total of 21,623 amino acids, for an average length

Table 5. Mapping the Chou–Fasman algorithm into the FSKBANN framework.

Domain theory	=	the Chou–Fasma algorithm
Goal	=	assign a secondary structure to each amino acid
External input	=	a sliding window of amino acids
Current state	=	the predicted secondary structure for the previous amino acid
Results	=	the predicted secondary structure for the current amino acid
Next state	=	*ditto*

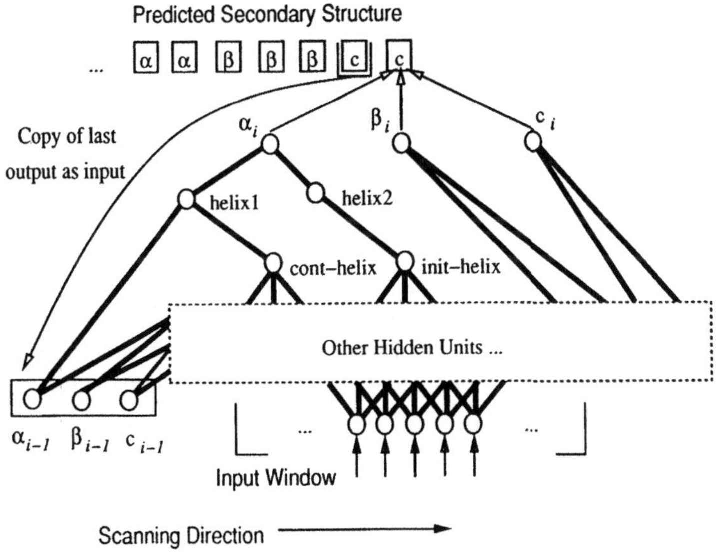

Figure 7. General neural-network architecture used to represent the Chou–Fasman algorithm.

of 169 amino acids per segment. Of these amino acids, 54.5% are part of coil structures, 25.2% are part of α-helix structures, 20.3% are part of β-strand structures. We randomly divided the proteins ten times into disjoint training and test sets, which contained two thirds (85 proteins) and one third (43 proteins) of the original proteins, respectively.

We use backpropagation to train the neural networks in the two approaches (FSKBANN and standard ANNs). Training is terminated using *patience*[3] as a stopping criterion (Fahlman & Lebiere, 1990). During training, we divided the proteins used for training into two portions—a training set and a *tuning* set. We employ the training set to train the network and the tuning set to estimate the generalization of the network. For each epoch, the system trains the network on each of the amino acids in the training set; it then assesses accuracy on the tuning set. We retain the set of weights achieving the highest accuracy for the tuning set and use this set of weights to measure test-set accuracy.

FSKBANN randomly chooses a "representative" tuning set; it considers a tuning set to be representative if the percentages of each type of structure (α, β, and coil) in the tuning set roughly approximate the percentages of all the training proteins. Note that the system does not consider the *testing* set when comparing the percentages. Through empirical testing (not reported here), we found that a tuning set size of five proteins achieves the best results for both FSKBANN and ANNs. It is important to note that this style of training is different than the one reported by Qian and Sejnowski. They tested their network periodically and retained the network that achieved the highest accuracy for the test set.

FSKBANN uses 28 hidden units to represent the Chou–Fasman domain theory. Qian and Sejnowski report that their networks generalized best when they had 40 hidden units. Using the methodology outlined above, we compared standard ANNs containing 28 and 40 hidden units. We found that networks with 28 hidden units generalized slightly better; hence, for this article's experiments, we use 28 hidden units in our standard ANNs. This has the added advantage that the FSKBANN and standard networks contain the same number of hidden units.

4.2. *Results and analysis*

Table 6 contains results averaged over the 10 test sets. The statistics reported are the percent accuracy overall, the percent accuracy by secondary structure, and the correlation coefficients for each structure.[4] The correlation coefficient is good for evaluating the effectiveness of the prediction for each of the three classes separately. The resulting gain in overall accuracy for FSKBANN over both ANNs and the non-learning Chou–Fasman method is statistically significant at the 0.5% level (i.e., with 99.5% confidence) using a *t*-test.

The apparent gain in accuracy for FSKBANN over ANN networks appears fairly small (only 1.6 percentage points), but this number is somewhat misleading. The correleation coefficients give a more accurate picture. They show that the FSKBANN does better on both α-helix and coil prediction, and much better on β-strand prediction. The reason that the ANN solution still does fairly well in overall accuracy is that it predicts a large number of coil structures (the largest class) and does very well on these predictions.

The gain in accuracy for FSKBANN over the Chou–Fasman algorithm is fairly large and exhibits a corresponding gain in all three correlation coefficients. It is interesting to note that the FSKBANN and Chou–Fasman solutions produce approximately the same accuracy for β-strands, but the correlation coefficients demonstrate that the Chou–Fasman algorithm achieves this accuracy by predicting a much larger number of β-strands.

Also shown in table 6 are results for ANNs that included state information—networks similar to Qian and Sejnowski's, but ones in which the previous output forms part of the current input vector. These results show that state information alone is not enough to increase the accuracy of the network prediction.

To evaluate the usefulness of the domain theory as a function of the number of training examples and to allow us to estimate the value of collecting more proteins, we performed a second series of tests. We divided each of the training sets into four subsets: the first contained the first 10 of the 85 proteins; the second contained the first 25; the third contained the first 50; and the fourth had all 85 training proteins. This process produced 40 training sets. Each of these training sets was then used to train both the FSKBANN and ANN networks. Figure 8 contains the results of these tests. FSKBANN shows a gain in accuracy for each training set size (statistically significant at the 5% level, i.e., with 95% confidence).

The results in figure 8 demonstrate two interesting trends. First, the FSKBANN networks do better no matter how large the training set, and second, the shape of the curve indicates that accuracy might continue to increase if more proteins were used for training. The one anomaly for this curve is that the gain in accuracy for the 10 training proteins is not very

Table 6. Results from different prediction methods.

Method	Testset accuracy				Correlation coefficients		
	Total	Helix	Strand	Coil	Helix	Strand	Coil
Chou–Fasman	57.3%	31.7%	36.9%	76.1%	0.24	0.23	0.26
ANN	61.8	43.6	18.6	86.3	0.35	0.25	0.31
FSKBANN	63.4	45.9	35.1	81.9	0.37	0.33	0.35
ANN (w/state)	61.7	39.2	24.2	86.0	0.32	0.28	0.31

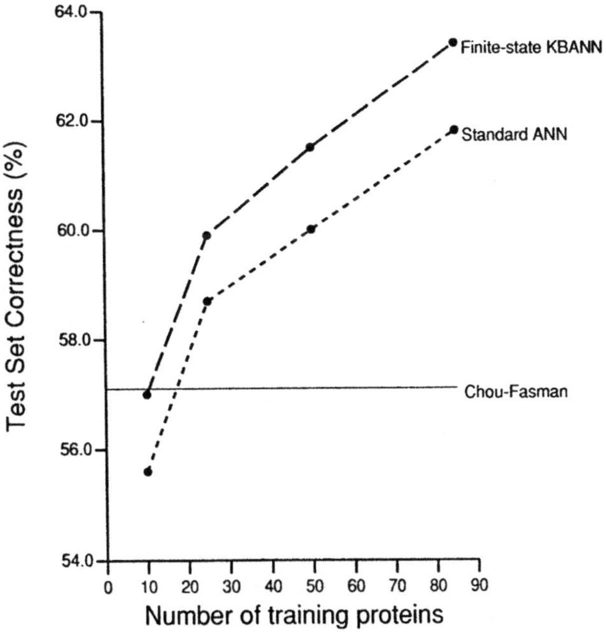

Figure 8. Percent correctness on test proteins as a function of training-set size.

large. One would expect that when the number of training instances is very small, the domain knowledge would be a big advantage. The problem here is that for a small training set it is possible to obtain random sets of proteins that are not very indicative of the overall population. Individual proteins generally do not reflect the overall distribution of secondary structures for the whole population; many proteins have large numbers of α-helix regions and almost no β-sheets, while others have large numbers of β-sheet regions and almost no α-helices. Thus in trying to learn to predict a very skewed population, the network may produce a poor solution. This problem is mitigated as more proteins are introduced, causing the training population to more closely match the overall population.

Finally, to analyze the detailed performance of the various approaches, we gathered a number of additional statistics concerning the FSKBANN, ANN, and Chou–Fasman solutions. These statistics analyze the results in terms of *regions*. A *region* is a consecutive sequence of amino acids with the same secondary structure. We consider regions because the measure of accuracy obtained by comparing the prediction for each amino acid does not adequately capture the notion of secondary structure as biologists view it (Cohen et al., 1991). For biologists, knowing the number of regions and the approximate order of the regions is nearly as important as knowing exactly the structure within which each amino acid lies. Consider the two predictions in figure 9 (adapted from Cohen et al., 1991). The first prediction completely misses the third α-helix region, so it has four errors. The second prediction is slightly skewed for each α-helix region and ends up having six errors, even though it appears to be a better answer. The statistics we have gathered try to assess how well each solution does on predicting α-helix regions (table 7) and β-strand regions (table 8).

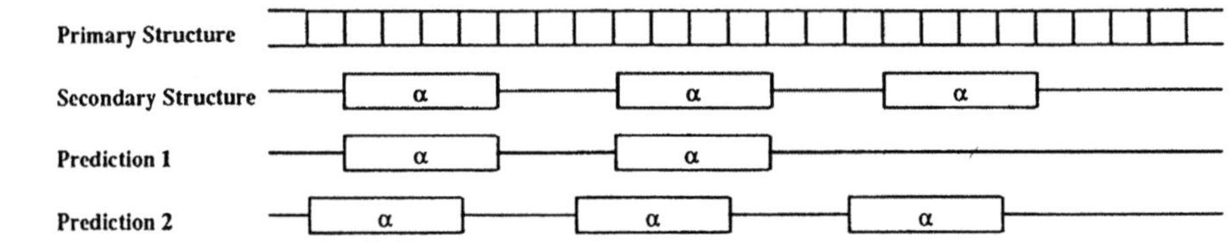

Figure 9. Two possible predictions for secondary structure.

Table 7. Region-oriented statistics for α-helix prediction.

Occurrence		Description	FSKBANN	ANN	Chou-Fasman
Actual	α-helix	Average length of an actual helix region (number of regions)	10.17 (1825)	10.17 (1825)	10.17 (1825)
Predicted	α-helix	Average length of predicted helix region (number of regions)	8.52 (1774)	7.79 (2067)	8.00 (1491)
Actual / Predicted	α-helix / α-helix	Percentage of time an actual helix region is overlapped by a predicted helix region (length of overlap)	67% (6.99)	70% (6.34)	56% (5.76)
Actual / Predicted	other / α-helix	Percentage of time a predicted helix region does not overlap an actual helix region	34%	39%	36%

Table 8. Region-oriented statistics for β-strand prediction.

Occurrence		Description	FSKBANN	ANN	Chou-Fasman
Actual	β-strand	Average length of an actual strand region (number of regions)	5.00 (3015)	5.00 (3015)	5.00 (3015)
Predicted	β-strand	Average length of predicted strand region (number of regions)	3.80 (2545)	2.83 (1673)	6.02 (2339)
Actual / Predicted	β-strand / β-strand	Percentage of time an actual strand region is overlapped by a predicted strand region (length of overlap)	54% (3.23)	35% (2.65)	46% (4.01)
Actual / Predicted	other / β-strand	Percentage of time a predicted strand region does not overlap an actual strand region	37%	37%	44%

Table 7 and table 8 give a picture of the strengths and weakness of each approach. Table 7 shows that the FSKBANN solution overlaps slightly fewer actual α-helix regions than the

ANNs, but that these overlaps tend to be somewhat longer. On the other hand, the FSKBANN networks *overpredict* fewer regions than ANNs (i.e., predict fewer α-helix regions that do not intersect actual α-helix regions). Table 7 also indicates that FSKBANN and ANNs more accurately predict the occurrence of regions than Chou–Fasman does.

Table 8 demonstrates that FSKBANN's predictions overlap a much higher percentage of actual β-strand regions than either the Chou–Fasman algorithm or ANNs alone. The overall accuracy for β-strand predictions is approximately the same for FSKBANN and the Chou–Fasman method, because the length of overlap for the Chou–Fasman method is much longer than for FSKBANN (at the cost of predicting much longer regions). The ANN networks do extremely poorly at overlapping actual β-strand regions. The FSKBANN networks do as well as the ANNS at not overpredicting β-strands, and both do better than the Chou–Fasman method. Taken together, these results indicate that the FSKBANN solution does significantly better than the ANN solution on predicting β-strand regions without having to sacrifice much accuracy in predicting α-helix regions.

Overall, the results suggest that more work needs to be done on developing methods of evaluating solution quality. A simple position-by-position count of correct predictions does not capture adequately the desired behavior. Solutions that find approximate locations of α-helix and β-strand regions and those that accurately predict all three classes should be favored over solutions that only do well at predicting the largest class. Most importantly, the results show that for difficult problems, such as the protein-folding problem, the FSKBANN approach of using neural learning to refine an existing algorithm can be worthwhile.

5. Future work

FSKBANN uses a domain theory to give a network a "good" set of initial weights, since search starts from that location in weight space. Therefore, augmenting the Chou–Fasman domain theory with other information may increase the solution's accuracy, because training will start from a "better" location. Information in tables 7 and 8 indicate the weaknesses of the present system. With this knowledge, we plan to develop domain-theory extensions addressing these weaknesses by studying the biological literature.

A second method of augmenting the knowledge is to use a more complex encoding scheme. At present each amino acid is represented by a single input unit. Hunter (1991) suggests a more complex encoding scheme that encodes a number of properties of each of the amino acids. Our preliminary tests with this encoding scheme on standard neural networks showed promising results. More recent domain theories (Garnier & Robson, 1989; Prevelige & Fasman, 1989) also include knowledge about a fourth type of secondary structure, β-turns, which in our data set are classified as random coils. This knowledge can be added to the present networks as a partial domain theory for coils, or in networks trying to predict the four different classes.

One interesting property of FSKBANN's networks is that the magnitude of each output is correlated with how accurate the prediction is. We plan to use this information in a more complex method: instead of predicting all of the protein's structure in one scan, we will predict only the strongest activated areas first, and then will feed these predictions back into the network for the next scan. In the first pass over the protein, the system could mark those amino acids with the largest predictions, and then these could be used in predicting for the next step. This is different from the existing method in that during the second pass the system would not only know the structure for the previous amino acid, but also might know what the structure is for the next amino acid, the amino acid two positions ahead, etc.

A basic problem with the KBANN approach is extracting information in a human-readable form from trained networks (Giles et al., 1992; Towell & Shavlik, 1992). We plan to address rule extraction for the augmented networks of FSKBANN by extending the existing method for extracting rules from KBANN networks (Towell & Shavlik, 1992). Our extension will extract refined FSAs rather than rules.

Jacobs et al. (1991) proposed a method for learning how to combine knowledge from a number of neural networks to produce a better solution. Since a number of different approaches to protein structure prediction have been investigated, we are working on a method to combine these strategies into a single prediction method. The combined solution will aggregate predictions from a number of different neural networks, plus the output of other machine learning approaches and biological approaches.

Another important area of focus is applying FSKBANN in other domains. We plan to apply FSKBANN to problems in molecular biology, such as the splice-junction problem (Noordewier et al., 1991), where the states of the network are *intron* and *exon*. Also of interest is evaluating this approach for problems in other fields, such as natural language (as in Elman, 1990). The task could involve learning to recognize simple sentences involving a simple (regular) grammar where some information about the grammar is known, but some is missing or incorrect.

6. Related research

Our work shares similarities with research in three areas: algorithms for predicting protein structure, neural networks that use state information, and systems that combine strategies for solving problems.

6.1. Methods of predicting protein secondary structure

There have been a number of algorithms proposed for predicting protein secondary structure. These can loosely be divided into those that use biological knowledge (and are non-learning methods) and those that use a learning mechanism.

6.1.1. Non-learning methods

The three most widely used approaches in the biological literature (Fasman, 1989) for predicting protein secondary structure are the Chou–Fasman (Chou & Fasman, 1978; Prevelige & Fasman, 1989), Robson (Garnier & Robson, 1989; Robson & Suzuki, 1976), and Lim (1974) algorithms. The Robson and Suzuki (1976) and the later GorII and GorIII (Garnier & Robson, 1989) solutions are based on information theory. These approaches, like neural networks, base prediction on a window of information around a central amino acid (from position −8 to +8 around the central amino acid). For every window position, the Robson algorithm determines the relevance of the amino acid for predicting each type of secondary structure. The computerized versions of the Chou–Fasman and Robson techniques that we implemented and tested on the Qian and Sejnowski test data exhibit 58% accuracy (see table 3). The Lim (1974) method is the only one that tries to account for long-range interactions; it uses a stereochemical theory of the secondary structure of globular proteins. Later solutions (Garnier & Robson, 1989; Prevelige & Fasman, 1989) include theories of a fourth type of secondary structure, β-turns, which usually are classified as coils. The main advantage of FSKBANN over these algorithms is that while FSKBANN contains biological information, it also has a mechanism for learning.

6.1.2. Learning methods

A number of investigators have used learning algorithms and sample folded proteins to try to predict secondary structure of new proteins. Holley and Karplus (1989) and Qian and Sejnowski (1988) use simple one-hidden-layer neural networks to try to predict secondary structure. Both studies focus on varying the hidden unit size and window size, achieving very different results (as shown in table 4) for these parameters, though both report test-set accuracies around 63%. Qian and Sejnowski also use a cascaded architecture, which produces a 1.6-percentage-point improvement in accuracy over their single-network results. Stolorz, Lapedes, and Xia (1991) use a perceptron architecture to evaluate a different error function, *mutual information*, which produces a one-percentage-point gain in accuracy over a standard perceptron. The interesting thing about the Stolorz measure is that it improves helix and strand prediction at the expense of coil prediction, a desirable effect, since coil (making up 54% of the training data) tends to be overpredicted in many other neural-network techniques.

Zhang et al. (1992) also uses machine learning. This method combines information from a statistical technique, a memory-based reasoning algorithm, and a neural network. Zhang and co-workers divide the training set into halves, where each of the three components is trained on one half of the training set. Further training is done using the other half of the training set to learn to combine results from the three different components, using a second neural network. The best results they report are 66.4% for a training set of 96 proteins (Zhang et al. (1992).

Another learning technique applied to this problem is the nearest-neighbor algorithm PEBLS (Cost & Salzberg, 1993). These authors report accuracy of approximately 64% for a training set similar in size to the one we used. Work by Muggleton and King (1991) applying inductive logic programming produced test-set results of 81% accuracy for proteins containing only α-helix and coil regions. Kneller, Cohen, and Langridge (1990) produced similar results (79% accuracy) on proteins consisting of α-helices and coils. Our domain theory, trained to solve a similar problem (predicting either α-helix or not), also showed approximately 81% accuracy.

The major difference between these learning approaches and FSKBANN is that only FSKBANN incorporates a complete algorithm. FSKBANN also differs from the above approaches in that the neural networks used in our studies incorporate state information.

6.2. Methods of representing state information in neural networks

Several researchers have proposed neural-network architectures for incorporating information about state. The idea of retaining a state or context across training patterns occurs primarily in work addressing natural language problems (Cleeremans, Servan-Schreiber, & McClelland, 1989; Elman, 1990). These approaches provide a mechanism for preserving one or more of the past activations of some units to use in processing of the next input.

Jordan (1986) and Elman (1990) introduced the particular recurrent network topology we use in FSKBANN. Their networks have a set of hidden units called *context units* that preserve the state of the network. At each time step, the previous value of the context units are copied back as input to the system. These networks allow for the possibility of keeping multiple past contexts as input to the system.

The idea of using the type of network introduced by Jordan to represent a finite-state automaton was discussed by Cleeremans et al. (1989). They show that this type of network can perfectly learn to recognize a grammar derived from a finite-state automaton. Giles et al. (1992) used a more complex recurrent network both to learn an FSA and to extract the learned FSA. The major difference between our research and that of Cleeremans et al. and Giles et al. is that we focus on using an initial domain theory expressed as a finite-state automaton, rather than attempting to learn it from scratch.

6.3. Methods of multistrategy learning

A number of researchers have recently addressed the problem of blending different strategies to produce more effective learners. Ourston and Mooney's (1990) EITHER system uses a domain theory to focus the corrections that an inductive learning system performs. Tecuci (this issue) describes a system that includes a number of different mechanisms such as induction, deduction, analogy, and abduction to correct a domain theory. In Pazzani's (this issue) Theory-Driven Learning system, the search for rules to explain incorrect examples is constrained by regularities observed between rules in the domain theory. Saitta and Botta (this issue) developed a system that combines abductive learning based on a domain model with inductive learning based on sample instances. The major difference between the above work and FSKBANN is that the above systems only use symbolic reasoning to learn. Each of these systems works directly on rules in some form. FSKBANN allows the integration of a symbolic representation with neural learning to take advantage of the generality and power of this type of learning.

7. Conclusion

This article presents and evaluates FSKBANN, a system that provides a mechanism for combining the knowledge from domain theories represented as generalized finite-state automata into neural networks. These networks can be further trained, using backpropagation, to refine the initial domain knowledge. The extension of KBANN to domain theories that include knowledge about state significantly enhances the power of the KBANN approach; rules expressed in the domain theory can take into account the current problem-solving context (i.e., the state of the solution).

We tested FSKBANN by refining the non-learning Chou–Fasman algorithm for predicting protein secondary structure, a task that is becoming a "challenge problem" in the machine learning and computational biology communities. The FSKBANN multistrategy approach of combining domain knowledge with a neural network proved to be more accurate than either a standard neural network approach or the non-learning Chou–Fasman algorithm. The FSKBANN solution proved even more effective when considered in terms of how well it does for each class of secondary structure.

The success of FSKBANN on the secondary-structure problem suggests it can be a useful tool for addressing other tasks that include state information. However, work must be done both in improving the neural-network refinement process and the extraction of symbolic knowledge from trained networks.

Appendix. The Chou–Fasman domain theory

The Chou–Fasman algorithm (1978) involves three activities: (1) recognizing nucleation sites, (2) extending sites, and (3) resolving overlapping predictions. This appendix provides more details of these three steps and describes the representation of their algorithm as a collection of rules.

To recognize nucleation sites, Chou and Fasman assign two *conformation* values to each of the 20 amino acids. The conformation values represent how likely an amino acid is to be part of either a helix or strand structure, with higher values being more likely. They also group the amino acids into classes of similar conformation value. The classes for helix are *formers*, *high-indifferent*, *indifferent*, and *breakers*; those for strand are *formers*, *indifferent*, and *breakers*. Table 9 defines the values for the various types of breakers and formers.

Table 10 contains the rules that represent the Chou–Fasman algorithm; x@N is true if x is the amino acid N positions from the one whose secondary structure the algorithm is predicting. The rules predict an α-helix nucleation site if for some consecutive set of six amino acids, at least four are helix formers and fewer than two are helix breakers. (Two helix high-indifferent amino acids count as a helix former.) A rule to determine if a location is a nucleation site simply adds the helix-former and helix-breaker values for a window six amino acids wide. If the totals are greater than four and less than two, respectively, the rule predicts a helix nucleation site (proposition init-helix in the rules). Nucleation of β-strands is similar to α-helix nucleation, except that the window is only five amino acids wide and a strand nucleation site is predicted if there are at least three strand formers and fewer than two strand breakers.

The third step of the algorithm—resolving overlaps—is the reason we use the numbers in table 9 rather than making the formers and breakers Boolean properties. Chou and Fasman suggest that the conformation values of regions be compared to resolve overlaps. This is done in FSKBANN's networks by weighting the links from various amino acids according to the numbers in table 9. For example, a combination of four alanines (A's) will produce a higher activation of the init-helix unit than a combination of four phenylalanines (F's).

Table 9. Former and breaker values‡ for the amino acids.

helix-former(E)	= 1.37	helix-former(A)	= 1.29	helix-former(L)	= 1.20
helix-former(H)	= 1.11	helix-former(M)	= 1.07	helix-former(Q)	= 1.04
helix-former(W)	= 1.02	helix-former(V)	= 1.02	helix-former(F)	= 1.00
helix-former(K)	= 0.54	helix-former(I)	= 0.50		
helix-former(*others*)	= 0.00				
helix-breaker(N)	= 1.00	helix-breaker(Y)	= 1.20	helix-breaker(P)	= 1.24
helix-breaker(G)	= 1.38				
helix-breaker(*others*)	= 0.00				
strand-former(M)	= 1.40	strand-former(V)	= 1.39	strand-former(I)	= 1.34
strand-former(C)	= 1.09	strand-former(Y)	= 1.08	strand-former(F)	= 1.07
strand-former(Q)	= 1.03	strand-former(L)	= 1.02	strand-former(T)	= 1.01
strand-former(W)	= 1.00				
strand-former(*others*)	= 0.00				
strand-breaker(K)	= 1.00	strand-breaker(S)	= 1.03	strand-breaker(H)	= 1.04
strand-breaker(N)	= 1.14	strand-breaker(P)	= 1.19	strand-breaker(E)	= 2.00
strand-breaker(*others*)	= 0.00				

‡We produced these values using the tables reported by Chou and Fasman (1978, p. 51). We normalized the values for formers by dividing the conformation value of the given former by the conformation value of the weakest former. So for example, the helix former value of alanine (A) is 1.29, since the helix conformation value of alanine is 1.45 and the conformation value of the weakest helix former phenylalanine (F) is 1.12. Breaker values work similarly except that the value used to calculate the breaker value is the multiplicative inverse of the conformation value.

We did not directly use the values of Chou and Fasman for two reasons. One, we wanted smaller values in order to decrease the number of times that three very strong helix-formers would add up to more than 4 (and similarly for strands). Two, breaker conformation values tend to be numbers between 0 and 1 with the stronger breakers being close to 0. We wanted the breaker value to be larger the stronger the breaker, so we used the inverse of the breaker's conformation value (restricting the result to not exceed 2).

The Chou–Fasman algorithm continues to predict α-helices as long as the predicate `cont-helix` is true. The rules define `cont-helix` mostly in terms of helix-breaking rules—a helix continues as long as a break region is not encountered. An α-helix break region occurs when a helix-breaker amino acid is immediately followed by either another helix-breaker or a helix-indifferent amino acid. A helix is also broken when encountering the amino acid proline (P). The process of extending β-strand structures works similarly. The algorithm predicts coil as the default.

Acknowledgments

This research was partially supported by National Science Foundation Grant IRI-9002413 and Office of Naval Research Grant N00014-90-J-1941. The authors would like to thank Terrence Sejnowski for providing the protein data used in testing. The domain theory and data used in testing are available by anonymous ftp from the University of California-Irvine archive maintained by David Aha and Patrick Murphy.

Table 10. The Chou–Fasman algorithm expressed as inference rules.

Rules for recognizing nucleation sites

$$\textit{init-helix} \leftarrow \left[\sum_{position=0}^{5} \textit{helix-former}\ (\textit{amino-acid@position})\right] > 4$$

$$\wedge \left[\sum_{position=0}^{5} \textit{helix-breaker}\ (\textit{amino-acid@position})\right] < 2$$

$$\textit{init-strand} \leftarrow \left[\sum_{position=0}^{4} \textit{strand-former}\ (\textit{amino-acid@position})\right] > 3$$

$$\wedge \left[\sum_{position=0}^{4} \textit{strand-breaker}\ (\textit{amino-acid@position})\right] < 2$$

Rules for pairs of amino acids that terminate helix structures

helix-break@0 ← *N@0* ∨ *Y@0* ∨ *P@0* ∨ *G@0*
helix-break@1 ← *N@1* ∨ *Y@1* ∨ *P@1* ∨ *G@1*
helix-indiff@1 ← *K@1* ∨ *I@1* ∨ *D@1* ∨ *T@1* ∨ *S@1* ∨ *R@1* ∨ *C@1*

break-helix ← *helix-break@0* ∧ *helix-break@1*
break-helix ← *helix-break@0* ∧ *helix-indiff@1*

Rules for pairs of amino acids that terminate strand structures

strand-break@0 ← *K@0* ∨ *S@0* ∨ *H@0* ∨ *N@0* ∨ *P@0* ∨ *E@0*
strand-break@1 ← *K@1* ∨ *S@1* ∨ *H@1* ∨ *N@1* ∨ *P@1* ∨ *E@1*
strand-indiff@1 ← *A@1* ∨ *R@1* ∨ *G@1* ∨ *D@1*

break-strand ← *strand-break@0* ∧ *strand-break@1*
break-strand ← *strand-break@0* ∧ *strand-indiff@1*

Rules for continuing structures

cont-helix ← ¬*P@0* ∧ ¬*break-helix*
cont-strand ← ¬*P@0* ∧ ¬*E@0* ∧ ¬*break-strand*

Rules for predicting a-helix: either by nucleation or propagating from the last state

$helix_i$ ← *init-helix*
$helix_i$ ← $helix_{i-1}$ ∧ *cont-helix*

Rules for predicting β-strand: either by nucleation or propagating from the last state

$strand_i$ ← *init-strand*
$strand_i$ ← $strand_{i-1}$ ∧ *cont-strand*

Rules for predicting coil (the default)

$coil_i$ ← $helix_{i-1}$ ∧ *break-helix*
$coil_i$ ← $strand_{i-1}$ ∧ *break-strand*
$coil_i$ ← $coil_{i-1}$

Notes

1. The notion of an FSA in FSKBANN is generalized in that rather than taking a single input value at each step, the FSA may take *a set* of input values.
2. FSKBANN actually scans each protein twice: from left-to-right and from right-to-left. It then sums the results to simulate extending nucleation sites in both directions.
3. The patience criterion states that training should continue until the error rate has not decreased for some number of training cycles. For this study we set the number of epochs to be four (a value determined by empirical testing).
4. The following formula defines the correlation coefficient for the secondary structure problem (Mathews, 1975):

$$C = \frac{P * N - F * M}{\sqrt{(P + F)(P + M)(N + F)(N + M)}}$$

where C is calculated for each structure separately, and P, N, F, and M are the number of true positives, true negatives, false positives, and misses for each structure, respectively.

References

Chou, P., & Fasman, G. (1978). Prediction of the secondary structure of proteins from their amino acid sequence. *Advances in Enzymology, 47,* 45–148.

Cleeremans, A., Servan-Schreiber, D., & McClelland, J. (1989). Finite state automata and simple recurrent networks. *Neural Computation,* (*3*), 372–381.

Cohen, B., Presnell, S., Cohen, F., & Langridge, R. (1991). A proposal for feature-based scoring of protein secondary structure predictions. *Proceedings of the AAAI-91 Workshop on Artitificial Intelligence Approaches to Classification and Pattern Recognition in Molecular Biology* (pp. 5–20). Anaheim, CA.

Cost, S., & Salzberg, S. (1993). A weighted nearest neighbor algorithm for learning with symbolic features. *Machine Learning, 10(1),* 57–78.

Elman, J. (1990). Finding structure in time. *Cognitive Science, 14*(*2*), 179–211.

Fahlman, S., & Lebiere, C. (1990). The cascade-correlation learning architecture. In D. Touretzky (Ed.), *Advances in neural information processing systems,* Vol. 2 (pp. 524–532). Denver, CO: Morgan Kaufmann.

Fasman, G. (1989). The development of the prediction of protein structure. In Fasman, G. (Ed.), *Prediction of protein structure and the principles of protein conformation.* New York: Plenum Press.

Garnier, J., & Robson, B. (1989). The GOR method for predicting secondary structures in proteins. In G. Fasman (Ed.), *Prediction of protein structure and the principles of protein conformation.* New York: Plenum Press.

Giles, C., Miller, C., Chen, D., Chen, H., Sun, G., & Lee, Y. (1992). Learning and extracting finite state automata with second-order recurrent neural network. *Neural Computation, 4,* 393–405.

Holley, L., & Karplus, M. (1989). Protein structure prediction with a neural network. *Proceedings of the National Academy of Sciences* (*USA*), *86,* 152–156.

Hopcroft, J., & Ullman, J. (1979). *Introduction to automata theory, languages, and computation.* Reading, MA: Addison Wesley.

Hunter, L. (1991). Representing amino acids with bitstrings. *Proceedings of the AAAI-91 Workshop on Artificial Intelligence Approaches to Classification and Pattern Recognition in Molecular Biology* (pp. 110–117). Anaheim, CA.

Jacobs, R., Jordan, M., Nowlan, S., & Hinton, G. (1991). Adaptive mixtures of local experts. *Neural Computation, 3*(*1*), 79–87.

Jordan, M. (1986). *Serial order: A parallel distributed processing approach* (Technical Report 8604). San Diego: University of California, Institute for Cognitive Science.

Kneller, D., Cohen, F., & Langridge, R. (1990). Improvements in protein secondary structure prediction by an enhanced neural network. *Journal of Molecular Biology, 214,* 171–182.

Lim, V. (1974). Algorithms for prediction of α-helical and β-structural regions in globular proteins. *Journal of Molecular Biology, 88,* 873–894.

Mathews, B. (1975). Comparison of the predicted and observed secondary structure of T4 Phage Lysozyme. *Biochimica et Biophysica Acta, 405*, 442–451.

Muggleton, S. (Ed.). (1992). *Inductive logic programming*. London: Academic Press.

Muggleton, S., & Feng, R. (1991). *Predicting protein secondary-structure using inductive logic programming*. (Technical Report). Glasgow, Scotland: Turing Institute.

Nishikawa, K. (1983). Assessment of secondary-structure prediction of proteins: Comparison of computerized Chou–Fasman method with others. *Biochimica et Biophysica Acta, 748*, 285–299.

Noordewier, M., Towell, G., & Shavlik, J. (1991). Training knowledge-based neural networks to recognize genes in DNA sequences. In R. Lippmann, J. Moody, & D. Touretzky, (Eds.), *Advances in neural information processing systems*, Vol. 3. Denver, CO: Morgan Kaufmann.

Ourston, D., & Mooney, R. (1990). Changing the rules: A comprehensive approach to theory refinement. *Proceedings of the Eighth National Conference on Artificial Intelligence* (pp. 815–820). Boston, MA: MIT Press.

Pazzani, M. (1993). Learning causal patterns: Making a transition from data-driven to theory-driven learning. *Machine Learning, 11* (this issue).

Prevelige, P. Jr., & Fasman, G. (1989). Chou–Fasman prediction of the secondary structure of proteins: The Chou–Fasman–Prevelige algorithm. In G. Fasman (Ed.), *Prediction of protein structure and the principles of protein conformation*. New York: Plenum Press.

Qian, N., & Sejnowski, T. (1988). Predicting the secondary structure of globular proteins using neural network models. *Journal of Molecular Biology, 202*, 865–884.

Quinlan, J. (1990). Learning logical definitions from relations. *Machine Learning, 5(3)*, 239–266.

Richardson, J., & Richardson, D. (1989). Principles and patterns of protein conformation. In G. Fasman (Ed.), *Prediction of protein structure and the principles of protein conformation*. New York: Plenum Press.

Robson, B., & Suzuki, E. (1976). Conformational properties of amino acid residues in globular proteins. *Journal of Molecular Biology, 107*, 327–356.

Rumelhart, D., Hinton, G., & Williams, R. (1986). Learning internal representations by error propagation. In D. Rumelhart, & J. McClelland (Eds.), *Parallel distributed processing: Explorations in the microstructure of cognition. Volume 1: Foundations* (pp. 318–363). Cambridge, MA: MIT Press.

Saitta, L., & Botta, M. (1993). Multistrategy learning and theory revision. *Machine Learning, 11* (this issue).

Sejnowski, T., & Rosenberg, C. (1987). Parallel networks that learn to pronounce English text. *Complex Systems, 1*, 145–168.

Stolorz, P., Lapedes, A., & Xia, Y. (1991). Predicting protein secondary structure using neural net and statistical methods. *Journal of Molecular Biology, 225*, 363–377.

Tecuci, G. (1993). Plausible justification trees: A framework for deep and dynamic integration of learning strategies. *Machine Learning, 11* (this issue).

Towell, G., Shavlik, J., & Noordewier, M. (1990). Refinement of approximate domain theories by knowledge-based neural networks. *Proceedings of the Eighth National Conference on Artificial Intelligence* (pp. 861–866). Boston, MA: MIT Press.

Towell, G. (1991). *Symbolic knowledge and neural networks: Insertion, refinement and extraction*. Doctoral dissertation, Department of Computer Science, University of Wisconsin, Madison.

Towell, G., & Shavlik, J. (1992). Interpretation of artificial neural networks: Mapping knowledge-based neural networks into rules. In R. Lippmann, J. Moody, & D. Touretzky (Eds.), *Advances in neural information processing systems*, Vol. 4. Denver, CO: Morgan Kaufmann.

Watson, J. (1990). The Human Genome Project: Past, present, and future. *Science, 248*, 44–48.

Wilson, I., Haft, D., Getzoff, E., Tainer, J., Lerner, R., & Brenner, S. (1985). Identical short peptide sequences in unrelated proteins can have different conformations: A testing ground for theories of immune recognition. *Proceeding of the National Academy of Sciences (USA), 82*, 5255–5259.

Zhang, X., Mesirov, J. & Waltz, D. (1992). Hybrid system for protein secondary structure prediction. *Journal of Molecular Biology, 225*, 1049–1063.

Received December 11, 1991
Accepted January 16, 1992
Final Manuscript February 28, 1992

Machine Learning, 11, 217-235 (1993)

Balanced Cooperative Modeling

KATHARINA MORIK MORIK@KILO.INFORMATIK.UNI-DORTMUND.DE
University of Dortmund, Dept. Computer Science VIII, P.O. Box 500 500, 44227 Dortmund, Germany

Abstract. Machine learning techniques are often used for supporting a knowledge engineer in constructing a model of part of the world. Different learning algorithms contribute to different tasks within the modeling process. Integrating several learning algorithms into one system allows it to support several modeling tasks within the same framework. In this article, we focus on the distribution of work between several learning algorithms on the one hand and the user on the other hand. The approach followed by the MOBAL system is that of **balanced cooperation**, i.e., each modeling task can be done by the user or by a learning tool of the system. The MOBAL system is described in detail. We discuss the principle of mutli-functionality of one representation for the balanced use by learning algorithms and users.

Keywords: Multistrategy learning, balanced cooperative modeling, MOBAL

1. Introduction

The overall task of knowledge acquisition as well as that of machine learning has often been described as constructing a model of part of the world, on purpose. If a system is to support the person constructing a model, it must **accept new items** and integrate them into the knowledge base. It must present the state of the domain model and allow the user to **inspect** it. It must support **revisions** of all modeling decisions of the user. Finally, it must support the **refinement** of rules or rule sets because of additional knowledge and the introduction of **new features** or concepts.[1]

The first two requirements are fulfilled by most of the knowledge acquisition environments. Revisions are frequently supported only by a text editor. Then it is up to the user to check consistency and integrity of the revised domain model. The user is supported only in performing the addition of new items and the inspection of the domain model.

Machine learning algorithms are most often used for automating the construction of rules as additional items of the knowledge base. Recently, automatic refinement and automatic construction of new features or concepts (constructive induction) are also provided by some machine learning systems. Moreover, inspection can also make good use of machine learning. Hence, for all of the modeling tasks listed above, there exists a machine learning tool that automatizes at least parts of them.

A system that integrates several learning tools, each responsible for performing a different modeling subtask, is a multistrategy learning system (Michalski 1991). Questions concerning the **cooperation of tools** are whether one tool can use the results of another, whether several tools can use the same knowledge items, and whether one tool can call another one. MOBAL is such a multistrategy learning system, where the learning tools cooperate by means of input-output data so as to solve the global modeling task. But a multistrategy learning system also needs some information about the domain and the desired domain model given by the user. The **cooperation with the user** is necessary even for the most advanced learning system. This is not a disadvantage. On the contrary, the user should guide the learning and be in control of the modeling process. On the one hand, we appreciate machine learning to automate some tasks. On the other hand, we still want the users to perform their tasks—supported by the system. The question is how to organize the cooperation of user and system tools such that both system and user contribute to model building. For MOBAL, a synergistic effect can be stated that is the result of both the user and the learning tools contributing to the global modeling task.

2. Cooperation

There are different ways to use machine learning algorithms for knowledge acquisition. They correspond to a different distribution of work between system and user. The work share has consequences for the knowledge representation.

2.1. Work share between system and user

We may distinguish the following three prototypical ways of distributing the work between system and user in modeling a domain:

1. one-shot learning, where the user prepares examples and background knowledge and then runs an algorithm on the data (examples are ID3 (Quinlan, 1983), FOIL (Quinlan, 1991), or KLUSTER (Morik & Kietz, 1989; Kietz & Morik, 1991));
2. interactive learning, where the user prepares examples and background knowledge and then interacts with a learning system (examples are DISCIPLE (Kodratoff and Tecuci 1989) or CLINT (De Raedt, 1991); and
3. balanced interaction of system and user, where learning contributes to the preparation of background knowledge, enhancement of the domain knowledge, and inspection of the (learned) knowledge (an example is MOBAL, described in this article).

These options of how to use machine learning correspond to different **tasks** handled by a learning system. A learning task can be described by a certain type of input and the produced output. An additional characteristic of the learning task is whether the learning is performed incrementally (which can be the case in the second and third option above). Of course, the same learning task can be applied to various domains. In the first option above, the user calls a learning algorithm for one particular task. Most often, this task is to learn a set of rules from examples of complementary classes. The second two options have the learning system cover a broader range of tasks. Each learning task corresponds to a learning tool that solves it—regardless of whether implementation is in separate modules or in one module.

Whereas in the first two options the user is requested to give some particular **information**, in the third option the user can give any information and the system uses it. Of course, the information must be sensible. However, the user is free to enter, e.g., facts or rules or term sorts or predicate sorts. That is, the distribution of work between system and user is strictly prescribed in the first two options, whereas it is flexible in the third one.

The **control** of the modeling process is in the users' hands in the first option; the user call the learning tool. In the second option, the system is in control; the system prompts the user to give the needed information. In the third option, control is mixed. The users can call tools explicitly, as in the first option. If they do not want to do so, the flow of control between the tools is organized by the system. The users are never prompted to input a (counter-) example or a declaration of background knowledge. However, by setting some parameters they can state that they want to be asked by the system at certain decision points.

In the first option, **revisions** of the learning results are performed by the user in an edit-and-compile cycle with no more support than a text editor can give. If new, negative examples are acquired from the application, a new example set must be constructed, consisting of the new and some already known examples. The learning algorithm then constructs new rules that probably are better than the ones learned before. In the second option, some revision of rules is performed by a learning tool because of negative examples. In the third option, learning techniques are used for refinement and the construction of new features or concepts. Moreover, revisions of all modeling decisions that have been made are supported by some knowledge-editing tools.

The prototypical ways of using learning (cases 1 to 3 above) illustrate the aspects of work share between system and user:

- Which tasks are performed by the user, and which tasks are performed by the system?
- Which information is given by the user, and which information is constructed or derived by the system?
- Is the user, the system, or both in control of the modeling process?
- Which revisions are supported by the system, and which revisions are automatically done by a learning tool?

If the user as well as the system can perform a task, construct knowledge items of a certain kind, run (learning) tools, and revise given knowledge, then we call such a system **balanced cooperative**. MOBAL is such a balanced cooperative system. It will be described in detail in the next chapter.

2.2. Multifunctionality

The use of the system has consequences for the knowledge representation. In the first option for using a tool, the representation can easily be tailored for the needs of the one algorithm. The representation of a multistrategy learner (option 2 and 3) has to be designed with respect to several, possibly conflicting needs, or the different representations of different tools have to be integrated. The MOBAL system is a multistrategy learner that integrates various tools using a *uniform* representation. The integration problem with respect to knowledge representation is then to develop a formalism that is powerful enough to suit all tools well and that is still tractable. In contrast, the MLT system integrates several learning systems, each with its own representation (see Morik et al., 1991). The integration problem is then to integrate *given* representation formalisms.

Balanced cooperative modeling allows the user as well as the system to work on the evolving domain model. As a consequence, all knowledge sources (examples, background knowledge, declarations, rules) have to be represented such that the system as well as the user can easily input, modify, and inspect the knowledge. This constrains the representation to be designed. If revisions of all knowledge entities have to be processed and their consequences have to be maintained by the system, this constrains the design of a representation even further.

The bidirectional use of knowledge bases has been discussed in other fields of artificial intelligence. For instance, a grammar is supposed to be used by the parser as well as by the generator of natural language sentences. Some efforts have also been made to use the same knowledge for plan recognition as for plan generation. Analogously, we claim that the same knowledge should be of good use for the user building up a model as well as for the learning system enhancing the model and building parts of it.

3. Cooperation in MOBAL

All the knowledge needed for problem solving in a particular domain can be input by the user. In this case, all the information is given by the user, who performs all modeling tasks and completely controls the modeling process. The user is supported by an inference engine and a human-computer interface (see below). However, the user does not need to input almost everything. For each knowledge item that the user might input, there exists a corresponding learning tool that can acquire parts of that knowledge. The basic input that the system expects from the user is facts and rule models (see next section). Of course, a system cannot create a model without any given information! But with reference to those basic items there also exist corresponding capabilities of MOBAL, namely, the inference engine (deriving facts) and the model acquisition tool (producing rule models). Between the extremes of modeling by the user alone and some automatic contribution to the modeling by the system, all variations of work share are possible. This flexibility also has a disadvantage that should not be hidden: new users of the system miss the strict guidance that is given by interactive systems. They have difficulties selecting among all the possible choices.

3.1. MOBAL's representation

The MOBAL system is an environment for building up, inspecting, and changing a knowledge base. Before we present the learning tools, we describe the items that constitute a domain model in MOBAL.

The knowledge items integrated by the inference engine of MOBAL (Emde, 1991) are

- **facts**, expressing, e.g., relations, properties, and concept membership of objects;

  `owner(luc, dianel)` and `not(owner(luc,mercedes))` are facts

- **rules**, expressing, e.g., relations between concepts, necessary and sufficient conditions of concepts, hierarchies of properties;

  `owner(X,Y)&involved(Z,Y) --> responsible(X,Z)` is a rule

- **sorts**, expressing a structure of all the objects (constant terms) of the domain model;
- **topology of predicates**, expressing the overall structure of the rules of the domain; and
- **rule models**, expressing the structure of the rules to be learned.

The items are represented in a restricted higher-order logic that was proven to be tractable (Wrobel, 1987). The user does not need to know all about the meta-predicates and the meta-rules in which they appear. The user also does not need to know the internal representation format. The windows of the human-computer interface provide presentations, both graphical and as text, of the knowledge base that are understandable without knowing the internal data structures. The user beginning an application regularly starts with facts and rules that are easy to understand. In the following, the knowledge items are described.

3.1.1. Facts

Facts are used to state relations, properties of objects, and concept membership. Facts are represented as function-free literals without variables. The arguments of a predicate are of a particular *sort*. A fact `p(o1,o2,o3)` is only well formed if the constant terms of `o1`, `o2`, `o3` belong to the sorts of the first, second, or third argument place of `p`, respectively. For instance, the term at the first place of the predicate `involved` must be a member of the sort of events, the one at the second place must be a member of the vehicle sort. The form of a fact is $p(t_1, \ldots, t_n)$ where p is a n-ary predicate and t_j is a constant term or a number of the sort s_j.

The mapping from a fact to a truth value may obey a fuzzy logic because, in principle, the inference engine handles continuous truth values (Emde, 1991). But, usually, it is difficult for a user to assign a fuzzy truth value to a fact. Therefore, only the truth values `unknown`, `true`, `false`, `contradictory` are used. A derived or input fact without explicit negation is interpreted as `true`. Every fact that is to be interpreted as `false` must be explicitly negated. This explicit negation has some advantages compared with the closed-world assumption. It enables the user to input incomplete examples and to build up the model incrementally. The closed-world assumption requires the user to know in advance which statements are necessary to complete the description of an example. But, as was stated above, modeling does not start with such a precise idea. Therefore, leaving out some statements in one example does not mean the negation of these statements. Hence, MOBAL interprets missing information simply as `unknown`.

Explicit negation also allows us to explicitly contradict a derived fact of the system. Suppose, the inference engine has derived the fact

```
owner(luc, dianel)
```

and the user knows that this is not true. The user then inputs

```
not(owner(luc, dianel)).
```

As a result, the fact `owner(luc, dianel)` becomes `contradictory`. An explicit contradiction does not lead to the counterintuitive behavior of standard logic that all formulas become true. Instead, the contradictory parts of the knowledge-base are excluded from inference processes. Hence, facts that are not contradictory keep their truth values. Contradictions are resolved by a knowledge revision component (Wrobel, 1989).

3.1.2. Rules

In MOBAL, rules correspond to Horn clauses. In addition, the applicability of rules is maintained. For each variable occurring in a rule, its domain is represented as a *support set* (Emde, Habel, & Rollinger, 1983; Wrobel, 1989). In the normal case, the support set is a tuple of the sets of all objects. The rule

```
owner(X,Y) & involved(Z,Y) --> responsible(X,Z)
```

has a support set giving the domains for `X,Y,Z`. In the regular case, these are `all`. The support set then is `all x all x all`. But it is also possible to restrict the applicability of a rule to a more special support set. This can be done by exceptions of a variable's domain, by a tuple of exceptions of the support set, or by expressing a variable's domain by a concept. The above rule is only valid for events that are members of the concept `minor_violation`. The domain of variable `Z` is restricted to instances of minor (traffic law) violations: `all x all x minor_violation` is the correct support set for that rule.[2]

More formally, let `all` denote the set of all objects of a universe of discourse, D_i denote `all` or subsets of this set, T_j be a n-tuple of constant terms, and $t_1 \ldots t_k$ be constant terms (corresponding to particular objects in D), covered by a concept C; then the form of a support set for a rule with the variables $X_1, \ldots, X_n$ is

$$(X_1, \ldots, X_n) \text{ in } D_1 \times \ldots \times D_n \text{ except } \{T_1, \ldots, T_j\}$$

where the `except` part can be empty.

The T_j are tuples of objects that should not be instances of the variables $X_1, \ldots, X_n$ of the rule because the rule would then lead to a contradiction. In a tuple T_j, each term can be of a different subset of `all`. In our example, such a tuple is `(luc,renault2,event3)`.

A particular D_i can be restricted by a set of exceptions, $\{t_1, \ldots, t_k\}$, written D_i `except` $\{t_1, \ldots, t_k\}$, in our example `all except {event3, event12, event 13}`. Or, the variable's domain D_i is restricted to a particular concept such as `minor_violation` in the example above.

3.1.3. Sorts

Sorts are used to guarantee the (semantic) well-formedness of predicates in facts and rules. Sorts can be named and given by the user in a predicate declaration:

```
owner/2: <person>, <vehicle>.
```

This means that the two-place predicate `owner` accepts only terms of sort `person` as the first argument and terms of sort `vehicle` as the second argument. It is not well formed to state `owner(john, michael)`. A sort covers a subset D_i of `all`. The sorts that are built automatically by the sort taxonomy tool have constructed names, such as `argl(owner)`, denoting the set of terms occurring at the first place of the predicate `owner`.

Sorts with the same set of terms form a class. For instance, `argl(owner)` and `argl(responsible)` have the same constant terms, e.g., `[luc, yves , eve]`. So, together they form a class:

```
class21:  [argl(owner), argl(responsible)] [luc,yves,eve]
```

Classes are organized in a lattice. The most general class is `all`; the most special class is the empty class. There are subclasses and intersection classes. The lattice of classes gives an overview of all sorts and classes, their subset relations, and their intersections. In this way, the structure of an application domain can be presented with respect to the objects of that domain. Figure 1 shows an except of the lattice of sorts for the traffic law domain.

3.1.4. Topology of predicates

The topology of predicates is used to guarantee the (semantic) well-formedness of rules. Sets of predicates form a named node of a graph. For instance, the node called `violation` represented as

```
tnode:  violation -Preds:  [parking-violation, responsible,
unsafe_vehicle_violation] -Links:  [places,circumstances,behavior,
vehicle, obligations]
```

contains the predicates `parking-violation`, `responsible`, `unsafe_vehicle_violation`. In the graph, the subnodes of this node are called

```
[places,circumstances,obligations, vehicle, behavior].
```

In a well-formed rule, if the predicate symbol of the conclusion is a member of a node TN (e.g., `violation`), the premises can only use predicate symbols from a subnode of TN (e.g., `places,circumstances,obligations,vehicle,behavior`) or TN itself. So, for instance, it is not well formed to conclude from the assurance contract of a vehicle's owner to the evaluation of the owner's parking behavior.

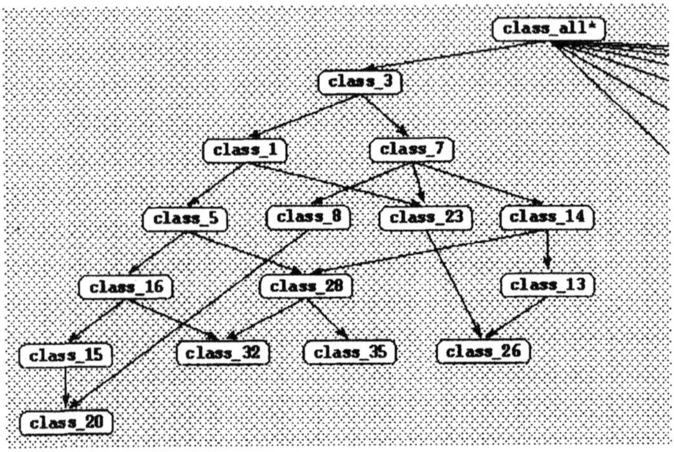

Figure 1. Excerpt of a lattice of sort classes.

The topology graph, where the nodes represent sets of predicate symbols that can be premises of the supernodes, gives an overview of possible rules in an application domain. Figure 2 shows the topology graph for the traffic law domain.

The topology graph can be viewed as a generalization of determinations (Davies & Russell 1987). There, it is stated that a rule is sensible if it relates some particular predicates. The topology generalizes this to sets of predicates: rules are sensible that use predicates of the same topology node TN or a predicate in TN for the conclusion, and predicates of subnodes of TN for the premises.

3.1.5. Rule models

A rule model is a rule in which predicate variables are used instead of actual predicates of an application domain. A predicate variable can be instantiated by a predicate symbol of the same arity. There is a substitution Σ for predicate variables. Let RS be a rule model; then RSΣ is a (partially) instantiated one. If all predicate variables are substituted by predicate symbols, the rule RSΣ is a predicate ground. Hence, a fully instantiated rule model is a rule. The rule model

```
R1(X,Y)&R2(Z,Y)  --> Q(X,Z)
```

can be instantiated

```
Σ: {R1/owner, R2/involved, Q/responsbile}
```

thus becoming our example rule. Rule models are ordered with respect to their generality such that the generality of fully instantiated rule models is given by theta-subsumption (Plotkin 1970). RS1 is more general than RS2 iff for all Σ there exists a substitution of terms σ such that $RS2\Sigma \subseteq RS1\Sigma\sigma$. The above rule model is, for instance, more general than the rule model `R1(X,Y)&R2(Z,Y)&R3(X,Y)  --> Q(X,Z)`, because every fully instantiated rule of the first one is a subset of the second one.[3] Σ is not allowed to replace

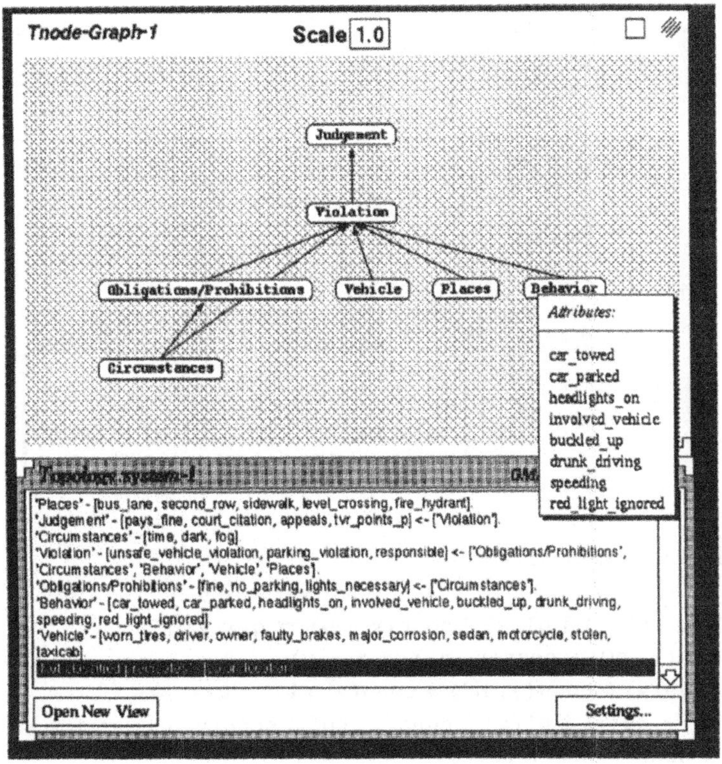

Figure 2. Topology graph.

different predicate variables by the same predicate symbol. Rule models are labeled by generated names such as, e.g., rl or l2. The generality structure is presented as a graph, where the labels of rule models are the nodes and the generality relations are the links (see figure 3).

Rule models can also be partially instantiated. All possible instantiations of all rule models together form the *hypothesis space* for rule learning in MOBAL. The hypothesis space is structured by the generality structure of rule models. This is used by RDT (see below) in order to prune branches of rule models where no instantiation can lead to an accepted rule.

The following rule models can be used to model neighborhood relations. The domain predicate symbol conn states a neighborhood relation; the predicate variables p0, p1, p2, p3, q can be instantiated to characterize the related objects. The most general rule model is the statement of a two-place predicate that always is true. The next general rule model has in addition a one-place premise.

```
r0(q) : → q(x,y).
r1(p0,q) : p0(y) → q(x,y).
r2(p1,p0,q) : p0(y) & p1(y) → q(x,y).
r3(q) : conn(y, n0) → q(x,y).
r4(p0,q) : p0(y) & conn(y, n0) → q(x,y).
```

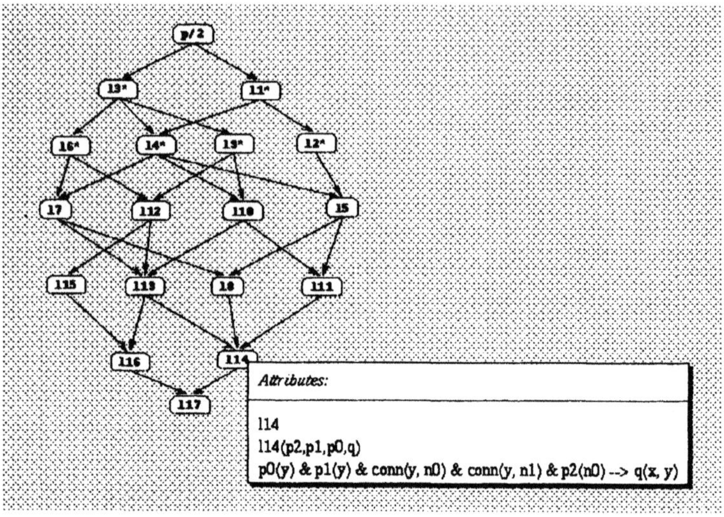

Figure 3. Generality structure of rule models.

r5(p1,p0,q) : p0(y) & p1(y) & conn(y, n0) → q(x,y).
r6(q) : conn(y, n0) & conn(y, n1) → q(x,y).
r7(p0,q) : p0(y) & conn(y, n0) & conn(y, n1) → q(x,y).
r8(p1,p0,q) : p0(y) & p1(y) & conn(y, n0) & conn(y, n1) → q(x,y).
r9(p0,q) : conn(y, n0) & p0(n0) → q(x,y).
r10(p1,p0,q) : p0(y) & conn(y, n0) & p1(n0) → q(x,y).
r11(p2,p1,p0,q) : p0(y) & p1(y) & conn(y, n0) & p2(no) → q(x,y).
r12(p0,q) : conn(y, n0) & conn(y, n1) & p0(n0) → q(x,y).
r13(p1,p0,q) : p0(y) & conn(y, n0) & conn(y, n1) & p1(n0) → q(x,y).
r14(p2,p1,p0,q) : p0(y) & p1(y) & conn(y, n0) & conn(y, n1) & p2(no) → q(x,y).
r15(p1,p0,q) : conn(y, n0) & conn(y, n1) & p0(n0) & p1(n1) → q(x,y).
r16(p2,p1,p0,q) : p0(y) & conn(y, n0) & conn(y, n1) & p1(n0) & p2(n1) → q(x,y).
r17(p3,p2,p1,p0,q) : p0(y) & p1(y) & conn(y, n0) & conn(y, n1) & p2(n0) & p3(n1) → q(x,y).

3.2. MOBAL's learning tools

The MOBAL system includes several learning tools:

- a rule discovery tool (RDT), which is a model-based, first-order logic learning algorithm inducing rules from facts
- a concept formation tool (CLT), which induces necessary and sufficient conditions for concepts from positive and negative examples

- a model acquisition tool (MAT), which abstracts rule models from rules
- a sort taxonomy tool (STT), which clusters constant terms occurring as arguments in facts
- a predicate structuring tool (PST), which abstracts rule sets to an overall structure of the knowledge base

To describe each of the learning tools in detail requires much more space than we have in this report. Since we want to concentrate on the use of the tools—either by the user or by another tool—it is sufficient to describe them as black boxes and only indicate the principle of how they work.

3.2.1. RDT

The rule discovery tool RDT helps the user to find regularities in facts. The *task* is that of learning from observations or discovering regularities in order to predict new events.

Input: a set of facts, a set of rule models
Output: a set of rules that are most general inductive generalizations of the facts.

The necessary *input* to this model-based inductive algorithm is facts and rule models. It is not necessary that the facts are complete descriptions of examples. If rules are already learned or given by the user, they are taken into account by the algorithm. In particular, they are not rediscovered, and they are not contradicted by a hypothesis for learning. Moreover, the inference engine performs forward inferences from (learned or given) rules, hence "saturating" the knowledge base for learning.

The learning *strategy* is top-down induction, i.e., the most general generalization is specialized until a rule is found that obeys a user-given acception criterion.

RDT can be *called* in different ways. It can be called with a time limit so that RDT learns within this CPU time limit and then stops. This allows us to use RDT incrementally. The aim is that RDT can learn in the background during the modeling activity of the user. RDT then tries to learn about the predicate that the user inputs as the predicate symbol of a fact. If the user wishes to focus on a particular predicate or a list of predicates. RDT looks for rules with these predicates in the conclusion. The set of predicates can be given by clicking on a node of the topology graph. RDT can also be called from CLT with a particular set of facts. The list of rule models is given by a parameter. The default is to use all rule models that are part of the domain model. The evaluation criteria for accepting a hypothesis can be set by the user. The basic building blocks for defining criteria are prepared. A default setting is given. But the user can define particular criteria and input them as parameter settings.

The *learning result* is a set of rules. The rules are not bound together in order to build sufficient and necessary conditions for concept membership, nor is there an ordering of rules, as in decision trees. Also, relations that hold between features are not distinguished from relations that hold between concepts or between features and concepts. The user may interpret the learned rules as characterizing concepts or as background knowledge. The learning result is used by the inference engine; hence, RDT performs *closed-loop learning*.

The basic idea behind this learning in predicate logic is to instantiate given rule models systematically and test the instantiations (i.e., rules) against ground facts. First, the most general rule model is instantiated. If an instance (i.e., a rule) is not accepted with respect to the acceptance criterion and yet enough facts are available, the next special rule model is instantiated. This procedure is similar to Shapiro's refinement operator (Shapiro 1981). But whereas the refinement operator builds up a complete hypothesis space, the hypothesis space of RDT is restricted by the rule models. Since the rule models regularly do not cover the forms of all possible Horn clauses, they restrict the hypothesis space.

For a rule model, each possible instantiation is tested. An instantiation is possible if the predicates that substitute predicate variables of the rule model have a compatible arity, sort restriction, and topology restriction. That is, the resulting rule hypothesis must be well formed with respect to the sorts and the topology of predicates (see above). This restricts the hypothesis space further. For instance, the most general rule models can be

```
P(X)-->Q(X), R(X,Y)-->Q(X,Y).
```

All 1-ary domain predicates with the same sort of an argument type that are in the same or linked topology node are tried as instances of the first rule model. If, for an instantiation Q/q and P/p there are many matching facts but not all of them justify the hypothesis, then the next special rule model is tried, e.g., `p(X)&R(X,Y) -->q(X)`. All compatible 2-ary predicates are tried as instantiations of R. Specializing hypotheses stops if a rule already exists, if it becomes accepted, or if there are not enough facts that could match the (more special) hypothesis. As is easily seen, RDT is much quicker than, e.g., FOIL(Quinlan, 1991) if the rule models are well suited for the desired learning results. If a rule model is missing that would correspond to the desired result, RDT will not find the desired rule.[4]

3.2.2. CLT

The concept learning tool CLT learns from positive and negative examples. The *task* is to define a concept on the basis of some concept instances

Input: a set of positive examples, a set of negative examples, a set of rule models
Output: a set of rules giving the sufficient and necessary conditions of a concept.

The new concept can serve as a feature for some other concepts. In other words; CLT can be used to construct new features. The *input* to CLT is a set of rule models, the name of the concept to be learned, and facts, among which are those with the target concept name as predicate symbol. If such a fact is positive, it contributes to a positive example. If such a fact is negated, it contributes to a negative example. The concept can be a relational one, i.e., a two-place predicate can be defined by CLT. As is the case for RDT and also for CLT, the user can input an acceptance criterion as a parameter of CLT. The list of rule models to be used by CLT needs not be identical with the list used by RDT.

CLT can be *called* by the user or by the knowledge revision module KRT.[5]

The *learning result* is a set of rules that represent the sufficient and necessary conditions for concept membership. The sufficient conditions are rules with the concept in the conclusion. The necessary conditions are rules with the concept as a premise.

CLT uses the RDT algorithm. It is the focused use of RDT with the additional requirement of finding necessary conditions for the concept.[6]

3.2.3. MAT

The model acquistion tool MAT abstracts rule models from rules. The *task* is to generate rule models.

Input: a set of rules, a set of rule models
Output: new, non-redundant rule models.

Since users prefer to input rules instead of rule models, the *inputs* to MAT are rules. The learning *strategy* is that of abstraction over rules. The rules are abstracted by turning predicate symbols from the application domain into predicate variables. It is checked whether a new rule model corresponds to an already existing one. If there are constant terms in the rule, these can be either turned into variables also or be introduced into the rule model. Rule models including a constant term as the argument of a predicate may be of good use if the desired learning result is to clarify all properties and relations concerning a particular object or attribute value. The *result* is a rule model that is not redundant to any given one.[7]

3.2.4. STT

The sort taxonomy tool STT organizes the objects (constant terms) of an application domain into sorts and classes of sorts. The *task* is to structure the constant terms or objects of a domain. In other words, the task is to learn types for a typed logic. If the fact base of MOBAL changes and the non-incremental mode has been selected, then the user can call the update of the sort taxonomy.

Input: a set of facts
Output: a lattice of classes of sorts.

The *input* to the algorithm is a set of facts. The *output* of it is a lattice of classes of sorts. STT can be used either incrementally or as a single-step learner. The lattice gives an overview of the actual state of the fact base. It is used by the user for inspection and by the system to check the sort compatibility of new facts and rules (rule hypotheses).[8]

The learning *strategy* is that of bottom-up induction, where the learned classes are described by their extensions. The basic idea of the algorithm is to produce sets of constant terms on the basis of their occurrence at particular argument places of predicates. These sets are inspected with respect to subset relations, identity, or intersections. The sets are sort extensions. Equivalence classes are built for these sorts. The classes are organized in a lattice based on their subset relations or intersections. The most time-consuming part of the algorithm is the calculation of intersections. The user can select whether intersections are to be built, or not. The algorithm is efficient, because it corresponds to learning in propositional logic.

3.2.5. PST

The predicate structuring tool PST organizes the predicate symbols of an application domain into linked sets of predicate symbols. The *task* is to structure the predicates of a domain.

Input: a set of rules
Output: an acyclic directed graph.

The *output* of it is an acyclic directed graph, the topology. The topology graph gives an overview of the rule base. It is used by the user for inspection and by the system to check the topology compatibility of rule hypotheses.

The learning *strategy* is that of abstraction over rule sets. The basic idea of the algorithm is to create a rule graph and then to perform abstraction on it. A rule graph is a graph where the predicates of rule conclusions are in one node and the predicates of the premises are in its subnodes. Since a predicate can only be in one node, the graphs for several rules can be combined easily to form the one rule graph for all rules of the rule base. This graph can be cyclic. It is transformed into an acyclic one by the first abstraction: for each cycle, a node is created with all the predicate symbols that occur in the cycle. The graph is further reduced by merging all nodes with the same successors or predecessors. In the *icterus* application, the rule graph had 127 nodes for about 200 rules, but the abstracted topology had only 50 nodes, thus giving a good overview of the rule base.[9]

3.3. Cooperating learning tools

The brief description of MOBAL's learning tools already indicated their task and their use by user and system. The cooperation of the tools is

- to use the results of another tool
- more particularly, to call another tool
- to use the same knowledge as does another tool.

In MOBAL, RDT uses the results of MAT, STT, and PST, if the user has not given the rule models, predicate declarations, or topology of predicates. In this way, the tools produce structures that on the one hand allow the user to inspect the evolving domain model. On the other hand, the tools produce prerequisites for another tool, namely, RDT. Moreover, in doing so, the tools take the burden of structuring, which otherwise would be on the back of the user. The results of STT and PST, in particular, illustrate the multifunctionality of represented knowledge. Figure 4 shows the interaction of the learning tools. The lines between tool names indicate the use of knowledge produced by a tool. The arrows denote a tool calling another one.

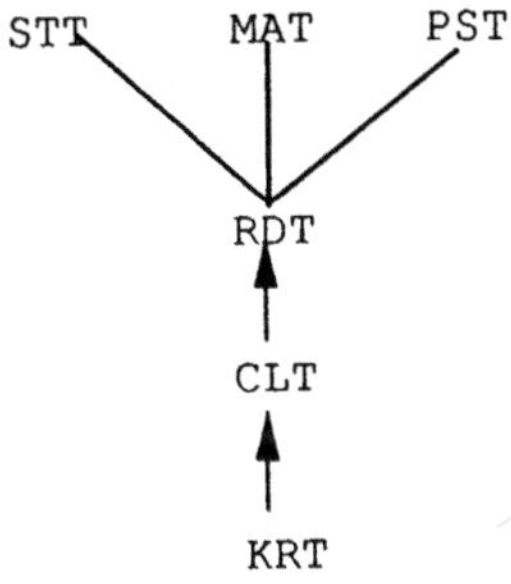

Figure 4. Learning tools cooperating.

CLT calls RDT with the name of the target concept and the list of rule models. CLT can be called by the user or by the knowledge revision. If a support set of a rule has too many exceptions (the criterion for "too many" given by the user or by default), CLT is called to define either a concept for the good rule applications or for the exceptions. The good and contradictive rule applications serve as positive and negative examples for CLT. In this way, the knowledge revision prepares the set of examples for CLT. The support sets are multifunctional in that they prohibit wrong inferences and can be used as examples for introducing new concepts.

The same knowledge, namely, facts, is used by RDT, CLT, and STT, where STT can use any set of facts and CLT needs positive and negative facts concerning a particular predicate, the target concept. Indirectly, via forward inferences (saturation), RDT, CLT, and STT use the rules also. In addition, RDT uses rules in order not to learn a known rule again. If background knowledge were represented differently from the (learned) rules—as is the case in many learning systems—RDT could not use its learning results for further learning. MOBAL's uniform representation of background knowledge and learning results enables RDT to use new facts that were derived from learned rules as additional descriptions (examples). In particular, negated facts can be derived from learned rules with a negative conclusion and serve as counterexamples for further learning.

3.4. MOBAL cooperating with the user

The user is supported in modeling by several capabilities of MOBAL. As was pointed out above, we include inspection, testing (validation), and revisions in the modeling process. The tools of MOBAL serve the overall modeling activity of the user. In addition to the learning tools described above, there is an inference engine, a programmer's interface, a user interface, and a knowledge-revision tool. In the following, first the user interface is sketched. Then, it is shown how each knowledge item can be input by the user or inferred by a tool. Finally, the opportunities of MOBAL for revising are indicated.

3.4.1. The interface

In general, all items are *input* using a edit-window named "scratchpad," where the user can edit the items before entering them into the system. A help window associated with the scratchpad shows the format of each item for input. If the data are available, they can also be read into the system as text files in the scratchpad format. Using the programmer's interface, which offers high-level system calls, MOBAL can be coupled with another system directly. Data can be exchanged between the systems using the commands of the programmer's interface.

All items can be displayed as texts in windows. The windows reflect changes of the knowledge base immediately. The content of a window can be *focused* so that only items containing a particular predicate symbol or constant term are displayed. Several windows can be opened for facts, rules, or rule models, in parallel.

The windows are easily used for some *operations*. A double click with the mouse on a particular item pops up a menu from which the user can select an operation (e.g., delete) or can display the item *graphically*.

The user interface eases the inspection of the evolving domain model. But the overview, the consequences of changes, and the detection of contradictions are delivered by the tools and provide the real support for inspection.

3.4.2. Balanced adding of items

In this section, the balanced cooperation of system and user is described with respect to adding knowledge items. It is shown that for each type of knowledge there exists a tool that creates items of this type and an interface that supports the user in adding items of this type.

The user may input *predicate declarations* with named *sorts*. This is sometimes useful, e.g., when it is easy to forget what argument type was supposed to occur where in a predicate. The predicate declaration then serves as a reminder of, e.g., where to put the person name in the predicate owner. If, however, the facts are already electronically available, the user needs not input predicate declarations. STT will do the job.

The user may input a *topology of predicates* in order to structure the domain model beforehand, e.g., with respect to steps of problem solving, which uses the (learned) rules.[10] For instance, the leaf nodes of the topology may consist of predicates that refer to the given data (observations) in an application. Intermediate nodes may refer to intermediate problem-solving results. The root node may consist of predicates that refer to possible results of problem solving (possible solutions). In this way, the topology is a task structure for the performance element, which uses the built-up knowledge base in an application. If, however, the user does not know the overall domain structure, PST can construct it on the basis of the rules.

The user may input *rules* and set the parameter such that MAT is called in order to obtain rule models from them. Or, the user may set the parameter to "direct rule input" so that MAT is not called for an inputed rule. The user may also input some rule models and call RDT for discovering rules. Thus, here again, there is a flexible work sharing by system and user.

The user must input some *facts*. Facts are necessary for learning, inferring, and building the sort taxonomy. But facts can also be added by the system's inferences. By selecting an inference depth for forward and for backward inferences (parameter of the inference engine), the user can force the inference engine to derive as many facts as possible within the selected inference depth (inference path length).

Hence, for each knowledge item, there is a system tool adding it to the knowledge base, and there is the option that the user enters it. Balanced modeling is the flexible use of the tools in supporting the user to add items or to have the system adding items to the knowledge base.

3.4.3. Revisions

Revisions of all knowledge items are supported by MOBAL, and the consequences are immediately propagated. If a rule or fact is deleted, all its consequences are deleted, too. Consequences are the facts derived from this rule or fact. Also, updating the sort taxonomy and the abstracted topology reflects the change. It is not (yet) maintained, however, that a particular rule was learned because of facts that were deleted afterwards. This requires more bookkeeping and would slow down the inference engine.

The interface allows us to react to the displayed knowledge base. If, for instance, the user detects a (derived) fact that he wants to reject, he can either delete it in the fact window or, better, can input this fact with the explicit negation. In this case, the negated fact serves as a constraint and influences learning. No rule covering the rejected fact can be learned anymore. The knowledge revision detects contradictions of facts and displays graphically the inference paths leading to the contradiction (Wrobel, 1993). The user or the system may perform the blame assignment and repair the rule base. Also, the explicit representation of exceptions in support sets and the call of CLT to form a new concept if too many exceptions of a rule have occurred helps to refine the domain model. In this way, MOBAL integrates inspecting, inputting, and revising a domain model.

4. Conclusion

There are some typical ways of using MOBAL. The extremes are to begin with facts and rule models and to have the system learning rules, the sort taxonomy, and afterwards calling the topology tool. This is the "automatic mode." The other extreme is to begin with some known rules, declare the predicates, build up the topology, then input some facts, and call the learning tools RDT or CLT. This is the "manual mode" where STT and PST are called for inspection purposes. The revision options of inference engine and knowledge revision are frequently used. Usually, modeling is performed using the system manually and automatically. The applications of MOBAL are

- traffic law domain—a self-made knowledge base with a rich structure and not so many facts; the knowledge base evolved in the automatic mode.
- icterus—facts and rules were provided by Dr. Mueller-Wickop, and the knowledge base was built up in the manual mode, using the tools for inspection only.
- maldecensus testis—data were provided by the Foundation of Research and Technology, Hellas (FORTH); the data do not reflect the diagnosis model, which was manually input by us in collaboration with a medical expert (Prof. Charisis).

- SPEED—knowledge about the supervision of security policy in distributed systems was provided by Alcatel-Alsthom Recherche, Marcoussis (AAR); the domain offers a rich structure where CLT successfully invented a new concept for rule refinement.

Some lessons have already been learned from the applications. Becoming acquainted with a system as complex as MOBAL takes some time. Setting the evaluation criteria, for instance, seems to be a skill that requires some experience with MOBAL. If users are familiar with attribute-value learning systems such as ID3, for instance, they tend not to input relations and not to use all the options that MOBAL offers. In this case, the users have already done beforehand what could have been learned using MOBAL. More naive users (with respect to computers) more easily exploit the opportunities of MOBAL. The main advantage of MOBAL was the ease of inputting background knowledge or learning parts of the background knowledge. Users also employed the inspection and revision abilities of MOBAL. Moreover, MOBAL offers all advantages of a first-order logic learning tool as opposed to a propositional logic one.

In conclusion, MOBAL indeed accepts new items and integrates them into the knowledge base, supports the user in inspecting the knowledge base, detects contradictions, and refines the rules. All these tasks can be performed by the user or by a tool of the system. The users choose when to let the system do a task and when doing the task themselves. In both cases, the same knowledge representation and operations are applied. Therefore, MOBAL is a balanced cooperative system.

Acknowledgments

Work reported in this article has partially been conducted within the project MLT, which is funded by the ESPRIT programme of the European Community under P2154.

The MOBAL system is developed at the German National Research Center for Computer Science by (in alphabetic order) Joerg-Uwe Kietz, Volker Klingspor, Katharina Morik, Edgar Sommer, and Stefan Wrobel. It is a successor of the BLIP system, which was developed at the Technical University, Berlin. The author of this article wishes to thank the colleagues from the Berlin days as well as the colleagues from the Bonn days.

Notes

1. For details of the modeling process see Morik (1989, 1991).
2. In Germany, the owner of a car has to pay a fine for a minor violation, even if he was not driving the car.
3. The more general rule model must be instantiated to become a subset of the more special one. This is the underlying meaning of theta-subsumption: a more general rule must be instantiated to become a subset of a more special rule.
4. For a detailed description of RDT see (Kietz, Wrobel 91).
5. Only the learning tools are described in this paper. The knowledge revision is a tool which handles contradictions, selects a rule to be deleted, or to be refined. The rule refinement is then performed either by the user or by the system. If a concept is missing which restricts the support set appropriately, KRT calls CLT to learn that concept.
6. For a detailed description of CLT see Wrobel (1989).
7. For a detailed description of a previous version of MAT, see Thieme (1989).

8. For a more detailed description, see Kietz (1988).
9. For a detailed description of PST, see Klingspor (1991).
10. Learning serves the acquisition of a rule base for a particular application where the rules are put to use!

References

Davies, T.R., & Russell, S.J. (1987). A logical approach to reasoning by analogy. *Proceedings of IJCAI-87.* Morgan Kaufmann.

Emde, W., Habel, C., & Rollinger, C.-R. (1983). The discovery of the equator or concept-driven learning. *Proceedings of IJCAI-83.* Morgan Kaufmann.

Kietz, J.-U., & Morik, K. (1991). Constructive induction: Learning concepts for learning. *Arbeitspapiere der GMD*, No. 543.

Kietz, J.-U., & Wrobel, S. (1991). Controlling the complexity of learning through syntactic and task-oriented models. In S. Muggleton (Ed.), *Inductive logic programming*, London: Academic Press.

Kietz, J.-U. (1988). Incremental and reversible acquisition of taxonomies. In M. Linster, J. Boose, & B. Gaines (Eds.), *Proceedings of EKAW-88.* GMD-Studien 143.

Klingspor, V. (1991). MOBAL's predicate structuring tool. *Deliverable 4.3.2/G* of the MLT project (MLT-Report, No. GMD/P2154/22/1).

Kodratoff, Y., & Tecuci, G. (1989). The central role of explanations in DISCIPLE. In K. Morik (Ed.), *Knowledge Representation and Organization in Machine Learning.* New York: Springer.

Michalski, R.S. (1991). Inferential learning theory as a basis for multistrategy task-adaptive learning. In R.S. Michalski & G. Tecuci (Eds.), *First International Workshop on Multistrategy Learning.* West Virginia.

Morik, K. (1989). Sloppy modeling. In K. Morik (Ed.), *Knowledge Representation and Organization in Machine Learning.* New York: Springer.

Morik, K., & Kietz, J.-U. (1989). A bootstrapping approach to conceptual clustering. In A. Serge (Ed.), *Proceedings of 6th IWML.* San Mateo: Morgan Kaufmann.

Morik, K. (1991). Underlying assumptions of knowledge acquistion and machine learning. *Knowledge Acquisition Journal, 3*, 137–156.

Morik, K., Causse, K., & Boswell, R. (1991). A common knowledge representation integrating learning tools. In R.S. Michalski & G. Tecuci (Eds.), *First International Workshop on Multistrategy Learning*, West Virginia.

Quinlan, R. (1983). Learning efficient classification procedures and their application to chess end games. In R.S. Michalski, J.G. Carbonell, & T. Mitchell. *Machine learning—An artificial intelligence approach*, vol. I, Palo Alto, CA: Tioga.

Quinlan, R. (1990). Learning logical definitions from relations. *Machine Learning Journal, 3*, 239–266.

Shapiro, E.Y. (1981). Inductive inference from facts. (*Yale Research Report* No. 192). Yale University, New Haven, CT.

Thieme, S. (1989). The acquisition of model knowledge for a model-driven machine learning approach. In K. Morik (Ed.), *Knowledge representation and organization in machine learning.* New York: Springer.

Wrobel, S. (1987). Higher-order concepts in a tractable knowledge representation. In K. Morik (Ed.), *Proceedings of the German Workshop on AI.* Berlin, Heidelberg: Springer .

Wrobel, S. (1989). Demand-driven concept formation. In K. Morik (Ed.), *Knowledge representation and organization in machine learning.* New York: Springer.

Wrobel, S. (1993). On the proper definition of minimality in specialization and theory revision. In P. Brazdil (Ed.), *Machine learning-ECML-93*, New York: Springer.

Received September 30, 1991
Accepted December 19, 1991
Final Manuscript February 28, 1992

Machine Learning, 11, 237-261 (1993)

Plausible Justification Trees: A Framework for Deep and Dynamic Integration of Learning Strategies

GHEORGHE TECUCI TECUCI@AIC.GMU.EDU
Center for Artificial Intelligence, Department of Computer Science, George Mason University, 4400 University Drive, Fairfax, VA 22030-4444, USA, and Romanian Academy, 125 Calea Victoriei, Bucharest 1, Romania

Abstract. This article describes a framework for the deep and dynamic integration of learning strategies. The framework is based on the idea that each single-strategy learning method is ultimately the result of certain elementary inferences (like deduction, analogy, abduction, generalization, specialization, abstraction, concretion, etc.). Consequently, instead of integrating learning strategies at a macro level, we propose to integrate the different inference types that generate individual learning strategies. The article presents a concept-learning and theory-revision method that was developed in this framework. It allows the system to learn from one or from several (positive and/or negative) examples, and to both generalize and specialize its knowledge base. The method integrates deeply and dynamically different learning strategies, depending on the relationship between the input information and the knowledge base. It also behaves as a single-strategy learning method whenever the applicability conditions of such a method are satisfied.

Keywords. Multistrategy task-adaptive learning, plausible justification trees, theory revision, concept learning

1. Introduction

Research in machine learning has elaborated and investigated in detail several single-strategy learning methods such as empirical induction, explanation-based learning, learning by abduction, learning by analogy, case-based learning, and others (Michalski, Carbonell & Mitchell, 1983, 1986; Kodratoff & Michalski, 1990; Shavlik & Dietterich, 1990). However, as this field evolves and concentrates more and more on solving complex real-world learning problems, it becomes more and more clear that the single-strategy learning methods provide solutions to overly simplified problems. One kind of oversimplification consists of specific requirements imposed on the input information and on the content of the KB. For instance, empirical induction requires many input examples and a small amount of background knowledge. Explanation-based learning requires one input example and a complete background knowledge. Learning by analogy and case-based learning require background knowledge analogous with the input. Learning by abduction requires causal background knowledge related to the input. Another kind of oversimplification consists of the limited result of the single-strategy learning process. This is a hypothetical generalization of several input examples (in the case of empirical induction), or an operational generalization of an input example (in the case of explanation-based learning), or new knowledge about the input (in the case of learning by analogy or case-based learning), or new background knowledge (in the case of learning by abduction).

From the above characterization, however, one may notice the complementarity of the requirements and of the results of the single-strategy learning methods. This complementarity naturally suggests that by properly integrating these methods, one could obtain a synergistic effect in which different strategies mutually support each other and compensate for each other's weaknesses. This hypothesis has been confirmed by the many multistrategy learning methods and systems that have been developed in the past several years (e.g., Bergadano & Giordana, 1990; Cox & Ram, 1991; Danyluk, 1987; DeRaedt & Bruynooghe, 1991; Flann & Dietterich, 1989; Genest, Matwin, & Plante, 1990; Hirsh, 1989; Lebowitz, 1986; Minton & Carbonell, 1987; Mooney & Ourston, 1991; Morik, 1993; Pazzani, 1988; Reich, 1991; Saitta & Botta, 1993; Shavlik & Towell, 1990; Tecuci & Kodratoff, 1990; Whitehall, 1990; Widmer, 1991; Wilkins, 1990).

After the development of many methods and techniques for the integration of learning strategies, the research in multistrategy learning started to address the problem of defining general principles and frameworks for the design of advanced multistrategy learning systems (Michalski, 1993; Tecuci & Michalski, 1991). One such framework for a multistrategy learning system consists of a cascade of single-strategy learning modules, in which the output of one module is an input to the next module. Another framework consists of a global control module and a tool box of single-strategy learning modules, all using the same knowledge base. The control module analyzes the relationship between the input and the knowledge base and decides which learning module to activate.

In this article we propose another general framework for multistrategy learning. This framework is based on the idea that each single-strategy learning method is ultimately the result of certain elementary inferences (such as deduction, analogy, abduction, generalization, specialization, abstraction, concretion, etc.). As a consequence, instead of integrating learning strategies at a macro level, we propose to integrate the different inference types that generate individual learning strategies. By this we achieve a deep integration of the learning strategies. The article presents a concept learning and theory revision method that was developed in this framework. It allows the system to learn from one or from several (positive and/or negative) examples, and to both generalize and specialize its knowledge base. The method integrates deeply and dynamically different learning strategies, depending on the relationship between the input information and the knowledge base. It is therefore a multistrategy task-adaptive learning (MTL) method (Michalski, 1990, 1993; Tecuci & Michalski, 1991a,b). An important feature of this MTL method is that it is also a generalization of the integrated single-strategy methods in that it behaves like any of these methods whenever their applicability conditions are satisfied.

This article is organized as follows. Section 2 defines and illustrates the general learning task of the MTL method. Section 3 contains a general presentation of the proposed MTL method. Sections 4, 5, and 6 present in more detail and illustrate the main stages of the MTL method. Next, section 7 presents the cases in which the MTL method behaves as a single-strategy learning method. The last section of the article analyzes the strength and the limitations of our approach to multistrategy learning and indicates what we consider to be the most promising directions of the future research.

2. The learning task

The learning task of a system is defined by the input information, the background knowledge, and the learning goal. We are considering a general learning task for multistrategy learning that subsumes the learning tasks of the integrated single-strategy methods. In particular, it is both a theory revision task and a concept learning task, as indicated in table 1.

By generalization of the KB we mean any transformation that results in an increase of knowledge inferable from the KB. The KB may be generalized by generalizing knowledge pieces or by simply adding new knowledge pieces. Similarly, by specialization of the KB we mean any transformation that results in a decrease of knowledge inferable from the KB. The KB may be specialized by specializing knowledge pieces or by simply removing knowledge pieces from the KB. These operations are also associated with an increase in the plausibility of the knowledge pieces inferable from the KB.

As stated in the above formulation of the learning task, our approach is based on the following assumptions:

- The input to the learning system consists of concept examples that are noise-free. However, the system may learn from a single positive example, or from a sequence of positive and negative examples.
- The KB is considered to be both incomplete and partially incorrect. It may also contain different types of knowledge pieces expressed as first-order predicate formulas.
- The goal of the learning system is to learn as much as possible from any input it receives. This is a general goal that consists in learning different types of concept definitions, and in performing different types of improvements of the KB. In a specific application of this learning method, this goal would need to be specialized. For instance, some of the learnable concept definitions may not be useful and, consequently, will not be learned.

In order to illustrate this learning task and the corresponding learning method, we shall consider the case of a learning system in the area of geography. The purpose of the system is that of acquiring geographical data and rules in order to answer questions about geography. Throughout this article, we use ::> to denote concept assignment, ⇒ to denote certain (deductive) implication, → to denote plausible implication, and --> to denote plausible determination (see section 4.3).

Table 1. The learning task.

***Input:** one or several (positive and/or negative) examples of a concept.*
The examples are represented as conjunctions of first-order predicates, are considered noise-free, and are presented in sequence.

***Background knowledge:** incomplete and partially incorrect knowledge base (KB).*
The KB may include a variety of knowledge types (facts, examples, implicative or causal relationships, determinations, etc.), represented with first-order predicates.

***Goal:** learn different concept definitions from the input example(s) and improve the KB.*
The learned concept definitions may be operational or abstract, and the KB is improved by both generalizing and specializing it, so as to entail these definitions.

Let us consider, for instance, that the knowledge base is the one shown in table 2. It contains several ground facts, two examples of fertile soil, a plausible determination rule, and three deductive rules.

Let us also consider that the input consists of the sequence of examples shown in table 3. The left-hand side of each positive example (negative example) is the description of a country that grows rice (does not grow rice), and the right-hand side is the statement that the respective country grows rice (does not grow rice).

The different types of knowledge pieces learned from the above KB and input examples are presented in table 4.

One result of learning consists of several concept definitions (Michalski, 1990):

- The first definition in table 4 is an operational definition of "grows(x, rice)," expressed with the features present in the input examples.
- The second definition is an abstract definition of "grows(x, rice)," expressed with more general features, derived from those present in the input examples (since this rule was already known, the new knowledge is just that it represents an abstract definition).
- The third definition is an abstraction of example 1 that was obtained by instantiating the previous abstract definition.

Table 2. A sample of an incomplete and partially incorrect KB.

Facts:
Terrain(Philippine, flat), rainfall(Philippine, heavy), water-in-soil(Philippine, high)

***Examples** (of fertile soil):*
soil(Greece, red-soil) ::> soil(Greece, fertile-soil)
terrain(Egypt, flat) & soil(Egypt, red-soil) ::> soil(Egypt, fertile-soil)

Plausible determination:
rainfall(x, y) --> water-in-soil(x, z)

Deductive rules:
∀ x, soil(x, loamy) ⇒ soil(x, fertile-soil)
∀ x, climate(x, subtropical) ⇒ temperature(x, warm)
∀ x, water-in-soil(x, high) & temperature(x, warm) & soil(x, fertile-soil) ⇒ grows(x, rice)

Table 3. Positive and negative examples of "grows(x, rice)."

Positive Example 1:
rainfall(Vietnam, heavy) & climate(Vietnam, subtropical) & soil(Vietnam, red-soil) & terrain(Vietnam, flat) & location(Vietnam, SE-Asia) ::> grows(Vietnam, rice)

Positive Example 2:
rainfall(Madagascar, heavy) & climate(Madagascar, subtropical) & soil(Madagascar, loamy) & terrain(Madagascar, flat) & in(Madagascar, Pacific-Ocean) ::> grows(Madagascar, rice)

Negative Example 3:
rainfall(Nepal, heavy) & climate(Nepal, subtropical) & soil(Nepal, loamy) & terrain(Nepal, abrupt) & location(Nepal, Central-Asia) ::> ¬grows(Nepal, rice)

Table 4. The learned knowledge.

Concept definitions

Operational definition of "grows(x, rice)":
{rainfall(x, heavy) & terrain(x, flat) & climate(x, subtropical) & (soil(x, red-soil) ∨ soil(x, loamy))}
::> grows(x, rice)

Abstract definition of "grows(x, rice)":
water-in-soil(x, high) & temperature(x, warm) & soil(x, fertile-soil) ::> grows(x, rice)

Abstraction of Example 1:
water-in-soil(Vietnam, high) & temperature(Vietnam, warm) & soil(Vietnam, fertile-soil)
::> grows(Vietnam, rice)

Improved KB

New facts:
water-in-soil(Vietnam, high), water-in-soil(Madagascar, high)

New rule:
∀ x, soil(x, red-soil) → soil(x, fertile-soil)
with the positive examples: (x<-Greece), (x<-Egypt), (x<-Vietnam).

Improved (specialized) plausible determination:
rainfall(x, y) & terrain(x, flat) --> water-in-soil(x, z)
with the positive examples: (x<-Philippine, y<-heavy, z<-high),
(x<-Vietnam, y<-heavy, z<-high),
(x<-Madagascar, y<-heavy, z<-high).
with the negative example: (x<-Nepal, y<-heavy).

The other result of learning is the improvement of the KB so as to entail the learned concept definitions:

- The KB was generalized by learning two new facts and a rule.
- It was also specialized, by conjunctively adding a literal to the left-hand side of the plausible determination.

As indicated in table 4, the system also keeps all the examples of the learned knowledge pieces in order to update them when new knowledge becomes available. These instances have been generated through different forms of plausible reasoning and have been validated during the learning process. Therefore, they also constitute an improvement of the KB.

3. General presentation of the learning method

The learning method consists in building, generalizing, and/or specializing plausible justification trees of the input examples, and in generalizing and/or specializing the KB so as to entail these trees.

A plausible justification tree is a demonstration that the input is a plausible consequence of the KB. It is like a proof tree, except that the inference steps that compose it may be the result of different types of reasoning (not only deduction, but also analogy, inductive prediction, abduction, etc). For instance, a plausible justification tree of example 1 in table 3 is the one from figure 1. It shows that, in the context of the current KB, example 1 is indeed a positive example of "grows(x, rice)."

In the following, we shall associate with each elementary inference step from a plausible justification tree (for instance, from A infer B), an implication (A $\rightarrow$ B or A $\Rightarrow$ B, depending on whether the inference is plausible or certain).

The main steps of the learning method are the following ones (more details are given in the next sections):

- ***For the first positive example I_1:***
  1. *Build a plausible justification tree T of I_1*
     The plausible justification tree T demonstrates that the input I_1 is a plausible consequence of the knowledge from the KB. The inference steps in the tree T may be the result of different types of inference: deduction, analogy, inductive prediction, abduction, etc.
  2. *Build the plausible generalization T_u of T*
     First build an explanation structure ES by replacing each implication from T with a plausible generalization of it. The generalization of each implication will depend on the type of inference, and on the knowledge used to derive it. It will correspond to the least general generalization of all the similar implications that the system would consider plausible.
     Then determine the most general unification of the general implications from ES. The obtained tree T_u is the most general plausible generalization of T.
  3. *Generalize the KB so as to entail T_u*
     Introduce into the KB the knowledge pieces hypothesized (through analogy, inductive generalization and prediction, abduction, etc.) during the building of the plausible justification tree T and the explanation structure ES.
- ***For each new positive example I_i:***
  1. *Generalize T_u so as to cover a plausible justification tree of I_i*
     Determine the instance T_i of T_u (which, in general, is an AND/OR tree) corresponding to the current input I_i. Analyze the leaf predicates and the implications from T_i and remove the false ones. If the resulting T_i is a plausible AND/OR tree (i.e., it contains a plausible justification of I_i), then T_u already covers a plausible justification tree of I_i. This ends the processing of the current example. Otherwise, make minimum modifications to T_i, so that it contains a plausible justification of the current positive example, and generalize T_u, as little as possible, so as to cover the updated justification tree T_i.
  2. *Generalize the KB so as to entail the new T_u*
     Introduce into the KB the knowledge pieces hypothesized (through analogy, inductive generalization and prediction, abduction, etc.) during the updating of the plausible justification trees T_i and T_u.

- ***For each new negative example I_i:***
  1. *Specialize T_u so as not to cover any plausible justification tree of I_i*
     Determine the instance T_i of T_u corresponding to the current input I_i. Analyze the leaf predicates and the implications from T_i and remove the false ones. If the resulting T_i is not a plausible AND/OR tree (i.e., it does not contain any plausible justification of I_i) then T_u does not cover any plausible justification tree of I_i. This ends the processing of the current example. Otherwise, T_i is a wrong AND/OR justification tree that is covered by T_u. Indeed, T_i "proves" that the current input is a positive example, although it is known that it is a negative example. Hypothesize that the implications $R_{k1}, \ldots, R_{kn}$ from T_i are false. The selection of the implications $R_{k1}, \ldots, R_{kn}$ is based on the following criteria:
     — if all the implications $R_{k1}, \ldots, R_{kn}$ are false, then T_i is not a plausible AND/OR tree (i.e., it does not contain any plausible jusitification of I_i);
     — prefer the weakest implications (first abduction, then inductive prediction, then analogy, and then deduction);
     — prefer the implications for which the specializations of the KB and of T_u cause the minimum loss of coverage of previous examples;
     — prefer the implications for which the specializations of the KB and of T_u produce a minimum increase in the complexity of the modified knowledge pieces.
     Specialize T_u as little as possible, so as no longer to cover the implications $R_{k1}, \ldots, R_{kn}$.
  2. *Specialize the KB so as to entail the new T_u without entailing the previous T_u*
     Specialize, as little as possible, the knowledge pieces from the KB that generated the implications $R_{k1}, \ldots, R_{kn}$, so as no longer to entail them.
- ***Learn different concept definitions***
  Extract several knowledge pieces from the tree T_u, such as operational definitions of the concept illustrated by the input examples, abstract definitions of the concept illustrated by the input examples, or abstractions of different input examples.

4. Learning from the first example

4.1. Building the plausible justification tree

In order to determine a plausible justification of the input, the system builds an AND/OR tree by conducting a top-down uniform-cost search (Nilsson, 1971).

The developed AND/OR tree contains several AND trees, each having a cost that estimates its global plausibility. The cost of a partial AND tree is computed as a tuple (m, n), where m represents the number of the deductive inference steps in the tree, and n represents the number of the non-deductive inference steps (which, in the present verison of the MTL system, could be made by analogy, inductive prediction, or abduction). The ordering relationship for the cost function is defined as follows:

$$(m1, n1) < (m2, n2) \textit{ if and only if } n1 < n2 \textit{ or } (n1 = n2 \textit{ and } m1 < m2)$$

This cost function guarantees that the system will find the justification tree with the fewest number of non-deductive inference steps. In particular, it will find a deductive tree (if one exists) and the deductive tree with the fewest inference steps (if several exist).

As a general strategy, the system always tries to justify a given predicate (for instance, "grows(Vietnam, rice)" in figure 1) by deduction. If it succeeds, then it tries to justify the resulting predicates ("water-in-soil(Vietnam, high)," "temperature(Vietnam, warm)," and "soil(Vietnam, fertile-soil)"). However, if it fails, then it tries to justify the predicate by using as many plausible reasoning methods as possible. It will try these methods in order: first analogy, then inductive prediction, and lastly abduction. If one of them produces a plausible inference step, then the system tries the remaining ones in order to confirm or to contradict it. If no contradiction is found, the inference step is accepted. This method (although quite simple, and definitely a necesssary topic of future research) is related to that employed by humans (Collins & Michalski, 1989). Indeed, Collins and Michalski argue that people solve problems by pursuing different "lines of reasoning." They estimate the "strength" of each line of reasoning, and make their conclusion on the basis of this evaluation. If the lines lead to the same conclusion, they have a strong belief in the result. If the lines lead to different conclusions, and the associated "strengths" are roughly similar, people refrain from making any decisive conclusion.

It should be noticed that, although at the level of a given inference step, the current MTL system applies the different reasoning methods in a predefined order, globally (at the level of the resultant justification tree) there is no predefined order. For instance, in the case of the justification tree in figure 1, the order of the inference steps was deduction, analogy, deduction, inductive prediction, and abduction. In general, this order depends on the relationship between the KB and the input. Therefore, the MTL method is an example of a dynamic and deep (i.e., at the level of individual inference steps) integration of single-strategy learning methods (each learning method corresponding to a specific type of inference).

The next sections present briefly the way the different inference steps in figure 1 have been made.

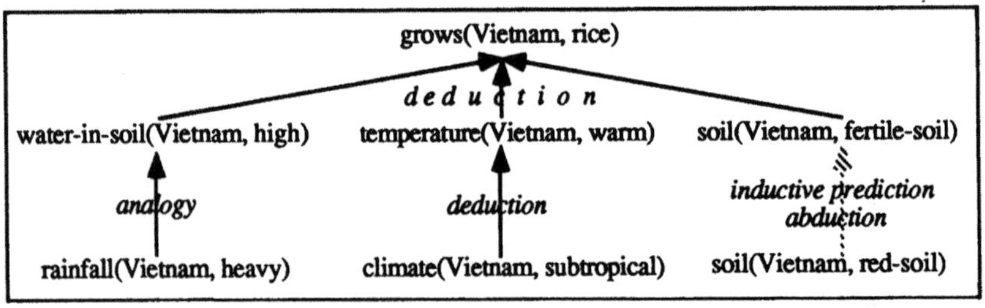

Figure 1. A plausible justification of example 1.

Table 5. The justifications of the deductive steps in figure 1.

Deduction 1:
∀ x, water-in-soil(x, high) & temperature(x, warm) & soil(x, fertile-soil) ⇒ grows(x, rice)
water-in-soil(Vietnam, high) & temperature(Vietnam, warm) & soil(Vietnam, fertile-soil)

---

grows(Vietnam, rice)

Deduction 2:
∀ x, climate(x, subtropical) ⇒ temperature(x, warm)
climate(Vietnam, subtropical)

---

temperature(Vietnam, warm)

4.2. Deduction

Two inference steps in figure 1 are the results of deductions based on the deductive rules in table 2, as shown in table 5.

4.3. Analogy

Analogical inference is the process of transferring knowledge from a known entity S to a similar but less known entity T. S is called the *source* since it is the entity that serves as a source of knowledge, and T is called the *target* since it is the entity that receives the knowledge. The central intuition supporting this type of inference is that if two entities, S and T, are similar in some respects, then they could be similar in other respects as well. Therefore, if S has some feature, then one may infer by analogy that T has a similar feature.

In the present version of MTL we use a simple form of analogy based on plausible determinations defined as follows:

P(x, y) --> Q(x, z) (P plausible determines Q) meaning
∀S, ∀T {If ∃y [P(S, y) & P(T, y)] then it is probably true that ∃z [Q(S, z) & Q(T, z)]}
where P and Q are first-order logical expressions.

Otherwise stated, if the source S and the target T are characterized by the same feature P (i.e., P(S, y_0) = true and P(T, y_0) = true), then it is probably true that they are also characterized by a same feature Q. Therefore, if Q(S, z_0) = true, then one may infer by analogy that Q(T, z_0) = true.

We use the term "probably true" to express that the determination-based analogy we are considering is a weak method that does not guarantee the truth of the inferred knowledge. This is similar to the mutual dependency rules introduced by Collins and Michalski (1989) and Michalski (1993), but different from the determination rules introduced by Davies and Russell (1977), which guarantee the truth of the inferred knowledge.

The analogical inference step in figure 1 was made by using the plausible determination

rainfall(x, y) --> water-in-soil(x, z)

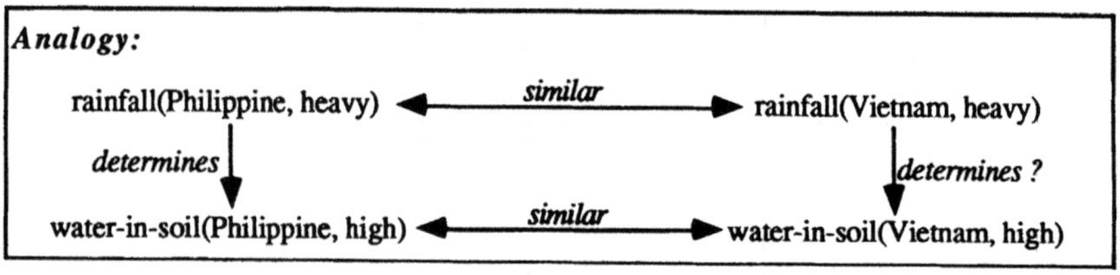

Figure 2. Hypothesizing Vietnam's water-in-soil through analogy.

(i.e., the rainfall of an area determines the quantity of water in the soil of that area) as illustrated in figure 2.

As can be seen in figure 2, the Philippines and Vietnam are similar from the point of view of "rainfall" (in both cases this is heavy). Therefore, one may infer by analogy that the two countries are also similar from the point of view of "water-in-soil." Thus, the system concluded that "water-in-soil(Vietnam, high)" from the fact "water-in-soil(Philippine, high)."

One should notice that a plausible determination rule indicates only what kind of knowledge could be transferred from a source to a target (knowledge about "water-in-soil," in the case of the considered determination), and in what conditions (the same type of "rainfall"). It does not indicate, however, the exact relationship between the type of the rainfall (for instance, "heavy") and the quantity of water in soil ("high"). The exact relationship is indicated by the source entity ("Philippine"). Therefore, a plausible determination rule alone (without such a source entity) cannot be used in the inference process.

The determination rules have been previously used in an explanation-based learning framework by Mahadevan (1989) and Widmer (1989). In MTL, however, these are only one way of implementing analogical reasoning. In general, the MTL method is intended to incorporate different forms of analogy, based on different kinds of similarities, such as similarities among causes, relations, and meta-relations (Carbonell, 1986; Gentner, 1983; Kedar-Cabelli, 1985; Kodratoff, 1990; Michalski, 1993; Porter, Bareiss, & Holte, 1990; Winston, 1986).

4.4. Inductive prediction

Inductive prediction consists in finding an inductive generalization of a set of examples of a concept and in applying it in order to predict whether a new instance is (or is not) a positive example of the concept.

The generalization of the examples could be obtained through a process of empirical or constructive generalization. The generalization process is empirical if it involves only descriptors from the description space of the examples, and is constructive if it introduces new descriptors that do not belong to the description space of the examples. A detailed characterization of empirical and constructive generalization is given in Michalski (1993).

In the current verison of MTL, we use an inductive generalization method that determines the most specific generalization of a set of positive examples that does not cover

Table 6. Making an inference through inductive prediction.

Examples from KB:
soil(Greece, red-soil) ::> soil(Greece, fertile-soil)
terrain-type(Egypt, flat) & soil(Egypt, red-soil) ::> soil(Egypt, fertile-soil)

Inductive generalization:
∀ x, soil(x, red-soil) → soil(x, fertile-soil)
with the positive examples: (x<-Greece)(x<-Egypt)

Predicted inference:
soil(Vietnam, red-soil) → soil(Vietnam, fertile-soil)

any of the negative examples. In general, the result will be a disjunction of conjunctive expressions. Moreover, the system is keeping all the examples in order to update the generalization when new examples become available.

One inference step in figure 1 was the result of inductive prediction. Indeed, in order to prove that "soil(Vietnam, fertile-soil)" is true, the system looked into the KB for examples of "fertile-soil." Then it inductively generalized them to a rule that was used to predict the inference step from figure 1, as indicated in table 6.

It is important to stress that the system keeps the learned rule in the KB as an inductive generalization. Therefore, future applications of this rule are also inductive predictions. Let us also notice that the rule in table 6 was obtained through an empirical generalization process because it is expressed only in terms of the descriptors used in the examples.

4.5. Abduction

In general, abduction is defined as follows (Josephson, 1991):

D is a collection of data;
H explains D;
No other hypothesis is able to explain D as well as H does;

Therefore, H is probably true.

In general, abduction involves two steps: generation of explanatory hypotheses and selection of the "best" hypothesis.

In the current version of MTL we consider two forms of abduction:

a) tracing backward a deductive rule
If D is to be explained and $H \Rightarrow D$*, then hypothesize H.*
In particular, *if* $H = H_1 \,\&\, H_2 \,\&\, \ldots \,\&\, H_n$ *and* $H_2 \,\&\, \ldots \,\&\, H_n$ *is true, then hypothesize* H_1.
b) hypothesizing an ISA relationship (i.e., d_1 ISA d_2)
If $P(a, d_2)$ *is to be explained and* $P(a, d_1)$ *is true, then hypothesize that* $P(a, d_1) \rightarrow P(a, d_2)$.

Table 7. Abducing an ISA relationship.

Abduction: soil(Vietnam, red-soil) → soil(Vietnam, fertile-soil)

Choosing the "best" abductive hypothesis is the most difficult problem of abductive learning. This is somewhat simplified in the context of MTL because the system is trying to make an inference step through as many plausible inference methods as possible, and abduction is the last one to try (as shown in section 4.1). Therefore, if an inference "H → D" has been made through some other form of reasoning, abduction is used only to confirm this inference or to contradict it (i.e., to prove "H → C," where D & C = false).

In the absence of the above criterion, the system chooses among the abductive hypotheses in the following order:

— prefer the ISA abductions;
— prefer to backtrace the rule H_1 & H_2 & . . . & H_n ⇒ D with the highest number of true antecedents;
— prefer to backtrace the rule that has the highest number of known instances;
— prefer the simplest hypothesis.

In the case of the plausible justification tree in figure 1, the system made an ISA abduction confirming the previously made inductive prediction from table 6. Indeed, "soil(Vietnam, fertile-soil)" needed to be proven and "soil(Vietnam, red-soil)" was known to be true. Therefore, the system abduced the ISA relationship from table 7.

4.6. Generalization of the plausible justification tree

Once a justification tree was successfully created, the system analyzes the individual implications associated with the elementary inference steps to determine if these implications could be locally generalized within the constraints of the KB that were used to make the inference steps. After the implications are generalized locally, the system unifies them globally, and builds a generalized justification tree. This technique is an extension of the one elaborated by Mooney and Bennet (1986). The extension concerns the way individual implications are generalized, by using the knowledge from which they were derived. The idea is to replace each implication A → B (or A ⇒ B) with the least general generalization of all the similar implications that could be obtained from the knowledge that produced it (Tecuci & Michalski, 1991b).

A deductive implication is replaced by the deductive rule that generated it. This is a deductive generalization.

An analogical implication is generalized by considering the knowledge used to derive it. In our example, the implication

rainfall(Vietnam, heavy) → water-in-soil(Vietnam, high)

was obtained by analogy with "rainfall(Philippine, heavy)" and "water-in-soil(Philippine, high)," based on the determination rainfall(x, y) --> water-in-soil(x, z).

Because the system would infer "water-in-soil(x, high)" for any x such that "rainfall(x, heavy)," the analogical implication is generalized to

$\forall$, rainfall(x, heavy) $\rightarrow$ water-in-soil(x, high).

This is a generalization based on analogy.

An implication obtained through inductive prediction is generalized to the rule that produced it. Therefore, the implication from table 6 obtained through inductive prediction would be replaced with the inductive generalization from table 6.

An abductive implication obtained by tracing backward a deductive rule would be generalized to that rule. However, for an abduced ISA relationship there is no knowledge that could be used to generalize it. Therefore it would remain unchanged in the explanation structure.

An implication obtained through several forms of reasoning is generalized to the least general expression that covers the generalizations corresponding to individual reasoning methods. Therefore, the implication from figure 1, which was obtained both through inductive prediction and abduction, is generalized to

$\forall$ x, soil(x, red-soil) $\rightarrow$ soil(x, fertile-soil)

which is the least general generalization of the rule in table 6 and the abduced ISA relationship in table 7.

The generalization of the implications from figure 1 form the explanation structure shown in figure 3.

The most general unification of the connection patterns in figure 3 is (x1 = x2 = x3 = x4 = x). By making these unifications, one obtains the tree in figure 4, which represents the most general plausible generalization of the justification tree from figure 1.

An interesting research direction suggested by the generalization of the plausible justification tree is to investigate different forms of generalizations, not only deductive and inductive, but possibly also analogical, abductive, etc.

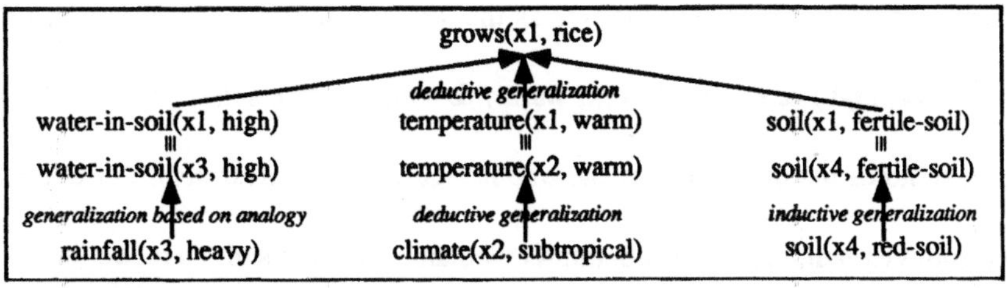

Figure 3. Explanation structure.

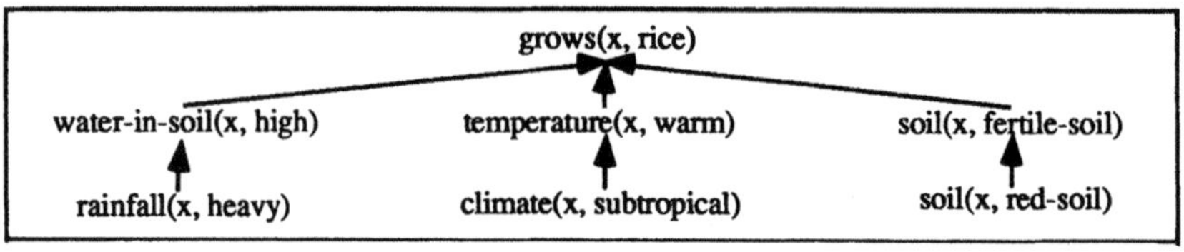

Figure 4. A generalization of the plausible justification tree from figure 1.

4.7. Generalization of the KB

As indicated in table 1, the system may improve the KB by learning different types of knowledge.

In this case it generalized the KB by learning a new fact (by analogy)

water-in-soil(Vietnam, high),

positive examples of the determination

rainfall(x, y) --> water-in-soil(x, z)
(x<-Philippine, y<-heavy, z<-high),
(x<-Vietnam, y<-heavy, z<-high).

and a rule (by empirical generalization)

∀ x, soil(x, red-soil) → soil(x, fertile-soil)
with the positive examples: (x<-Greece), (x<-Egypt), (x<-Vietnam).

If example 1 is the only input, then the system also extracts several concept definitions from the trees in figures 1 and 4. For instance, it stores the leaves of the general tree in figure 4 as an *operational definition* of the concept "grows(x, rice):"

rainfall(x, heavy) & climate(x, subtropical) & soil(x, red-soil) ::> grows(x, rice)

It also stores the upper part of the tree as the *abstract definition* of "grows(x, rice):"

water-in-soil(x, high) & temperature(x, warm) & soil(x, fertile-soil) ::> grows(x, rice)

Finally, it stores the upper part of the tree in figure 1 as an *abstraction* of example 1:

water-in-soil(Vietnam, high) & temperature(Vietnam, warm) & soil(Vietnam, fertile-soil)
::> grows(Vietnam, rice)

5. Learning from a new positive example

5.1. Generalization of the plausible justification tree

Let us now consider that the system receives example 2 in table 3. As indicated in section 3, the system tries to generalize the current justification tree T_u in figure 4 so as to cover a justification of the new positive example. At the same time, it may also generalize the KB if this is needed in order to entail the new T_u.

First of all, the system determines the instance of the general tree in figure 4, corresponding to example 2 in table 3 (see figure 5).

Then the system analyzes the leaf predicates and the inference steps from this proof tree. If the leaf predicates are true and the inference steps are plausible, then the tree in figure 5 is a plausible justification of the new positive example that is already covered by the general justification tree in figure 4. This ends the processing of the current example.

However, the tree in figure 5 is not a correct justification of example 2 because the leaf predicate "soil(Madagascar, red-soil)" is not true. Therefore, the system uses the deductive rule "∀x, soil(x, loamy) ⇒ soil(x, fertile-soil)" from table 2, and builds the plausible justification tree in figure 6.

It is important to notice that the plausible justification tree of example 2 has been built by using the plausible justification tree of the previous example. This not only facilitates the process of building the justification tree, but also the process of generalizing the general

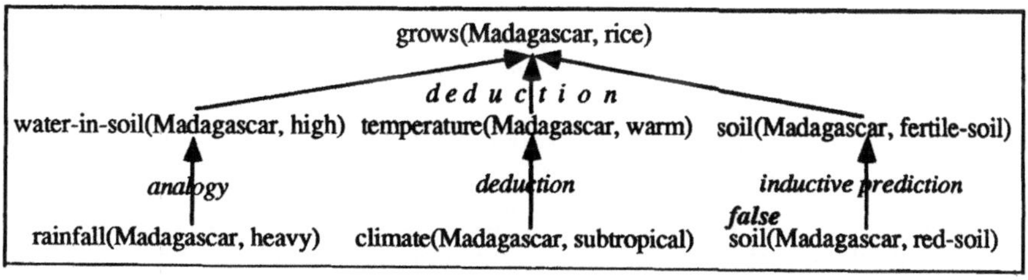

Figure 5. Instance of the general justification tree corresponding to example 2 in table 3.

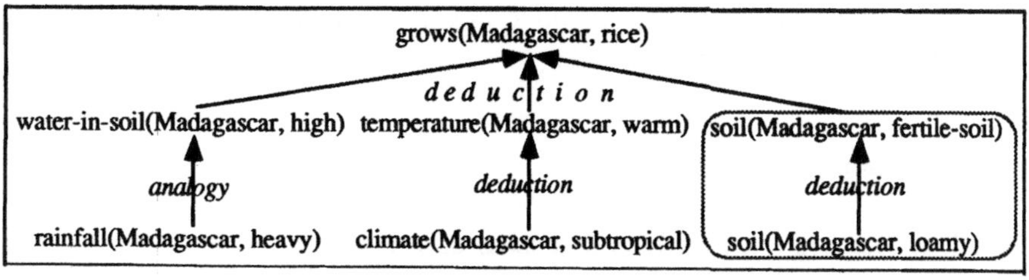

Figure 6. Plausible justification of example 2 in table 3.

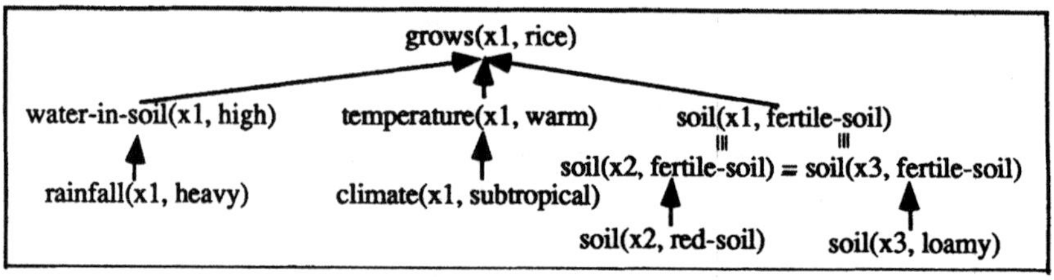

Figure 7. Explanation structure covering the plausible justification in figure 6.

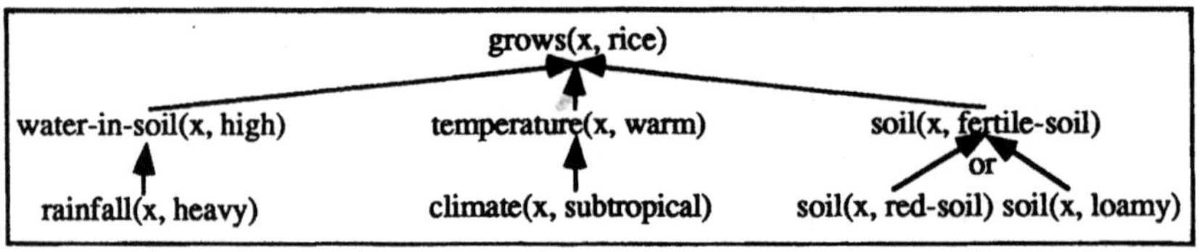

Figure 8. General justification tree covering the justifications of example 1 and example 2.

tree T_u, as will be shown in the following. Moreover, it shows some similarities between our method and human learning, which involves the use of the explanations of previous examples in the process of building an explanation for a new example (Wisniewski & Medin, 1991).

The next step of the learning process is to build the explanation structure (shown in figure 7), which has three general components to be unified:

— the part of the tree in figure 4 that covers part of the tree in figure 6,
— the part that is specific to the tree in figure 4, and
— the generalization of the part of the tree in figure 6 that is specific to it (this generalization being made according to the procedures described in section 4.6).

As the result of the unification of the connection patterns in figure 7, one obtains the general justification tree in figure 8 that covers the justification trees of both example 1 and example 2. It should be noticed that, although the justification trees of individual positive examples are AND trees, the generalization of these trees is, in general, an *AND/OR tree*. This is also the case with the tree in figure 8. Indeed, "grows(x, rice)" is an AND node and "soil(x, fertile-soil)" is an OR node.

5.2. Generalization of the KB

The result of learning from example 2 consists of a new fact,

water-in-soil(Madagascar, high),

and a new positive example of the determination "rainfall(x, y) --> water-in-soil(x, z),"

(x<-Madagascar, y<-heavy, z<-high).

If example 2 is the last example, then the system extracts the abstract and operational definitions of "grows(x, rice)" from the tree in figure 8. In particular, the operational definition would be

terrain(x, flat) & climate(x, subtropical) & (soil(x, red-soil) or soil(x, loamy))
::> grows(x, rice)

6. Learning from negative examples

6.1. Specialization of the general justification tree

Let us now consider that the system receives Negative Example 3 from table 3. As indicated in section 3, the system tries to specialize the general justification tree T_u so as not to cover any justification of the negative example. At the same time, it may need to specialize the KB so as to entail the new T_u while rejecting the previous T_u.

Again the system builds the instance of the general justification tree in figure 8, corresponding to this new example (see figure 9). This tree would lead to the wrong conclusion that the current input is a positive example of "grows(x, rice)." Therefore, the tree must contain some false leaf facts or false implications. These have to be detected, and both the general justification tree in figure 8 and the KB should be specialized, so as no longer to contain them. One should notice that this is a limited specialization of the KB. Further specializing the KB so as no longer to entail *any* plausible justification of the negative example does not seem to be an obvious goal for a plausible reasoner that, by definition, may also reach some false conclusions.

Because the tree in figure 9 is an AND/OR tree, one should make sure to prove that enough of the leaf facts and implications are false. For instance, "soil(Nepal, red-soil)" in figure 9 is false. However, because the node "soil(Nepal, fertile-soil)" is an OR node, the tree may still entail "grows(Nepal, rice)." Therefore, one should show that an implication is false.

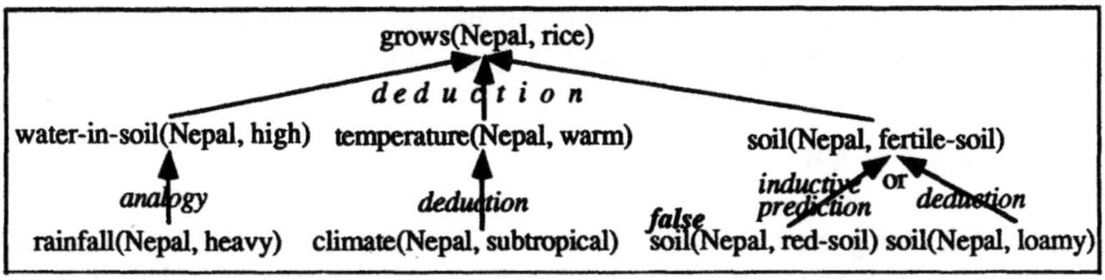

Figure 9. The instance of the justification tree in figure 8, which is a wrong proof tree.

Deciding which is the false implication is a difficult problem. In the current version of MTL, the implications hypothesized to be false are selected according to the following criteria:

— select the weakest implications (first abduction, then inductive prediction, then analogy, and lastly deduction);
— among the selected implications select those for which the corrections of the KB and of the general justification tree cause the minimum loss of coverage of the known instances;
— among the selected ones, select those for which the corrections produce a minimum increase in the complexity of the modified knowledge pieces;
— choose arbitrarily from the remaining hypotheses.

In the considered example, hypothesizing which is the false implication was simple because the justification tree from figure 9 contains one analogical implication and three deductive implications. Therefore, the analogical implication was considered to be the false one:

rainfall(Nepal, heavy) -/-> water-in-soil(Nepal, high) (1)

The corresponding implication from the current general justification tree is

rainfall(x, heavy) → water-in-soil(x, high) (2)

which was derived from the determination

rainfall(x, y) --> water-in-soil(x, z) (3)

Consequently, the system will try to specialize rule (3) so as no longer to cover implication (1), by taking into account the known instances of rules (2) and (3):

rainfall(Philippines, heavy) → water-in-soil(Philippines, high)
rainfall(Vietnam, heavy) → water-in-soil(Vietnam, high)
rainfall(Madagascar, heavy) → water-in-soil(Madagascar, high)

together with the known properties of the involved objects (Nepal, Philippine, Vietnam, and Madagascar).

The inductive learner of MTL will suggest, in this case, to specialize the determination (3) by adding the left-hand side predicate "terrain(x, flat):"

rainfall(x, y) & terrain(x, flat) --> water-in-soil(x, z)

The same specialization is applied to the implication (2). Thus, the general justification tree in figure 8 is specialized, as indicated in figure 10.

6.2. Specialization of KB

As a result of learning from the Negative Example 3, the system discovered a negative example of the plausible determination rule in table 2, and specialized it, by conjunctively adding a left-hand-side predicate:

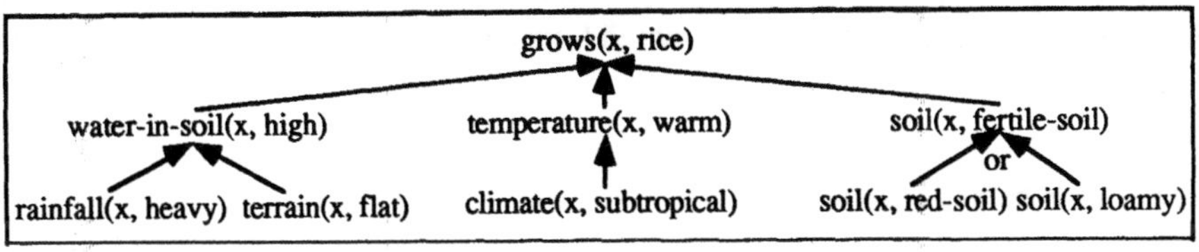

Figure 10. Specialization of the general justification tree.

rainfall(x, y) & terrain(x, flat) --> water-in-soil(x, z)
with the positive examples: (x<-Philippine, y<-heavy, z<-high),
(x<-Vietnam, y<-heavy, z<-high),
(x<-Madagascar, y<-heavy z<-high).
with the negative example: (x<-Nepal, y<-heavy).

It has also specialized accordingly the general justification tree T_u.

Because Negative Example 3 is the last input example, the system extracts from the tree T_u the operational and abstract definitions indicated in table 4.

7. Basic cases

An important feature of the presented method is that it behaves as a single-strategy learning method whenever the applicability conditions of such a method are satsified, and the learning task of MTL is specialized to the learning task of the single-strategy method.

This feature is important because it shows that the MTL method is a generalization of the integrated learning strategies that not only takes advantage of the complementarity of the integrated strategies (as has been shown in the previous sections), but also inherits the features of these strategies.

The next sections show that the MTL method may behave as

- explanation-based learning, learning by abduction, or learning by analogy, when the input consists of only one positive example;
- multiple-example explanation-based generalization, when the input consists of a sequence of positive examples;
- empirical or constructive inductive generalization when the input consists of a sequence of positive and negative examples.

7.1. Explanation-based learning

Let us suppose that, in addition to the rules in table 2, the KB also contains the following deductive rules:

∀x, rainfall(x, heavy) ⇒ water-in-soil(x, high)
∀x, soil(x, red-soil) ⇒ soil(x, fertile-soil)

In such a case, the justification trees in figures 1 and 4 become logical proofs, and the result of learning from example 1 is an operational definition of "grows(x, rice)." Thus, the MTL method reduces to explanation-based learning (DeJong & Mooney, 1986; Mitchell, Keller, & Kedar-Cabelli, 1986).

7.2. *Learning by abduction*

Let us now suppose that the relationship between "rainfall" and "water-in-soil" is not a determination, but a deductive implication

$\forall$x, rainfall(x, heavy) $\Rightarrow$ water-in-soil(x, high)

and the KB does not contain examples of the predicate "soil." In this case, in order to build the justification tree of example 1, the system needs only to create the explanatory hypothesis

soil(Vietnam, red-soil) $\rightarrow$ soil(Vietnam, fertile-soil)

as shown in figure 11. Therefore, the result of learning is the created explanatory hypothesis, and the MTL method reduces to abductive learning.

7.3. *Learning by analogy*

If the only background knowledge that is related to example 1 is

Facts:
rainfall(Philippine, heavy),
water-in-soil(Philippine, high)
Determination:
rainfall(x, y) --> water-in-soil(x, z)

then the system can only infer that "water-in-soil(Vietnam, high)," by analogy with "water-in-soil(Philippine high)," as shown in figure 2. Thus, in this case, the MTL method reduces to analogical learning.

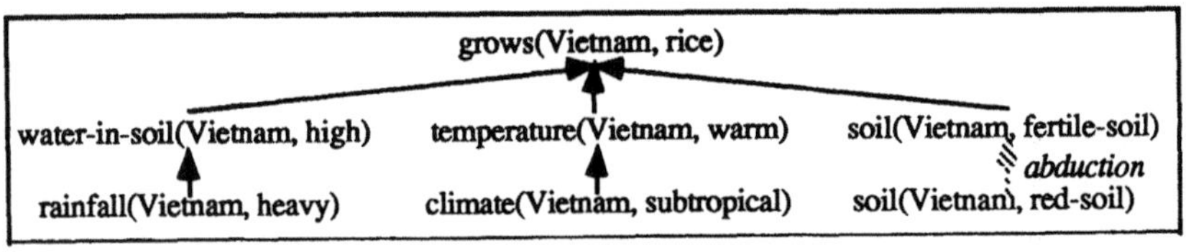

Figure 11. Using abduction to build a justification tree of the input.

7.4. Multiple-example explanation-based generalization

If the input of the system consists only of positive examples that are deductively entailed by the KB, then the presented MTL method behaves as the multiple example explanation-based generalization (mEBG) that was developed, among others, by Hirsh (1989), Kedar-Cabelli (1985), and Pazzani (1988).

7.5. Empirical and constructive inductive generalization

Finally, let us assume that the KB does not contain the determination and the deductive rules shown in table 2, and the input consists of all the examples from table 3. In this case, each input is new, neither confirming nor contradicting the KB. Therefore, each example is interpreted as representing a single inference step that define a tree, as shown in the top part of figure 12.

The MTL method will compute the least general generalization of the trees corresponding to the positive examples, a generalization that does not cover the trees corresponding to the negative examples (see the bottom of figure 12). The result of learning is therefore an operational definition of "grows(x, rice)" that represents the common properties of the positive examples that are not properties of the negative examples. Thus, in this case, the MTL method behaves like an empirical or constructive inductive generalization (Michalski, 1993).

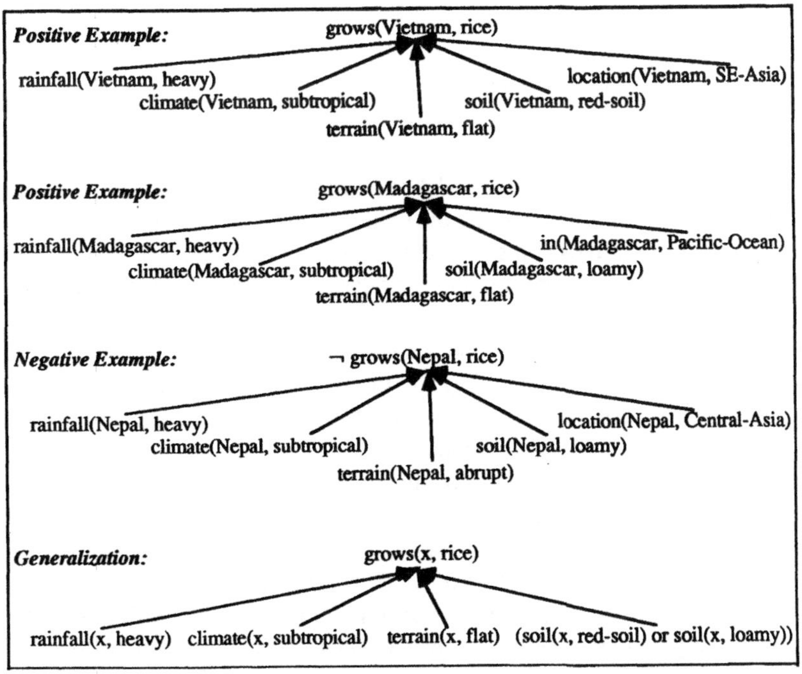

Figure 12. Empirical (or constructive) inductive generalization of examples.

8. Discussion and conclusion

In this article we have proposed a general framework for multistrategy learning that is based on a dynamic integration of the elementary inference steps employed by the single-strategy learners. This framework was illustrated with a specific multistrategy task-adaptive learning (MTL) method. There are several dimensions of generality of this framework. First of all, it is extensible in that new types of inference, and therefore learning strategies, could naturally be added to the MTL method. Secondly, it allows the use of different search strategies in the process of building plausible justification trees. The strategy employed in the current MTL method is a uniform-cost search of an AND-OR tree. However, one could employ any other search strategy (not only exhaustive but also heuristic). Thirdly, it is general with respect to the knowledge representation, allowing learning from a great variety of knowledge pieces. Finally, it is not only a framework for the integration of single-strategy learning methods, but also for the generalization of these strategies, due to the following reasons:

- the learning task subsumes the learning tasks of the integrated learning strategies;
- the MTL method behaves as a single-strategy learning method, whenever the applicability conditions for such learning are satisfied.

This approach to multistrategy learning has also revealed a new research direction in the theory of generalization by suggesting that a certain type of generalization may be associated with each type of inference. Consequently, one could perform not only deductive and inductive generalizations, but also generalizations based on analogy, on abduction, etc.

The presented framework and method is also an illustration of a synergistic combination of learning strategies. Indeed, the MTL method may learn in situations in which none of the integrated single-strategy methods would be sufficient.

Obviously, humans learn through a kind of multistrategy method. Although we do not claim that the presented method is a model of human learning, some features are similar to those employed by humans. These are the building of the justification tree of an example by using the justification trees of the previous examples (Wisniewski & Medin, 1991), and the use of multiple lines of reasoning in the justification of a plausible inference step (Collins & Michalski, 1989).

There are also several limitations and necessary developments of the presented framework and method that need to be addressed by the future research. One limitation has already been mentioned in section 6.1: during learning from a negative example, the KB is not specialized enough to be able to guarantee that it no longer entails any justification tree that would prove that the example is positive. Also, the presented method does not yet deal with noisy input. This is an intrinsically difficult problem for a plausible reasoner that may itself make wrong inferences. However, because the MTL method is a generalization of methods that could deal with noisy input, it inherits these capabilities. For instance, as in EBL, it may reject as noisy a negative example if it can build a deductive proof showing that the example is positive. Or, it may reject the negative example if the required specializations of the KB would determine a significant loss of coverage of instances of the knowledge pieces to be specialized.

The present versions of the integrated learning strategies (especially learning by analogy) are simple and should be replaced by more powerful ones. Also new symbolic and even subsymbolic methods (as, for instance, reinforcement learning or neural network learning) should be integrated into the MTL method. This will also require elaboration of generalization techniques specific to each new strategy. The method may also be extended so that to learn also from other types of input (like general pieces of knowledge, or input already known).

Another important research direction regards the extension and the application of the MTL method to the problem of knowledge acqusition from a human expert. In this case, the method would be extended with an important interactive component that would allow the system to ask different questions to the human expert, in order to decide on the best learning actions to take (Tecuci, 1991, 1992). In general, the human expert would be asked to solve the problems that are intrinsically difficult for a learning system such as *the credit-assignment problem* (i.e., assigning credit or blame to the individual decisions that led to some overall result) and *the new terms problem* (i.e., extending the representation language with new terms when this cannot represent the concept or the rule to be learned).

Acknowledgments

I have benefited from many useful discussions with Ryszard Michalski and from his work on the inferential theory of learning. I am also grateful to Ray Mooney and the reviewers for many useful comments and criticisms. This research was done in the GMU Center for Artifical Intelligence. Research of the Center is supported in part by the National Science Foundation Grant No. IRI-9020266, in part by the Office of Naval Research Grant No. N00014-91-J-1351, and in part by the Advanced Research Projects Agency Grant No. N00014-91-J-1854, administered by the Office of Naval Research.

References

Bergadano, F., & Giordana, A. (1990). Guiding induction with domain theories. In Y. Kodratoff & R.S. Michalski (Eds.), *Machine learning: An artificial intelligence approach* (Vol. 3), San Mateo, CA: Morgan Kaufmann.

Carbonell, J. (1986). Derivational analogy: A theory of reconstructive problem solving and expertise acquisitions. In R.S. Michalski, J.G. Carbonell, & T.M. Mitchell (Eds.), *Machine learning: An artificial intelligence approach* (Vol. 2). San Mateo, CA: Morgan Kaufmann.

Collins, A., & Michalski, R.S. (1989). The logic of plausible reasoning: A core theory. *Cognitive Science, 13*, 1–49.

Cox, M., & Ram, A. (1991). Using introspective reasoning to select learning strategies. *Proceedings of the First International Workshop on Multistrategy Learning* (pp. 217–230). Harpers Ferry, WV, AI Center, George Mason University.

Danyluck, A.P. (1987). The use of explanations for similarity-based learning. *Proceedings of the International Joint Conference on Artificial Intelligence* (pp. 274–276). Milan, Italy: Morgan Kaufmann.

Davies, T.R., & Russell, S.J. (1987). A logical approach to reasoning by analogy. *Proceedings of the International Joint Conference on Artificial Intelligence* (pp. 264–270). Milan, Italy: Morgan Kaufmann.

DeJong, G., & Mooney, R. (1986). Explanation-based learning: An alternative view. *Machine Learning, 1*, 145–176.

De Raedt, L., & Bruynooghe, M. (1991). CLINT: A multistrategy interactive concept learner and theory revision system. *Proceedings of the First International Workshop on Multistrategy Learning* (pp. 175–190). Harpers Ferry, WV, AI Center, George Mason University.

Flann, N., & Dietterich, T. (1989). A study of explanation-based methods for inductive learning. *Machine Learning, 4,* 187–266.

Genest, J., Matwin, S., & Plante, B. (1990). Explanation-based learning with incomplete theories: A three-step approach. In B. Porter & R. Mooney (Eds.), *Machine Learning: Proceedings of the Eighth International Workshop.* Austin, Texas: Morgan Kaufmann.

Gentner, D. (1983). Structure-mapping: A theoretical framework for analogy. *Cognitive Science, 7,* 155–170.

Hirsch, H. (1989). Incremental version-space merging: A general framework for concept learning. Doctoral dissertation, Department of Computer Science, Stanford University, Stanford, CA.

Josephson J. (1991). Abduction: Conceptual analysis of a fundamental pattern of inference (Technical Research Report 91-JJ). Columbus, Laboratory for Artificial Intelligence Research, The Ohio State University.

Kedar-Cabelli, S. (1990). Toward a computational model of purpose-directed analogy. In J.W. Shavlik & T. Dietterich (Eds.), *Readings in machine learning.* San Mateo, CA: Morgan Kaufmann.

Kodratoff, Y. (1990). Using abductive recovery of failed proofs for problem solving by analogy. In B. Porter & R. Mooney (Eds.), *Machine Learning: Proceedings of the Eighth International Workshop.* Texas: Morgan Kaufmann.

Kodratoff, Y., & Michalski, R.S. (Eds.). (1990). *Machine learning: An artificial intelligence approach* (Vol. 3). San Mateo, CA: Morgan Kaufmann.

Lebowitz, M. (1986). Integrated learning: Controlling explanation. *Cognitive Science, 10,* 219–240.

Mahadevan, S. (1989). Using determinations in explanation-based learning: A solution to incomplete theory problem. *Proceedings of the Sixth International Workshop on Machine Learning.* Ithaca, NY: Morgan Kaufmann.

Michalski, R.S. (1983). A theory and methodology of inductive learning. In R.S. Michalski, J.G. Carbonell, & T.M. Mitchell (Eds.), *Machine learning: An artificial intelligence approach* (Vol. 1). Palo Alto, CA: Tioga Publishing Co.

Michalski, R.S. (1990). Toward a unified theory of learning: Multistrategy task-adaptive learning. *Reports of Machine Learning and Inference Laboratory* (MLI 90-1). Fairfax, VA: Center for Artificial Intelligence, George Mason University.

Michalski, R.S. (1993). Inferential learning theory as a conceptual basis for multistrategy learning. *Machine Learning, 11* (this issue).

Michalski, R.S. Carbonell, J.G., Mitchell, T.M. (Eds.). (1983). *Machine learning: An aritficial intelligence approach* (Vol. 1). Palo Alto, CA: Tioga Publishing Co.

Michalski, R.S., Carbonell, J.G., Mitchell, T.M. (Eds.). (1986). *Machine learning: An artificial intelligence approach* (Vol. 2). San Mateo, CA: Morgan Kaufmann.

Minton, S., & Carbonell, J.G. (1987). Strategies for learning search control rules: An explanation-based approach. *Proceedings of the International Joint Conference on Artificial Intelligence* (pp. 228–235). Milan, Italy: Morgan Kaufmann.

Mitchell, T.M. (1978). Version spaces: An approach to concept learning. Doctoral dissertation, Department of Computer Science, Stanford University, Stanford, CA.

Mitchell, T.M., Keller, T., & Kedar-Cabelli, S. (1986). Explanation-based generalization: A unifying view. *Machine Learning, 1,* 47–80.

Mooney, R., & Bennet, S. (1986). A domain independent explanation based generalizer. *Proceedings of the Fifth National Conference on Artificial Intelligence* (pp. 551–555). Philadelphia: PA: Morgan Kaufmann.

Mooney, R., & Ourston, D. (1991). A multistrategy approach to theory refinement. *Proceedings of the first International Workshop on Multistrategy Learning* (pp. 115–130). Harpers Ferry, WV, AI Center, George Mason University.

Morik, K. (1993). Balanced cooperative modeling. *Machine Learning, 11,* (this issue).

Nilsson, N. (1971). *Problem solving methods in artificial intelligence.* New York: McGraw-Hill.

Pazzani, M.J. (1988). Integrating explanation-based and empirical learning methods in OCCAM. *Proceedings of the Third European Working Session on Learning* (pp. 147–166). Glasgow, Scotland: Pitman.

Porter, B., Bareiss, R., & Holte, R. (1990). Concept learning and heuristic classification in weak-theory domains. In J.W. Shavlik & T. Dietterich (Eds.), *Readings in machine learning.* San Mateo, CA: Morgan Kaufmann.

Reich, Y. (1991). Macro and micro perspectives of multistrategy learning. *Proceedings of the First International Workshop on Multistrategy Learning* (pp. 97–112). Harpers Ferry, WV.

Saitta, L. & Botta, M. (1993). Multistrategy learning and theory revision. *Machine Learning, 11* (this issue).

Shavlik, J.W., & Towell, G.G. (1990). An approach to combining explanation-based and neural learning algorithms. In J.W. Shavlik & T. Dietterich (Eds.), *Readings in machine learning*. San Mateo, CA: Morgan Kaufmann.

Tecuci, G. (1988). DISCIPLE: A theory, methodology, and system for learning expert knowledge. Ph.D. thesis, LRI, University of Paris-South.

Tecuci, G. (1991). Steps toward automating knowledge acquisition for expert systems. *Proceedings of the AAAI-91 Workshop on Knowledge Acquisition: From Science to Technology to Tools*. Anaheim, California: AAAI.

Tecuci, G. (1992). Automating knowledge acquisition as extending, updating, and improving a knowledge base. *IEEE Transactions on Systems, Man and Cybernetics*, 22, 1444–1460.

Tecuci, G. & Kodratoff, Y. (1990). Apprenticeship learning in imperfect theory domains. In Y. Kodratoff & R.S. Michalski (Eds.), *Machine learning: An artificial intelligence approach* (Vol. 3). San Mateo, CA: Morgan Kaufmann.

Tecuci, G., & Michalski, R.S. (1991a). A method for multistrategy task-adaptive learning based on plausible justifications. In L. Birnbaum & G. Collins (Eds.), *Machine Learning: Proceedings of the Eighth International Workshop* (pp. 549–553). Chicago, IL: Morgan Kaufmann.

Tecuci, G., & Michalski, R.S. (1991b). Input understanding as a basis for multistrategy task-adaptive learning. In *Proceedings of the International Symposium on Methodologies for Intelligent Systems* (pp. 419–428). Charlotte, NC: Springer-Verlag.

Whithall, B.L. (1990). Knowledge-based learning: Integration of deductive and inductive learning for knowledge base completion. Ph.D. Thesis, Computer Science Department, University of Illinois at Champaign-Urbana.

Widmer, G. (1989). A tight integration of deductive and inductive learning. *Proceedings of the Sixth International Workshop on Machine Learning*. Ithaca, NY: Morgan Kaufmann.

Widmer, G. (1991). Learning by plausible reasoning and its application to a complex musical problem. *Proceedings of the First International Workshop on Multistrategy Learning* (pp. 411–418). Harpers Ferry, WV, AI Center, George Mason University.

Wilkins, D.C. (1990). Knowledge base refinement as improving an incorrect and incomplete domain theory. In Y. Kodratoff & R.S. Michalski (Eds.), *Machine learning: An artificial intelligence approach* (Vol. 3). San Mateo, CA: Morgan Kaufmann.

Winston, P.H. (1986). Learning by augmenting rules and accumulating censors. In R.S. Michalski, J.G. Carbonell, & T.M. Mitchell (Eds.), *Machine learning: An artificial intelligence approach* (Vol. 2), San Mateo, CA: Morgan Kaufmann.

Wisniewski, E.J., & Medin, D.J. (1991). Is it a pocket or a purse? Tightly coupled theory and data driven learning. In L. Birnbaum & G. Collins (Eds.), *Machine Learning: Proceedings of the Eighth International Workshop* (pp. 564–568). Chicago, IL: Morgan Kaufmann.

Received September 30, 1991
Accepted September 30, 1991
Final Manuscript February 28, 1992

INDEX

GPSR Compliance

The European Union's (EU) General Product Safety Regulation (GPSR) is a set of rules that requires consumer products to be safe and our obligations to ensure this.

If you have any concerns about our products, you can contact us on ProductSafety@springernature.com

In case Publisher is established outside the EU, the EU authorized representative is:

Springer Nature Customer Service Center GmbH
Europaplatz 3
69115 Heidelberg, Germany

Batch number: 10755292

Printed by Printforce, the Netherlands